The

XML
Schema

companion

The
XML
Schema
companion

Neil Bradley

✦Addison-Wesley

Boston • San Francisco • New York • Toronto • Montreal
London • Munich • Paris • Madrid
Capetown • Sydney • Tokyo • Singapore • Mexico City

Many of the designations used by manufacturers and sellers to distinguish their products are claimed as trademarks. Where those designations appear in this book, and Addison-Wesley was aware of a trademark claim, the designations have been printed with initial capital letters or in all capitals.

Java is a trademark of Sun Microsystems, Inc. W3C is a registered trademark of the World Wide Web Consortium.

The author and publisher have taken care in the preparation of this book, but make no expressed or implied warranty of any kind and assume no responsibility for errors or omissions. No liability is assumed for incidental or consequential damages in connection with or arising out of the use of the information or programs contained herein.

The publisher offers discounts on this book when ordered in quantity for bulk purchases and special sales. For more information, please contact: U.S. Corporate and Government Sales, (800) 382-3419, corpsales@pearsontechgroup.com. For sales outside of the U.S., please contact: International Sales, (317) 581-3793, international@pearsontechgroup.com.

Visit Addison-Wesley on the Web: www.awprofessional.com

Library of Congress Cataloging-in-Publication Data

Bradley, Neil.
  The XML schema companion / Neil Bradley.
    p. cm.
  Includes index.
  ISBN 0-321-13617-9
  1. XML (Document markup language). 2. Database management. I. Title.

  QA76.76.H94B772 2003
  006.7'4—dc22

                                                    2003063011

ISBN: 0-321-13617-9

Text printed on recycled paper

First printing

Preface

XML Schemas

The *XML Schema Standard* is a powerful eXtensible Markup Language (XML) document modeling technology that was released in 2001 by the *World Wide Web Consortium* and aims to replace the Document Type Definition (DTD) feature of the core XML standard. The XML Schema standard performs the same role and is fully backward compatible in terms of the modeling tools at its disposal, but also includes many additional features.

This book

The XML Schema Companion serves the **programmer**, **analyst**, or **consultant** involved in the modeling of XML documents. It provides a concise, compact yet thorough examination of *every* feature of the XML Schema standard. It also covers document modeling techniques in general, to assist those who need to amend or create new document models.

This book assumes knowledge of the XML standard in general but does not assume an understanding of the DTD language or any other document modeling language. In addition, it does not require any prior knowledge of namespaces and XPath expressions (they are both exploited to support features of the XML Schema language).

Acknowledgments

Thanks to Michael Will for reviewing the first draft, and once again to Adobe for *FrameMaker+SGML* (which was used both in the preparation and publication of this book).

Feedback

Comments and suggestions for a possible future edition are welcome. They should be sent to the author at *neil@bradley.co.uk*. Also, *www.bradley.co.uk*, the author's Web site, contains more information on the author and links to various XML-related sites.

Neil Bradley
September 2003

Contents

The
XML
Schema
companion

1. Using This Book

Assumptions about the reader are outlined in this chapter, along with a description of the scope and structure of the book, and explanations of the conventions used in the text.

1.1 Assumptions

It is assumed that the reader is interested in gaining a detailed understanding of the XML Schema standard in order to develop new schema definitions or to be able to read and interpret schema definitions written by others.

Some familiarity with XML markup is assumed. The reader should be comfortable with the meaning and syntax of XML elements and attributes. Familiarity with namespaces would also be helpful, though not necessary because an overview of this topic is provided (see Chapter 21). Similarly, it is not necessary to understand DTDs (but see Chapter 19 for a brief description).

1.2 Book Structure

This book is divided into three parts. The first part, *Document Models*, shows how the XML Schema standard defines a template that document instances must conform to. The second part, *Creating Data Types*, shows how to define reusable building blocks that specify the allowed content of attributes and elements and includes an in-depth explanation of the powerful pattern language included in the standard. The *Reference* section contains chapters on various related topics, such as namespaces and DTDs, offers tips on how to create effective document models, and includes a DTD for XML Schema documents.

1.3 Style Conventions

The use of bold, italic, and monospaced fonts within the text requires explanation, along with the meaning of special codes and the way that element and attribute name letter-case issues are dealt with.

Bold and italic text

A name or term that appears in bold style has specific meaning in **XML Schemas** or one of the other standards covered in this book, and is widely used by experts in the field, or it is defined within this book for convenience. Such a term is emphasized in this way each time its use is significant (and, for this reason, not necessarily on its first occurrence) because the term is being explained or qualified. Note that all of these highlighted occurrences are referenced in the *Index* at the end of this book.

Words displayed in italic style are highlighted only to ensure that they are *not* missed.

Element and attribute names

When element and attribute names are mentioned in the text, they are presented in a monospaced font. Each significant occurrence of an element or attribute defined in the XML Schema standard is highlighted as described above ('the `element` element is very significant'). To help distinguish elements and attributes that belong to the XML Schema standard from elements and attributes that belong to example document models, the latter generally have names that begin with an uppercase letter, whereas all elements and attributes defined in the XML Schema standard have names that begin with a lowercase letter. It is therefore clear that the phrase 'the `element` element declares the `Book` element' includes one reference to an XML Schema element (`element`) and one reference to an example element (`Book`). But note that examples from real-world standards are not modified to fit this convention, and in some cases (such as XHTML), the element and attribute names also start with lowercase letters.

Example text

Other text appearing in a monospaced font represents example data (usually an XML fragment, such as '`<schema>...</schema>`'). But substantial examples are separated from the text, like this:

```
This is a sample line of text.
```

Although bold typeface is often used to emphasize part of an example, such highlighted text does not have the significance described above. Emphasis is used in this context to highlight particularly significant parts of the example (the remaining text simply provides some useful context):

```
The only part of this sentence of particular signifi-
cance is this part; the remainder is only here to give
some context.
```

Three dots ('...') denote omitted material, such as missing attributes and element content:

```
<schema ...>...</schema>
```

When an entire XML document is shown and it is important to appreciate this fact, an XML declaration appears above the root element:

```
<?xml ... ?>
<book>...</book>
```

Replaceable and invisible text

Italic styling in a code fragment indicates that the text never appears as seen because it represents a value of the type it describes:

```
<element ... type="data-type" />

    <element ... type="integer" />
    <element ... type="string" />
```

When it is necessary to show the location of whitespace characters, which are not normally visible, they are represented by the following codes:

```
[TAB]  = Tab character
[LF]   = Line-feed (end of line) character
[SP]   = Space character
```

2. Essential Concepts

The ability to validate well-formed XML document instances against a document model is very important. Initially, DTDs provided the only mechanism to define a document model. However, DTDs are showing their age, and many of the newer alternatives are either not yet widely supported or are destined to fall by the wayside. The XML Schema standard is powerful, well supported, and capable of modeling both data and narrative XML document structures. This chapter introduces XML markup structures, document models, and alternatives to the DTD feature, with emphasis on the XML Schema standard, and includes some example document types that will be developed in later chapters. This chapter also includes an introduction to data types.

2.1 Well-Formed Documents

Although XML documents can contain comments and processing instructions, the most interesting components of any XML document instance are the elements and attributes that combine to carry items of information, and the meaningful relationships between these items. Some sensible limitations on the use of these components are specified in the XML standard to ensure that the document is intelligible. Specifically, an XML document must be **well formed** to be accepted as valid.

In well-formed documents, elements can contain other elements, nested to an unlimited number of levels, though an XML document can contain only one element at the top level (this is the 'root' element):

```
<Root>
  <EmbeddedElement>
    <FurtherEmbeddedElement>
      ...
    </FurtherEmbeddedElement>
  </EmbeddedElement>
</Root>
```

Elements may directly contain more than one element. When this is the case, the embedded elements naturally form a sequence, regardless of whether the order of elements in the sequence is meaningful. For instance, there must always be a first element and a last element:

```
<AnElement>
  <FirstEmbeddedElement>...</FirstEmbeddedElement>
  ...
  <LastEmbeddedElement>...</LastEmbeddedElement>
</AnElement>
```

Elements must not overlap. Apart from the root element, all elements must begin and end in the same parent element.

An element may contain an attribute (but an attribute must not contain an element). If several attributes are present on an element, then they must have unique names within that element:

```
<AnElement AttributeOne="..." AttributeTwo="...">
  ...
</AnElement>
```

Both elements and attributes can hold text:

```
<AnElement AnAttribute="Attribute Value" >
  Text Content
</AnElement>
```

Well-formedness constraint checking is an essential part of the process of reading and interpreting an XML document. A document that claims to be an XML document but that does not comply with these rules is not well formed and is therefore not an XML document at all (however closely it might resemble one). Such a document may be corrupted or truncated, or, if complete, it may include invalid characters, incorrect tagging syntax, or overlapping elements.

A well-formed XML document is easy to create. A document author needs no particular preparation before starting to create one and can invent elements and attributes as they are needed, while organizing the elements in any way that the author desires. There are few restrictions on the names of elements and attributes and no constraints on where text and elements can appear within a parent element. The text content of an element and the text that constitutes an attribute value are also unconstrained.

2.2   Document Classes and Instances

The flexibility permitted by well-formed documents sounds ideal, but it introduces a serious problem when the document is just one member of a large number of XML document instances that are intended to be similar.

When a number of documents are created for the same purpose, they are said to belong to a **document class**, and each document is properly termed a **document instance** (or **instance document**). In general, a great many document instances belong to a single document class. It is rare for an application of XML to involve the creation of a single XML document. For example, many document instances (in this case, Web pages) belong to the XHTML document class.

Document instances belonging to a particular class are inevitably processed by software that has been specifically designed to read, interpret, and act upon their content. Some of these programs may need to modify documents or format them for display or publication (for example, Web browsers understand and present XHTML document instances), and others may need to copy the content of the documents into database records. Such software will break if it discovers unfamiliar elements, attributes, or element structures in a document instance. If authors were allowed to create new elements and attributes and to organize element structures at will, then software applications would be likely to receive data structures that they could not recognize and interpret. Any XML document may claim to belong to a particular document class, but such a claim should be tested, and a mechanism is needed to perform such tests.

2.3 Document Class Rules

One obvious approach to testing the claim made by a document instance that it belongs to a particular document class is to create a set of rules that precisely define the characteristics of that document class, then test that the document obeys these rules.

Word processor rules

Regardless of the applications to which XML is commonly put today, this technology emerged out of earlier attempts to provide a suitable platform for creating self-describing documents. It is therefore relevant to take a look at word-processing concepts, which show how XML first shadows then builds on common word-processing techniques.

The concept of a document **stylesheet** is now familiar to users of popular word processors. Users of such stylesheets select a descriptively named style, such as 'title,' 'paragraph,' or 'note,' from a list of options. The selected style is mapped to a set of formatting instructions that are immediately applied to highlighted text or to text that the author is about to type. Stylesheets are popular because the author does need to apply each of the formatting characteristics individually and does not even have to learn which characteristics to apply. A stylesheet approach would at least present an XML document instance author with a list of allowed elements, and perhaps a list of allowed attributes, thus informing the author of the **vocabulary** of the model. But formatting efficiency is not relevant in this case. Also, authors are never obliged to use a stylesheet and are given no guidance as to the order in which specific styles should be selected.

Some word processors allow a **document template** to be defined in order to ensure that required information is supplied and to gain precise control over the placement of this information in the document. The word processor takes care of positioning and styling the text entered into a form by the author. In XML terms, a document template approach would not only define the elements and attributes that could be used but would strictly control the order in which they could occur. However, such templates are only useful for small, nonrepeating items, such as a document title, author name, and creation date. They cannot be used to control repeating items, such as paragraphs and lists, especially when these objects can be mixed in any combination.

Document models

While a stylesheet or document template could, in XML terms, state the elements that may be used and, in simple cases, the order in which they can occur, it cannot specify that an element

- must be empty;
- can only contain text;
- can only contain specific elements, possibly in a strict sequential order, in some cases requiring their presence or allowing them to repeat;
- can contain both text and subelements;
- can hold specific attributes (in some cases with restrictrictions on their possible values).

These characteristics, when applied to relevant elements of a document class, form the basis of a **document model** for that class. For a set of documents that represent email, for example, it makes sense to say that every email will have an originator, that a single element called 'From' must be used for this purpose, and that this element must always be present.

A document model can exist in electronic form, using a number of declarations that are defined by a **document modeling language**. Among many applications of XML, document models have been created to represent Web pages (XHTML), books (DOCBOOK), mathematical structures (MathML), news items (NewsML), vector graphics (SVG), and data interchange over the Internet (SOAP).

When such a model exists, it becomes necessary to distinguish between an element that is present within a document instance (in the form of an empty element tag or a pair of tags with enclosed content) and the declaration of that element in the document model. To avoid confusion between the two, the term **element type** is used to describe the declaration, and **element instance** to describe an instance of that element in a document instance.

Note that XML is derived from an older markup language called SGML (Standard Generalized Markup Language), which officially only recognizes a document instance that conforms to the constraints of a document model. When XML was developed, one of its major selling points was that, unlike its older brother, it did not need to create a document model. The concept of the well-formed document was born. Many people who had struggled with SGML document models imagined that they would get all of the advantages of SGML without the pain of creating, using, and maintaining document models. But this was always an unrealistic expectation. In truth, many people had long been processing and presenting SGML documents without actually referring to a model, but usually only after the document had already been checked against a model. The XML standard simply made this activity legal. XML models are just as important as SGML models ever were and exist for the same good reasons.

Document instance validation

Once a document model has been encoded with a document modeling language, it can validate, using a **validating parser**, any document instance that claims to conform to this model.

Note that it may not always be appropriate to use a validating parser to check a document as it is processed. If the document has already been validated or if the document was generated automatically by fully tested software, it may be better to avoid validation, if only because it takes time to perform.

Despite an earlier observation that well-formed documents are easy to create because no preparation is needed, there are compensations for document authors in having access to a document model. An XML-sensitive word processor that can read and interpret a document model provides some obvious benefits. It makes sense for such a word processor to continually refer to the document model and allow insertion only of elements allowed in the current context by presenting a menu of only these elements to the author. The tags do not then have to be keyed, a benefit that is faster and prevents typing errors from corrupting the document. In the following example, the cursor is placed in the middle of a paragraph, and the document model allows only the `Emph` and `Keyword` elements to appear in this context. Note the availability of a number of XML-sensitive word processors that take this approach to authoring XML documents (and that vaguely resemble the illustration below):

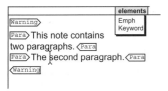

2.4 Narrative Documents and Data Documents

The term **document** has some confusing and contradictory connotations. There are two main categories to consider: the original domain of markup languages and the new arena into which XML has been pitched.

Narrative data

An XML document can be used to represent and describe, in electronic form, many written document types that existed long before computers were invented. These types include letters, memos, forms, policies, contracts, deeds, reports, guides, and published products such as journals, textbooks (including this book), and encyclopedias. These document types generally contain a **narrative** (a sequence of connected events) and are text based. Typically, a **narrative document** includes such structures as headings, paragraphs, lists, and tables. A model that describes one of these document types can be described as a **narrative document model**.

As mentioned earlier, XML emerged out of earlier technologies that were specifically targeted at these kinds of documents. Elements can therefore be arranged in sequential order and may form hierarchical structures. The following example illustrates the point. In this example, it would certainly make a difference if the order of the steps in the procedure were changed (and be embarrassing to anyone following the modified instructions):

```
<Procedure>
  <Step>get out of bed</Step>
  <Step>shower</Step>
  <Step>get dressed</Step>
  <Step>leave house</Step>
</Procedure>
```

Document models of this type are likely to include **mixed content** models, in which the content of an element is a mixture of elements and text and in which each embedded element is considered to be an **inline element** (an element at the paragraph level or higher in the document structure is a **block element**):

```
<Para>This paragraph contains a mixture of
both <emphasis>text</Emphasis> and
<emphasis>elements</Emphasis>.</Para>
```

Datacentric documents

Alternatively, an XML document can be used to hold highly structured data. This includes information traditionally found in a card index and more recently in the records of a computer database. A **datacentric document** has very different characteristics than those of a narrative document. XML tends to be used as an interchange or publishing format here, typically for data extracted from a relational database or generated by a software application. Interestingly, some published products, including many directories, catalogues, and the smaller dictionaries, also fall into this category.

Mixed content is rare in this case. Also, sequential relationships tend to be unimportant. On the other hand, rules governing the structure of the text itself tend to be tighter. For example, databases and programming languages both distinguish between text and numbers and between decimal and integer numbers.

Data and narrative combinations

Some document models can include both narrative and data structures. Typically, datacentric **metadata** identifies, classifies, and describes a narrative structure. Traditionally, attributes have been used to hold this metadata, while the narrative has been held as element content. For example, a `Book` element may contain further elements that hold the content of a book, while `Author`, `Date`, and `ISBN` attributes on this element may hold important information *about* the book.

2.5   Example Document Classes

The following three examples focus on an organization called the MegaTVi Corporation and specifically on the email that its employees generate, the books that they write about TV programs, and program broadcast details that they distribute to other organizations. Careful study of these three example document instances is recommended because they form the basis of many other examples that appear in later chapters.

EMail example

As an example of a simple datacentric document, consider the need to represent an archive of email in XML form:

```
<EMail Importance="urgent">
  <From>j.smith@MegaTVi.com</From>
  <To>p.jones@MegaTVi.com</To>
  <Title>Schema wars episode</Title>
  <Date>2002-07-20</Date>
  <Message>We need a description of this episode
  immediately!</Message>
</EMail>
```

A document model for such instances might require the `From`, `To`, `Title`, `Date`, and `Message` elements to be present, while allowing the `To` element to repeat and the `Title` element to be absent. The model might also place tight constraints on the text within the `Date` element and the `Importance` attribute (which must either hold the value 'normal' or the value 'urgent').

Some variant examples will later include an optional `CarbonCopy` element and an optional `BlindCarbonCopy` element (often seen as CC and BCC fields in email forms).

This book example

A model that represents the structure of this book can be used as an example of a narrative document type (and this entire book can be treated as a sample document instance). This model consists of the `Book`, `Title`, `Part`, `Chapter`, `Section`, `SubSection`, `DisplayExample`, `Para`, `List`, and `Table` block elements, and the `Emphasis`, `ImportantTerm`, and `InlineExample` inline elements, though only a subset of the mostly optional elements appear in the following example. Attributes are used to hold the International Standard Book Number (ISBN), publishing date, and author name:

```
<Book ISBN="0-201-77059-8"
      PublishDate="2002-12-30"
      Author="N Bradley">
  <Title>The XML Saga</Title>
  ...
  <Chapter>
    <Title>Schema Wars</Title>
    ...
    <Section>
      <Title>A New Hope - XML Schemas</Title>
      ...
      <SubSection>
        <Title>Introduction</Title>
        <Para>Perhaps the most promising schema
        language, called the XML Schema
        standard ...</Para>
        ...
      </SubSection>
      ...
    </Section>
    ...
  </Chapter>
  ...
</Book>
```

Among many other rules, a document model might reasonably specify that subsections can only occur within sections, that sections can only occur within chapters, and that the `Title` element must always be the first child of the `Book`, `Chapter`, `Section`, and `SubSection` elements. Also, the `ISBN` attribute on the `Book` element might be contstrained to contain only characters that are allowed in an ISBN.

Program broadcast example

As an example of a reasonably complex document class that contains both data and narrative structures, consider a document instance that contains details of the broadcasting of a TV program:

```
<ProgramBroadcast>
  <ProgramDetails>
    <Ratings DegreeOfViolence="1"
             StrengthOfLanguage="5"
             AdultThemes="0" />
    <SeriesTitle>The XML Saga</SeriesTitle>
    <EpisodeTitle>Schema Wars</EpisodeTitle>
    <EpisodeNumber>5</EpisodeNumber>
    <Description>The inadequacy of the
    <Name>DTD</Name> feature led to a plethora
    of proposals for a new <Stress>schema</Stress>
    language, which led to the advent of the
    XML Schema standard, Schematron,
    RelaxNG, and others.</Description>
  </ProgramDetails>
  <BroadcastDetails>
    <Country>UK</Country>
    <Channel>BBC 2</Channel>
    <Date>2002-07-21</Date>
    <StartTime>19:00</StartTime>
    <EndTime>20:00</EndTime>
  </BroadcastDetails>
</ProgramBroadcast>
```

A suitable document model might reasonably specify the following:

- The Ratings element must be present, along with all of the attributes it holds.
- There must be either a single ProgramTitle element, or a SeriesTitle element and both an EpisodeTitle element and EpisodeNumber element.
- The Country element must contain a standard two-letter country code.
- The Channel element must contain a recognized TV channel name.
- The Date element must contain a valid date.
- Both the StartTime element and the EndTime element must contain a valid time.
- The Description element may contain text while also allowing the Name and Stress elements to be mixed with this text.

2.6   Document Type Definitions

A document model can take many forms. This book is dedicated to just one of the means available for creating document models, but an earlier modeling language, defined in the XML standard itself, deserves some attention for its long history and widespread use and for its influence on the XML Schema standard.

An alternative name for a document model is a **document type**. This name forms part of the title behind the abbreviation **DTD**, which stands for **Document Type Definition**. Until the advent of the XML Schema standard, the DTD feature was the only widely supported mechanism for creating a document model.

A DTD is constructed from a set of instructions that conform to a syntax vaguely resembling that of XML element tags. The following instruction adds a Chapter element to the document model; it further specifies that this element must contain a Title element followed by any number of Section elements (other instructions would similarly add these elements to the model):

```
<!ELEMENT Chapter (Title, Section+)>
```

2.7   Alternative Modeling Languages

The DTD feature was inherited from the SGML standard, though the **SGML DTD** language is more sophisticated than the XML DTD modeling language. During the development of the XML standard, there was little agreement about the precise scope of the DTD feature, which was conceived at the start to be a simplified version of the SGML DTD language (dropping many features that were either redundant or never much used in the first place, and others that were considered too complex for prospective XML parser developers to support). Some contributors and interested parties thought that DTDs were not needed at all. Others thought that they were not only needed but that they should be *more* powerful than SGML DTDs. Although neither group won this argument and the XML standard was released with its simplified, backward-compatible DTD feature, the latter group continued to argue their cause. Alternatives to the DTD were proposed even before the XML standard was released, and several attempts to develop separate standards have since matured.

Some basic principles are shared by most of the efforts to replace DTDs, and it has been widely accepted that any replacement should

- be functionally backward compatible with DTD features (so that it could be applied to existing documents and so that old DTDs could be automatically converted to the new modeling language);
- use XML document syntax so that XML tools could be used to create, validate, process, and present document models;
- resurrect useful features from SGML DTDs that were dropped from the XML version;
- extend functionality to model datacentric documents.

A number of proposals have been put forward. Some have fallen by the wayside or have been incorporated into other attempts. The field is now largely reduced to these:

- XML Schemas
- RELAX NG (a merger of earlier proposals called RELAX and TREX)
  (see http://oasis-open.org/committees/relax-ng/spec-20011203.html)
- Schematron (an XPath-based validation approach)
  (see http://www.ascc.net/xml/resource/schematron/)

Note that the advent of competing modeling languages does not necessarily mean that DTDs are redundant right now, though in time they almost certainly will be.

The word '**schema**' has appeared in the names of various proposals (including two of those listed above). This term is defined in *The New Oxford Dictionary of English* as '*a representation of a plan or theory in the form of an outline or model.*' Within the field of computing, this term has been used to describe database models. XML document models are sufficiently similar in concept to database schemas to make the adoption of this term inevitable.

2.8 XML Schemas

The **XML Schema recommendation** is one of the latest attempts to improve upon the DTD feature. It was released in 2001 by the **W3C** (*World Wide Web Consortium*) and is now supported by a wide range of parsers and XML applications.

This sophisticated standard employs 42 elements and 37 attributes (see Section 20.2 and Section 20.3 for lists of the elements and attributes), defined in a large specification developed by a committee of 47 (with 35 additional contributors). It is, arguably, not an especially elegant standard, but it is undoubtedly powerful. This standard is defined in three parts, of which the first serves as an introduction to the other two, and is relatively easy to read but is not exhaustive in its coverage of the features of this language (see http://www.w3.org/TR/xmlschema-0/).

XML Schema characteristics

The XML Schema standard was developed to meet most of the major design goals listed earlier. It is backward compatible with DTD features, uses XML syntax, resurrects some SGML DTD features, and adds features to validate values in datacentric documents.

A schema instruction looks very different from a DTD rule. The XML Schema standard is an XML application, and each rule is therefore an XML document fragment. The DTD fragment shown above would translate into the following equivalent schema fragment:

```
<element name="Chapter">
  <complexType>
    <sequence>
      <element ref="B:Title" />
      <element ref="B:Section" minOccurs="1"
                                maxOccurs="unbounded" />
    </sequence>
  </complexType>
</element>
```

Any document model that can be encoded with a DTD can now be specified with the XML schema standard instead. It is always possible to automate the conversion of a DTD into an equivalent XML Schema document (using widely available tools).

Schema definitions

An **XML schema definition (XSD)**, or just **schema definition** for short, is a document model that conforms to the XML Schema standard.

Note that people who create schema definitions are typically not the same people who create conformant document instances. The term **schema definition author** can be used to describe the former, and **document instance author** to describe an example of the latter, generally much larger, community (this book is clearly aimed at the former kind of author).

A schema definition contains rules to *declare* element and attribute types. Each element is specified by an **element declaration** and each attribute is specified by an **attribute declaration**. A schema definition may also *define* data types (introduced in Section 2.9) and reusable groups of declarations, by means of rules that create **definitions** of objects that will help build element and attribute declarations.

Schema definitions can be created, edited, and viewed with tools that hide the declaration markup shown above. The following illustration shows a typical view of a schema definition that hides some of the complexity of these models:

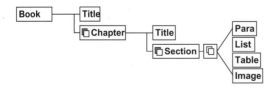

However, there is no standard graphical notation for schema definition models, so the XML syntax (as described in this book) is therefore the only standard way to illustrate the features of this language.

The following schema definition could be used to validate document instances that contain email exported for archiving purposes from an email system. It could be used to validate the example email document instance shown earlier:

```
<xsd:schema
        xmlns:xsd="http://www.w3.org/2001/XMLSchema">
  <xsd:element name="EMail" type="xsd:string">
    <xsd:complexType>
      <xsd:sequence>
        <xsd:element ref="From" />
        <xsd:element ref="To" maxOccurs="unbounded" />
        <xsd:element ref="Title" minOccurs="0" />
        <xsd:element ref="Date" minOccurs="0" />
        <xsd:element ref="Message" />
      </xsd:sequence>
      <xsd:attribute name="Importance">
        <xsd:restriction base="xsd:string">
          <xsd:enumeration value="normal" />
          <xsd:enumeration value="urgent" />
        </xsd:restriction>
      </xsd:attribute>
    </xsd:complexType>
  </xsd:element>

  <xsd:element name="From"    type="xsd:anyURI" />
  <xsd:element name="To"      type="xsd:anyURI" />
  <xsd:element name="Title"   type="xsd:string" />
  <xsd:element name="Date"    type="xsd:date" />
  <xsd:element name="Message" type="xsd:string />
</xsd:schema>
```

This schema definition forms the basis of others that can validate example document fragments in later chapters, so it can be usefully copied in preparation for experimenting with these examples.

Schema processors

A validating XML parser that includes a **schema processor** can validate a document instance against a schema definition. Typically, the schema processor is so tightly integrated into the parsing software that the distinction is too subtle to be useful, and the terms 'parser' and 'schema processor' are therefore often used interchangeably. A clearer separation would require the parser to perform only a well-formed validation while it creates an in-memory representation of the entire document instance before it tells the schema processor to validate this representation against a specified schema definition. The processor might also validate against a DTD before validating against a schema definition.

2.9   **Data Types**

A significant feature of the XML Schema language is its ability to create and utilize **data types**. A data type constrains values to a range or set of suitable possibilities. This concept does not add new markup constructs to the XML language, so a value that conforms to a data type is still expressed as an attribute value or as element content. Consider the Date element in the BroadcastDetails element of the program broadcast example, the Date element in the email example, and the PublishedDate attribute on the Book element in the third example document type. These elements and attributes may have different names and are found in different document models, yet they share the single important characteristic that the values they contain must conform to identical rules. In this case, the values must be valid and recognizable dates.

Two kinds of data types are supported by the standard.

A **simple data type** does not allow any XML markup to occur within a compliant value and is the only kind of data type that can be assigned to an attribute. The standard includes a number of 'built-in' simple data types, including 'string' ('hello world'), 'integer' (123), and 'date' ('2002-05-17'), but a schema definition author may create more specific simple data types.

A **complex data type** *does* allow XML markup to occur and may also include attribute declarations and so can be assigned to an element. An element declares that it conforms to the given complex data type and may also specify that its content, or any of its attributes, conforms to a simple data type constraint. There are no built-in complex data types, so the schema definition author must create one before it can be used.

The presence of data types allows values to be checked for compliance with detailed rules. If a processing application is aware that some values do not conform to its expectations in advance, it can more easily recover from this error by simply refusing to process the document at all. This is much tidier than discovering halfway through processing that the document does not conform, resulting in the application either crashing, corrupting data, or having to undo the changes already made. In addition, a processing application that has no prior knowledge of the document model can extract useful information about that model. For example, a freetext searching application that accepts document instances conforming to many different document models might have different algorithms for indexing text and purely numeric data and would benefit from prior knowledge of where data of each kind appears.

Assuming that an application can access and interrogate a schema definition, it can then identify common structures even when they are defined in disparate element declarations. For example, it would be possible, using the XML Query standard,

to count all email addresses from email without knowing all of the elements used
to hold these addresses:

```
import schema "eMail.xsd"
declare namespace E="http://MegaTVi.com/NS/EMAIL"

count(
  document("emails.xml")//E:*[. instance of element of
  type E:eMailAddress]
)
```

Those familiar with XSLT stylesheets may also see the benefit of being able to
specify a template for all elements that conform to a given data type, as will be possible in XSLT 2.0:

```
<template match="*[. instance of eMailAddress]">
  ...
</template>
```

The fact that such useful information is contained in the document model rather
than the document instance is a little disconcerting, but there are precedents for this
approach (many XML documents cannot be interpreted without a DTD, perhaps
because it assigns default attribute values, and the 'standalone="no"' parameter
of the XML declaration identifies such documents).

However, despite their undoubted strengths, data types have their limitations. Just
because the value of an attribute or the content of an element is confirmed to be a
valid instance of the data type assigned to the attribute or element, this does not
mean that the value is actually correct. The value could be a valid date, for example, but still happen to be the wrong date, or even a meaningless string of characters that accidentally resembles a date.

3. Schema Definitions

A schema definition is an XML document that conforms to a document model defined in the XML Schema standard. This model includes XML structures that declare elements and attributes, define data types, and allow comments to be added. It adopts a number of conventions that one should appreciate before delving into specific features.

3.1 Schema Documents

A schema definition is an XML document (or several linked documents) that conforms to the XML Schema standard. It can therefore be created by any XML authoring application. Also available are a number of schema definition authoring tools that, in many cases, hide the XML markup described below behind a visual user interface.

Naming conventions

In general, the names of elements and attributes defined by the XML Schema standard employ lowercase letters. When a name is composed of two or more words, the second and subsequent words have an initial capital letter (such as `complexType`), though there are exceptions (the `appinfo` and `keyref` elements, and the `xpath` attribute).

Root element

The root element is called **schema**:

```
<schema ...>
   ...
</schema>
```

An XML declaration may precede the root element, and a document type declaration may be included to reference a DTD for schemas (see Chapter 20) or to hold entity definitions (that perhaps help construct the model).

Schema definition version

The `schema` element has an optional **version** attribute. This attribute can be used by schema definition authors to identify the version of the schema definition when the definition undergoes periodic updates:

```
<!-- MyDoc Version 1.6 - Author N. Bradley -->
<schema version="1.6" ...>...</schema>
```

This attribute is therefore *not* used to identify the version of the XML Schema standard to which the model conforms, and indeed there is no mechanism to do this. It must be hoped that future versions of this language will either be fully backward compatible or will introduce such a mechanism.

Schema definition namespace

Schema definition documents belong to the XML Schema namespace (see Chapter 21 for more on namespaces) and must identify themselves as such. Therefore, the xmlns attribute must be added and given the value 'http://www.w3.org/2001/XMLSchema':

```
<schema xmlns="http://www.w3.org/2001/XMLSchema">
...
</schema>
```

Typically, the default namespace is not used, and when this is the case the elements usually have a prefix of '**xsd**' (standing for 'XML Schema Definition'):

```
<xsd:schema
        xmlns:xsd="http://www.w3.org/2001/XMLSchema">
...
</xsd:schema>
```

Indeed, it is essential that the default namespace *not* be used for a schema definition if it is going to be employed to validate documents that do not belong to a namespace (for reasons that are discussed in Section 6.2).

Top-level elements

Within the schema element, a number of **top-level elements** can occur. They fall into two groups, and all elements from one group must appear before any elements from the second group.

The first group of elements manage the schema definition itself when it is spread across a number of data files, or include rules from other schema definitions (see Chapter 13). The following elements must appear before the elements shown later (and import elements should appear before any of the others):

```
<schema>
  <!-- SCHEMA MANAGEMENT -->
  <import>...</import>
  <include.../>
  <redefine>...</redefine>
  ...

</schema>
```

The second group of elements includes element and attribute declarations, and data type definitions, among other model-building instructions. Each one creates a **component** of the document model:

```
<schema>
  <!-- SCHEMA MANAGEMENT -->

  ...

  <!-- MODEL-BUILDING COMPONENTS -->

  <notation>...</notation>
  <simpleType>...</simpleType>
  <complexType>...</complexType>
  <attributeGroup>...</attributeGroup>
  <attribute ... />
  <group>...</group>
  <element>...</element>
</schema>
```

The ordering of the elements in the second group is not important, and they may be mixed in any combination.

3.2 **Annotations**

Because a schema definition is an XML document, it can include XML comments:

```
<!-- This is a comment -->
```

Comments are very important when the schema definition is large and complex. Indeed, they are so important that a more sophisticated alternative **annotation** technique is available. This feature allows annotations to be divided into human-readable documentation (possibly with language-specific variants) and software-readable instructions. An annotation can apply to the schema definition as a whole, to individual components, or to any part of a component. The **annotation** element can occur before, after, or between elements from the two groups of elements introduced above:

```
<annotation>...</annotation>
```

This element directly contains any number and any mixture of the two other elements discussed below.

The **documentation** element contains human-readable documentation and is therefore equivalent to the basic XML comment feature:

```
<annotation>
  <documentation>This is a comment</documentation>
</annotation>
```

It can include elements from any namespace, such as XHTML formatting elements:

```
<annotation>
  <documentation>
    <html xmlns="http://www.w3.org/1999/xhtml">
      <body><p>This is a comment</p></body>
    </html>
  </documentation>
</annotation>
```

The `xml:lang` attribute can also be used, and the same documentation can then be provided in multiple languages:

```
<annotation>
  <documentation
      xml:lang="en">English comment</documentation>
  <documentation
      xml:lang="fr">commentaire Francais</documentation>
</annotation>
```

The **source** attribute can locate externally held documentation. It holds a URL reference. If this attribute is present, the `documentation` element it is on should be empty:

```
<annotation>
  <documentation xml:lang="en"
          source="http://MegaTVi.com/C/comm55.en" />
  <documentation xml:lang="fr"
          source="http://MegaTVi.com/C/comm55.fr" />
</annotation>
```

The **appinfo** element holds annotations that are aimed at software processing rather than human consumption (note that this element breaks the general rule in this standard that names consisting of two (-part) words use an uppercase letter to begin the second word). Possible content of this element includes software scripts and processing instructions. One popular use of this feature is to include validation instructions from another modeling language required to employ validation techniques that are beyond the capabilities of the XML Schema standard. XML elements conforming to a suitable namespace are expected to be used so that the application can determine whether it is receiving instructions that it can understand:

```
<annotation>
  <appinfo>
    <X:CheckPresentInDatabase
                  xmlns:X="http://MegaTVi.com/schema"
                  Attribute="CoName"
                  DatabaseField="CompanyName" />
  </appinfo>
</annotation>
```

Alternatively, the **source** attribute can hold a URL that locates the information. In the following example, a file called 'validate99.src' is referenced:

```
<annotation>
  <appinfo
      source="http://MegaTVi.com/c/validate99.src" />
</annotation>
```

3.3   Element and Attribute Declarations

The primary purpose of a schema definition is to declare the elements and attributes that constitute the document model.

The schema definition creates a new **element type** by using the **element** element, which includes a **name** attribute to give the element type its name:

```
<element name="Book" ... />

<element name="EMail" ... />

<element name="ProgramBroadcast" ... />
```

Similarly, the schema definition creates a new **attribute type** by using the **attribute** element, which includes a **name** attribute to give the attribute type its name:

```
<attribute name="Author" ... />

<attribute name="Importance" ... />

<attribute name="DegreeOfViolence" ... />
```

Both of these elements can occur directly within the schema element, and the order in which they appear is not important. Attribute types that are declared directly within the schema element can be shared by several element declarations, though there are complications concerning this approach that are explored later. However, attribute elements can also be embedded within element elements, which ties the attribute specifically to that element (the converse is not true, of course, because attributes cannot contain elements):

```
<element name="Book">
  ...
  <attribute name="ISBN" ... />
  <attribute name="Author" ... />
  ...
</element>
```

There are many options for specifying the legal content of an element or attribute type, using a variety of techniques (as explained in the following chapters).

3.4   Data Type Definitions

The **simpleType** element creates a **simple data type**. Its **name** attribute gives the data type a name that can be referenced from element and attribute declarations:

```
<simpleType name="channelNamesList" ... />
```

Some simple data types are so commonly needed that, for convenience, they are built in to the standard itself, so they do not need to be defined in this way. They are referenced by name in the same way, but this time the names are listed in the standard. For example, authors can reference the '**string**' data type (which allows any text string to occur, and is shown in many examples below) without creating a definition (see Section 7.5 for the full list of built-in data types).

The **complexType** element is used to create a complex data type, and the **name** attribute is used in the same way to name it:

```
<complexType name="contentOfTitles" ... />
```

There are no built-in complex data types. Their very complexity makes them too specific for any predefined complex model to be of practical use.

There are no constraints on the order in which data types are defined in the document, and they do not have to appear before the elements and attributes that reference them (though it is, arguably, good practice to define them first).

3.5   Common Attributes

A number of elements in the XML Schema standard have the same attributes, representing similar or identical concepts, and some of these attributes also have potentially confusing purposes. It is therefore worthwhile to have a quick look at these attributes in isolation.

Identifiers

All schema definition elements have an **id** (identifier) attribute. These attributes have no purpose within the schema language and are included only to support other technologies. For example, hypertext links can be created from an XML file that documents the schema definition, with each link targeting the specific component of the model being discussed at the time.

Names and references

The **name** attribute gives elements, attributes, data types, and other constructs an identity so that they can be referenced from elsewhere in the schema definition. But two attributes are commonly used, under different circumstances, to refer to a named definition or declaration, and the distinction between them can be confusing at first.

The **ref** attribute turns the component it is on into a reference to a named component of the same kind. Essentially, it becomes an alias for the named component. For example, when this attribute is used on an element element, it refers to another element element that has a name attribute with the same value:

```
<element name="AnElement"> <!-- DECLARATION -->
  ...
</element>

<element ref="AnElement" /> <!-- REFERENCE -->
```

The name and ref attributes are therefore mutually exclusive. For example, an attribute element cannot be both a declaration of an attribute and at the same time a reference to such a declaration.

The **type** attribute creates a reference to a data type from a component of a different kind, such as an element's declaration:

```
<complexType name="contentOfTitles">...</complexType>

<element name="Title" type="contentOfTitles" />
```

It is not logically possible for an object to both reference a definition elsewhere and also contain a reference to a data type to which it belongs, so the ref and type attributes should never appear together.

One simple way to determine when to use a ref attribute instead of a type attribute is to check that the element name of the target component is the same as the name of the current element. The other way is to recognize that the name of the type attribute refers to a data *type*, either built in to the language or defined by the simple*Type* or complex*Type* elements.

4. Validating Document Instances

A document instance can be validated against an appropriate schema definition in a number of ways, though the most popular approach involves the document instance directly referring to a schema definition that it claims to conform to. Yet there are variants of the same technique that are required to deal with scenarios that include documents or document fragments that belong to namespaces.

4.1 Validation Techniques

For a schema definition to be used to validate a document instance, a schema processor must be given access to both, and this can be achieved in various ways. One simple approach would be to pass both documents to a parser that includes a schema processor. The following imaginary but typical command-line invocation includes the name of the validating utility (in this case, 'validate'), the name of the XML document to be validated (in this case, 'broadcast08.xml'), and the name of the XML Schema definition to validate the document against (in this case, 'pB.xsd' in the 'schemas' directory):

```
C:> validate  broadcast08.xml  \schemas\pB.xsd
```

But it is common practice for a document instance to include an embedded reference to the document model that it claims to belong to. Traditionally, this has been done by the inclusion of the document type declaration that includes a reference to a DTD:

```
<!DOCTYPE ProgramBroadcast
                 SYSTEM "file:///C:/DTDs/pB.dtd">
<ProgramBroadcast>
  ...
</ProgramBroadcast>
```

However, this technique cannot be used to reference a schema definition. In any case, it has long been argued that this is a flawed technique because every document must be edited when the DTD is no longer present at the specified location. Many professionals therefore advised the use of the PUBLIC keyword instead of the SYSTEM keyword, because it is followed by a location-independent document type identifier. The idea is that the parser should look up the actual DTD location in a catalogue that matches identifiers to location paths. A change of DTD location then requires a single edit to be made to the catalogue.

Although a document type declaration cannot be used to reference a schema definition, a similar mechanism that uses attributes on the root element is available. This approach is similar to using the PUBLIC parameter, in that the URL held in the attribute is a permanent identifier that might act as a systemlike schema definition locator but need not do so.

The first approach shown above (the runtime explicit selection of a schema definition) avoids these complications. It is particularly suitable when an organization handles documents that always conform to the same schema definition, and when namespaces are not used. Readers who expect to use only this technique need not read the rest of this chapter, which is concerned with the schema equivalent of the second technique and requires the use of namespaces.

4.2   Namespace Complications

The **Namespaces standard** (http://www.w3.org/TR/REC-xml-names) allows documents to unambiguously contain fragments from different document models, or **namespaces**.

Although namespaces were primarily devised to identify the source of elements and attributes, the XML Schema standard introduces the concept of data types and the assignment of these data types to namespaces. In this book, the following conventions visually distinguish between the three main kinds of object that can be encompassed by a namespace. In the case of data types, the '>"' and '"<' delimiters are a reminder that text that is required to follow a data type constraint can be an attribute value or element content, and the italic text between the delimiters indicates that this is a name that stands in for a real value:

Note that for a standard that is specified in less than 11 printed pages, the Namespaces specification allows some surprisingly complex scenarios to arise (readers who are unfamiliar with namespace concepts and markup should read Chapter 21 before proceeding further).

Unqualified documents

A schema definition can easily create element and attribute declarations that do not belong to a namespace. For example:

```
<xsd:schema
       xmlns:xsd="http://www.w3.org/2001/XMLSchema">
  ...
  <xsd:element name="ProgramBroadcast">
    ...
  </xsd:element>
  ...
</xsd:schema>
```

This schema definition creates the `ProgramBroadcast` element, but this element is not associated with any namespace:

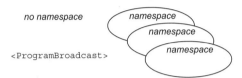

Note the 'xsd:' prefixes in the example above. Namespace prefixes for schema definition elements are essential when the schema definition is used to build a model for documents that do *not* belong to a namespace (which is quite ironic), but the prefixes are not essential when the documents described by the document model do belong to a namespace. Because prefixes make examples harder to read, they are omitted from most of the examples in this book, but in the real world, if only for the sake of consistency, it may be a good idea to always use explicit namespace prefixes, regardless of this distinction.

Foreign fragments

The Namespaces standard allows a document that conforms to one document model to contain elements that conform to other models. There must be a namespace for at least the 'root' element of the embedded fragment for a parser to recognize that the fragment is foreign and to determine its origins. In the following example, the program broadcast document includes metadata that conforms to the Dublin Core Metadata Initiative model (see dublincore.org). Each element beginning with 'dc:' is a fragment that belongs to the namespace associated with this model:

```
<ProgramBroadcast
       xmlns:dc="http://purl.org/dc/elements/1.1/">
  <dc:language>en-uk</dc:language>
  <dc:title>The XML Saga</dc:title>
  <dc:title>Schema Wars</dc:title>
  <dc:creator>MegaTVi Corporation</dc:creator>
  <dc:date>2002-07-21</dc:date>
  <dc:rights>All rights reserved by
  MegaTVi Corp.</dc:rights>
  ...
</ProgramBroadcast>
```

Entire documents can belong to a namespace too. The following example of a **qualified document** has a root element that belongs to the program broadcast namespace:

```
<PB:ProgramBroadcast
        xmlns:dc="http://purl.org/dc/elements/1.1/"
        xmlns:PB="http://MegaTVi.com/NS/PB">
    . . .
</PB:ProgramBroadcast>
```

Throughout this book, the term **unqualified document** indicates XML documents that do not belong to a namespace (even if they contain namespace-qualified fragments).

Namespace awareness of schema definitions

A schema definition can create a concrete implementation of a namespace (the Namespaces standard itself does not include such a feature) in addition to creating the actual document model associated with this namespace. The schema definition creates the elements, attributes, and other things, such as data types, that the namespace will contain, and these items are assigned to the **target namespace** as they are created. The schema definition can then be used to validate documents and document fragments that belong to this namespace.

To make the ProgramBroadcast element type declaration belong to a namespace, schema definition authors must first add the namespace declaration to the schema (note that the value of the namespace declaration matches the value of the declaration in the document instance above, though the prefix it maps to happens to be slightly different):

```
<schema xmlns="http://www.w3.org/2001/XMLSchema"
        xmlns:pB="http://MegaTVi.com/NS/PB">
    . . .
    <element name="ProgramBroadcast">
        . . .
    </element>
    . . .
</schema>
```

The **targetNamespace** attribute on the **schema** element holds the name of the namespace to which declarations and definitions within the schema definition will belong. This attribute must not be used in a schema definition for documents that do not conform to a namespace. As the following example demonstrates, the attribute's value should be the same as the value of one of the namespace declarations (in this case, the program broadcast namespace):

```
<schema xmlns:xsd="http://www.w3.org/2001/XMLSchema"
        xmlns:pB="http://MegaTVi.com/NS/PB"
        targetNamespace="http://MegaTVi.com/NS/PB">

  ...
  <element name="ProgramBroadcast">

    ...
  </element>
  ...
</schema>
```

It may appear that there is needless repetition of the target namespace in the xmlns and targetNamespace attributes and that only one of these attributes should be needed. But a single schema document could include references to elements or attributes from several other schemas, and namespace declarations similar to the 'xmlns:pB' declaration. The targetNamespace attribute therefore serves the necessary purpose of unambiguously identifying the particular namespace that the schema is dedicated to defining.

The ProgramBroadcast element is then assigned to the specified namespace. Of course, the actual element model is not added to the namespace (an ethereal entity incapable of holding such information), and the relevant schema definition is still needed to validate that an element that claims to conform to a namespace really does so.

Global attribute definitions are likewise assigned to this namespace:

```
<attribute name="Violence">...</attribute>
```

The same also applies to named data type definitions (and to other components):

```
<simpleType name="startOrEndTime">...</simpleType>
```

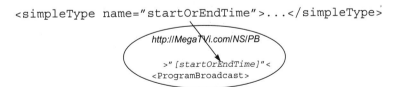

A schema definition can only have one target namespace. Theoretically, this means that there is a one-to-one relationship between a schema definition and a namespace, though many schema definitions actually in existence could target the same namespace, and a document instance could be verified using any one of them.

4.3   Document Instance Namespace Issues

The exact means by which a document instance refers to a schema definition or to multiple schema definitions depends on the way that namespaces are used. There are four scenarios to consider:

- The document does not belong to a namespace, and namespaces are not used for any of the elements and attributes within the document.
- The document belongs to a namespace.
- The document belongs to a namespace and contains at least one fragment from at least one other namespace.
- The document does not belong to a namespace but contains fragments that do.

Each of these scenarios requires in-depth analysis and is discussed in the following sections in the same order as listed above.

Documents without namespaces

The Namespaces standard was developed and released after the XML standard, and therefore many XML documents in existence do not conform to the Namespaces standard. Some of these unqualified documents reference a DTD, whereas others are merely well formed. Either way, it is possible to define a schema model for such documents, then validate these documents against this schema definition.

The concept of namespaces seems to be redundant in this simple scenario. However, one complication may arise, the solution to which introduces namespaces even to these documents.

Before schemas, a reference to a DTD model took the form of a document type declaration. This mechanism is optional, though rarely omitted from documents for which a suitable DTD exists:

```
<!DOCTYPE ProgramBroadcast SYSTEM "pB.dtd">
<ProgramBroadcast...>
  ...
</ProgramBroadcast>
```

This feature cannot be used for schema definitions. Instead, the reference must take the form of an attribute value. This value is interpreted as a URL reference that locates the schema definition. But the attribute containing this URL reference is not really part of the document model, because it belongs to the XML Schema standard instead. Of course, this is a classic example of the problem that raised the need for namespaces, so the Namespaces standard is employed to identify the purpose of the attribute. The namespace required is 'http://www.w3.org/2001/XMLSchema-instance':

```
<ProgramBroadcast
  xmlns:xsi="http://www.w3.org/2001/XMLSchema-instance"
  ...>
  ...
</ProgramBroadcast>
```

One of the attributes associated with this namespace contains the URL reference needed to locate the schema definition. This is the **noNamespaceSchemaLocation** attribute. If this attribute contains only the name of a document file, such as 'pB.xsd', then this is taken to be a relative reference to a file in the same directory as the document:

```
<ProgramBroadcast
  xmlns:xsi="http://www.w3.org/2001/XMLSchema-instance"
  xsi:noNamespaceSchemaLocation="pB.xsd">
  ...
</ProgramBroadcast>
```

Theoretically, this mechanism is optional, and other techniques can be used instead. These include the direct selection and catalog approaches discussed earlier, but in the latter case, the namespace name is equivalent to a public identifier.

Note that the noNamespaceSchemaLocation and xmlns:xsi attributes discussed above must not be defined in the schema model for the document type. A schema processor will understand that these attributes do not belong to that model, and will also recognize that one of the attributes belongs to one of the namespaces defined in the XML Schema standard, and the other belongs to the Namespaces standard itself.

Qualified documents

Many document instances now conform to the Namespaces standard. Only a single attribute needs to be added to the program broadcast document in order to turn it into a namespace-qualified document:

```
<ProgramBroadcast xmlns="http://MegaTVi.com/NS/PB"
                  ...>
  ...
</ProgramBroadcast>
```

In this case, the document instance must include the **schemaLocation** attribute in place of the noNamespaceSchemaLocation attribute. But this attribute does not contain a single value; a pair of values is required instead. The first value in the pair is the namespace name, and the second is the URL reference (in this case 'pB.xsd') that locates the schema document:

```
<ProgramBroadcast
  xmlns="http://MegaTVi.com/NS/PB"
  xmlns:xsi="http://www.w3.org/2001/XMLSchema-instance"
  xsi:schemaLocation="http://MegaTVi.com/NS/PB
                      pB.xsd">
  . . .
</ProgramBroadcast>
```

The namespace reference must exactly match the name in the namespace declaration. The reason why it is needed at all will become apparent later:

```
<ProgramBroadcast
  xmlns="http://MegaTVi.com/NS/PB"
  xmlns:xsi="http://www.w3.org/2001/XMLSchema-instance"
  xsi:schemaLocation="http://MegaTVi.com/NS/PB
                      pB.xsd">
```

Note that, in theory, the location can be a fragment identifier instead of a complete URL, thus allowing the schema definition to be embedded within the same document as the structure to be validated, but not all schema processors will understand this (at the time of this writing):

```
<wrapper>
  <!-- VALIDATE THIS -->
  <ProgramBroadcast
    xmlns:xsi="http://www.w3.org/2001/
               XMLSchema-instance"
    xsi:schemaLocation="http://MegaTVi.com/NS/PB
                        #embeddedSchema" ...>
    . . .
  </ProgramBroadcast>
  <!-- VALIDATE USING THIS -->
  <schema id="embeddedSchema"...>
    . . .
  </schema>
</wrapper>
```

Documents with multiple namespaces

Some qualified documents contain elements or attributes that belong to other namespaces. This is handled by addition of subsequent value pairs (namespace and location) to the **schemaLocation** attribute. In the following example, the Dublin Core namespace is referenced along with the program broadcast namespace. Note that it is not necessary to have a blank line between the pairs of values; a single space character is sufficient):

```
<ProgramBroadcast ...
   xsi:schemaLocation="http://MegaTVi.com/NS/PB
                       pB.xsd

                       http://purl.org/dc/elements/1.1/
                       DublinCore.xsd">
   ...
</ProgramBroadcast>
```

The parser then knows which schema definition to use, and where to find it, when it reaches an element or attribute from a namespace not previously encountered. The schema definition itself does not have to reference the other schema definition files (though it might do so anyway).

It should now be clear why the namespace name is needed. It clarifies which URL reference is associated with each namespace.

Qualified fragments in unqualified documents

There is one circumstance that demands the presence of *both* the **noNamespace-SchemaLocation** attribute *and* the **schemaLocation** attribute. This scenario applies when a document that does not belong to a namespace contains fragments that do. The schema definition for the whole document has no target namespace and is therefore referenced by the noNamespaceSchemaLocation attribute; but schema definitions for the fragments each have a target namespace and are therefore referenced by a value pair in the schemaLocation attribute:

```
<ProgramBroadcast ...
   xsi:noNamespaceSchemaLocation="pB.xsd">
   xsi:schemaLocation="http://purl.org/dc/elements/1.1/
                       DublinCore.xsd">
   ...
</ProgramBroadcast>
```

In another, much less common scenario, a namespace-qualified document can contain a fragment that does not belong to any namespace (an empty value in the namespace declaration is used to achieve this effect), and the same use of both attributes is involved in this case.

4.4   Schema for Schemas

The fact that an XML Schema definition document is itself an XML document raises the intriguing possibility that this application of XML could also be described by a document model. Every schema definition can be considered to be a document instance that belongs to such a model.

A schema definition could be validated by use of a DTD for schemas (see Chapter 20 for an example DTD that can be used for this purpose, and the URL in the SYSTEM parameter below for another):

```
<!DOCTYPE schema
      PUBLIC "-//W3C//DTD XMLSCHEMA 2001//EN"
      SYSTEM "http://www.w3.org/2001/XMLSchema.dtd">
<schema...>
  ...
</schema>
```

Alternatively, a schema definition could be validated by a schema for schemas:

```
<xsd:schema ...
        xmlns:xsd="..."
        xmlns:xsi="..."
        xsi:schemaLocation="
            http://www.w3.org/2001/XMLSchema
            http://www.w3.org/2001/XMLSchema.xsd">
  ...
</xsd:schema>
```

Note that there is a schema definition for schemas at http://www.w3.org/2001/ XMLSchema.xsd.

In practice, a schema definition does not have to refer to an actual schema for schemas. Indeed, this approach would suggest that the schema for schemas would also have to be parsed by another copy of itself, causing an infinite loop to occur. In reality, all the rules in the schema for schemas model are also hard-coded into the logic of every schema processor. The model for schema definitions is the one model that the processor should already understand. However, one good reason for acquiring a schema definition for schemas would be to pass it to a general-purpose XML editor so that it could be used to create schema definitions; thus it could guide the schema author in the same way that resulting schema definitions may be used to guide the authors of conforming document instances.

5. Simple Elements and Attributes

A schema definition declares element and attribute types that may have optional, default or fixed values, or a predefined list of possible values. Elements may also be empty or be allowed to contain text that conforms to a specified data type, and attributes can be either optional or required. This chapter covers the declaration of elements that have simple content (that do not have specific child elements) and attributes.

5.1 Element Declarations

The **element** element declares an element type. It is usually a container for a number of instruction elements that specify what the element can contain, but in one circumstance it has no contents and so may take the form of an empty element:

```
<element name="Book">...</element>

<element name="PageBreak" />
```

The schema definition author is free to create element declarations in any order within the schema element. Reversing the order of the Book and PageBreak element declarations above would have no impact on the model they help to build.

The content of the element element can be simple or complex and takes many possible forms, depending on whether the element that it declares

- is allowed to contain a combination of text and unconstrained child elements;
- is empty and has no attributes;
- has text content that must obey strict rules;
- has unconstrained text content;
- is empty and has attributes;
- has both text content and attributes;
- has both strictly controlled text content and attributes;
- has specific child elements (see Chapter 6);
- has a mixture of text content and specific child elements (see Section 7.3).

Apart from the final two possibilities, these scenarios are explored in the remainder of this section (in the same order as they are listed above).

Any content

The simplest possible construct is an empty `element` element:

```
<element name="Anything" />
```

This is shorthand for a larger declaration that allows any configuration of elements, mixed with text, to occur:

```
<Anything>Some Text and an <Emph>element</Emph>
here.</Anything>
```

At this point, it should be noted that the allowed content of an element can be defined elsewhere in the form of a **data type**, which is referenced from the **type** attribute. Any number of elements can specify that their content must conform to the constraints of a particular data type. The following declaration is equivalent to the one above, but explicitly references the '**anyType**' data type:

```
<element name="Anything" type="anyType" />
```

This data type specifies no constraints at all on the value, which may therefore consist of text, defined elements (from any declared namespace or from no namespace), or even a mixture of text with elements (as shown above). However, the content of each of these elements must be valid according to the relevant element declarations.

Note that the example above is itself shorthand for the following, much more complex, declaration, involving element structures that are explained later:

```
<element name="Anything">
  <complexType mixed="true">
    <sequence>
      <any minOccurs="0" maxOccurs="unbounded"/>
    </sequence>
  </complexType>
</element>
```

Empty 'placeholder' elements

With only a little more effort, an empty element that has no content and no attributes (a '**placeholder**' element) can be created. Its presence in a document instance would simply indicate the existence and location of something in the narrative text stream. For example, the schema definition for a book might include an element that forces a page break to occur at an earlier point than would happen by default.

This requirement involves the use of the **complexType** element. Normally, this element holds instructions that create or reference other element declarations while indicating where instances of these elements may be allowed to occur within the element currently being declared. However, in this case, child elements are not wanted, so the complexType element is empty:

```
<element name="PageBreak"><complexType/></element>
```

Despite the lack of content, the rules of the XML standard permit the use of a start tag and and end tag, but the meaning remains the same:

```
<element name="PageBreak">
  <complexType></complexType>
</element>
```

This construct allows the following empty element tag to appear in a document instance:

```
<PageBreak/>
```

Again, the following can also appear because the XML standard makes no distinction between these two ways of creating an empty element:

```
<PageBreak></PageBreak>
```

By including the complexType element but not adding any attributes or content to this element, this construct is stating that there must be no subelements and no text. This is shorthand for the following (the complexContent and restriction elements are described later):

```
<complexType>
<!-- NO TEXT CONTENT ALLOWED (mixed='false') -->
  <complexContent>
     <restriction base="anyType">
        <!-- NO ELEMENTS ARE REFERENCED -->
     </restriction>
  </complexContent>
</complexType>
```

Simple content

When an element is allowed to contain text, it can be stated that the content must conform to a **data type**, such as an integer value or a date that must follow a precise format (such as 'dd/mm/yyyy'). The **type** attribute is added to the element element for this purpose. For example, one of the least restrictive of the available data types is the '**string**' data type, and another data type that is popular is the '**integer**' data type (the full range of ready-made data types is listed in Section 7.5).

The 'string' data type is commonly used to specify that the element can contain any text string:

```
<element name="Title" type="string" />
```

```
<Title>Title Conforming To 'string' Type</Title>
```

The 'integer' data type is commonly used to specify that the element can contain a simple numeric value:

```
<element name="Score" type="integer" />
```

```
<Score>178</Score>
```

Recall that it is possible to create new simple data types (see Chapter 14), which can then be referenced within the same schema definition or even from within other schema definitions.

An alternative method uses an embedded **complexType** element to allow an element to contain text. This element holds a **mixed** attribute, which can be given the value '**true**' to give the declared element mixed content, thus allowing text to be 'mixed' with child elements. But, in this simple scenario, there happen to be no elements to mix with the text:

```
<element name="Title">
  <complexType mixed="true" />
</element>
```

This approach is too verbose for this simple requirement, but it is essential for other scenarios that are covered later.

Default element values

An element can be given a default value that applies only when the element is present but has no content. The **default** attribute gives an element this default value:

```
<element name="OneThousand" type="integer"
                            default="1000" />
```

The following three instances of the OneThousand element are then deemed to be equivalent:

```
<OneThousand/>
```

```
<OneThousand></OneThousand>
```

```
<OneThousand>1000</OneThousand>
```

However, this feature is only applicable to elements that do not have required child element content (it can still be used when all the child elements are optional). This is a necessary constraint because an attribute is used to specify the default value and element tags (in this case, to specify default required child elements) cannot be included in an attribute value.

This feature does not always work as might be expected, depending on the data type selected. It is obvious when an integer value is absent because all integers must include at least one digit, but it is not so obvious when a string value is missing, because it is also possible for a string to be present that just happens to contain no characters (software developers will be familiar with the concept of an empty string value or variable). Also, the default value will often be inserted when an element contains only whitespace, again depending on the data type, because many data types require whitespace characters to be removed before interpretation of the value (see Section 7.6).

Default values do not apply when the element is missing, and they do not apply if the xsi:nil attribute is added to the element and given the value 'true' (see Section 7.7). Note that attributes can also have default values, but the default *does* apply when the attribute is absent and does *not* apply when it is present but empty.

Fixed values

It is possible to specify a value for an element that cannot be changed in any document instance that includes the element, and the **fixed** attribute provides the value that will always apply. At first sight, this appears to be a superfluous feature. If the value of an element is always the same, then its presence in a document instance surely adds nothing useful to the document. But this feature could be used for important boilerplate content. For example, an organization that distributes program broadcast details may wish to see its name in every document instance that is created (or at least prevent other organization names from replacing it):

```
<element name="CreatedBy" type="notEmptyString"
                    fixed="MegaTVi Corp." />
```

In this case, the following examples in an instance document are all legal:

```
<CreatedBy/>
```

```
<CreatedBy></CreatedBy>
```

```
<CreatedBy>MegaTVi Corp.</CreatedBy>
```

But the following example is not legal:

```
<CreatedBy>AnotherTVi Corp.</CreatedBy>
```

However, if the document model allows the element to be omitted, then its absence remains acceptable even when a fixed value is defined.

As with default values, and for the same reason, this feature cannot be used if the element has required element content.

This approach will also not work for values that conform to the 'string' data type. The example above conforms to a data type called 'notEmptyString', which defines a string that must consist of at least one character. In this way, it becomes possible to detect the absence of a value of this type. This data type is not part of the standard. It needs to be created within the schema definition (by techniques described in Section 14.7 to restrict a 'token' data type to contain at least one non-whitespace character).

Another surprising aspect of this feature, again depending on the data type, is that the value might be present in the document instance in a form different from the value in the `fixed` attribute, yet still be considered to be a valid match. When the data type is 'integer', for example, the following instances are all valid (this topic is fully explored in Section 14.6):

```
<element name="Thirteen" type="integer" fixed="13" />

<Thirteen/>

<Thirteen></Thirteen>

<Thirteen>13</Thirteen>

<Thirteen>0013</Thirteen>

<Thirteen>   +13   </Thirteen>
```

It would not make sense to include both a default value and a fixed value in the same element declaration. Indeed, this is actually illegal, even if the same value appears in both the `default` and `fixed` attributes.

Confined set of possible values (enumeration)

The legal text content of an element can be constrained in various ways. One of the most popular requirements is to constrain the value to one of a list of possible options. For example, a list of country codes ensures that the country in which a program broadcast occurred is a real country (the elements used to construct this list are also used for many other purposes and are explained in Section 14.5):

```
<element name="Country">
  <simpleType>
    <restriction base="string">
      <enumeration value="uk" />
      <enumeration value="us" />
      <enumeration value="fr" />
      <enumeration value="de" />
      . . .
    </restriction>
  </simpleType>
</element>
```

Program broadcasts must occur on an actual TV station. In the UK, the list of valid values (for terrestrial stations) would be 'BBC1', 'BBC2', 'ITV1', 'Channel4', and 'Five'.

5.2 Attribute Declarations

An attribute declaration is similar to an element declaration. The **attribute** element may contain a **type** attribute that refers to a data type to be used to constrain its value. Again, the 'string' data type is appropriate when no constraints are required (beyond those set by the XML standard):

```
<attribute name="Author" type="string" />
```

If this attribute is associated with the book element, then the following example is legal:

```
<Book Author="J Smith">...</Book>
```

There are various ways of attaching an attribute to an element declaration. If the attribute declaration applies to only one element type, then it can be embedded within the element declaration (but only indirectly, and where it appears depends on various factors yet to be discussed).

Attributes on empty elements

The simplest scenario is that attributes need to be added to an empty element. The reason is that an element that contains attributes is considered to be a complex element. The element declaration must therefore contain a **complexType** element, which in turn contains the attribute declarations:

```
<element name="Image">
  <complexType>
    <!-- NO ELEMENTS (none referenced) -->
    <attribute name="Format" type="string"/>
    <attribute name="Ref" type="string"/>
  </complexType>
</element>
```

As soon as the complexType element is employed, it is no longer possible for the element element to refer to a simple data type in order to constrain its content. The type attribute is therefore absent in the example above, which is, of course, desirable when the element must be empty:

```
<Image Format="GIF" Ref="images/boat.gif" />
```

Attributes on elements with content

When elements have both attributes and content, it is not possible to simply put the type attribute back onto the element element in order to specify constraints on the nature of the content, but two very different techniques can be employed instead. One is simple to understand and create but does not include the ability to choose a data type. The alternative permits selection of a data type but involves some complex techniques to implement.

The first technique revives the mixed content concept and therefore requires the complexType element to be present and the mixed attribute to be added and set to the value 'true'. The declared element is then allowed to contain any text:

```
<element name="Para">
  <complexType mixed="true">
    <attribute name="Language" type="string" />
  </complexType>
</element>
```

This technique permits the following to occur in a document instance:

```
<Para Language="English">This is an English
paragraph.</Para>
```

Note, however, that it does not allow a data type to be referenced to place constraints on the possible content of the element.

The second technique is more complicated to implement but does allow a data type to be referenced. It exploits the fact that a complex element may be complex only because it has attributes and not because it needs to contain child elements. Although the complexType element is needed, as before, to allow the attributes to be declared, it now includes a simpleContent element:

```
<element name="Para">
  <complexType>
    <simpleContent>
      ...
        <!-- ATTRIBUTE DECLARATIONS -->
      ...
    </simpleContent>
  </complexType>
</element>
```

Unfortunately, attribute declarations cannot be embedded directly within the simpleContent element. They must be treated as an extension to whichever simple data type is wanted. Using the base attribute, the embedded extension element references the data type that will be extended to include the attribute. Finally, this element encloses the attribute declarations that are to constitute the nature of this extension (and possibly other extensions, as discussed in Section 16.7):

```
<element name="Para">
  <complexType>
    <simpleContent>
      <extension base="string">
        <!-- ATTRIBUTE DECLARATIONS -->
      </extension>
    </simpleContent>
  </complexType>
</element>
```

Required and prohibited attributes

An attribute is optional by default. If it happens not to be present, an application that is processing the element must interpret this as it sees fit. However, an attribute can be made mandatory or, at the other extreme, can even be prohibited. But the **use** attribute has a default value of '**optional**', so the following declarations are equivalent:

```
<attribute name="ISBN" ... />

<attribute name="ISBN" use="optional" ... />
```

If the use attribute is given the value '**required**', then a document instance author is not allowed to omit the attribute. The first of the two examples below is then invalid:

```
<Book>...</Book> <!-- ERROR -->

<Book ISBN="0 201 77059 8">...</Book>
```

When the use attribute is given the value '**prohibited**', it is the second example above that becomes invalid. The two main uses of this option are to temporarily comment out an attribute declaration from the document model and to restrict a derived complex data type so that the restricted variant cannot use an attribute that is allowed in the original (see Section 16.6).

Default attribute values

An attribute can be given a default value. This value applies only when the attribute is absent. The **default** attribute holds the value that is to be assumed when the attribute is not present:

```
<attribute name="ISBN" default="unknown" ... />
```

The following examples are then equivalent:

```
<Book ISBN="unknown">...</Book>

<Book>...</Book>
```

However, the default value does *not* apply if the attribute is present but has no content (regardless of the data type of the attribute value). Contrast this behavior with the default feature when it is applied to element content, in which an empty element *is* given the default value and a missing element is *not*, and in which the chosen data type has an impact on whether the default is applied when the value is present but empty.

When an attribute is required, it does not make sense to define a default value, because this default will never be given an opportunity to be used. Such a combination is therefore illegal.

Fixed attribute values

It is possible to specify a value for an attribute that cannot be changed in a document instance. The **fixed** attribute provides the value that will always apply. The reasons why this feature can be useful were explained earlier (because element declarations share this feature):

```
<attribute name="CreatedBy" type="string"
                    fixed="MegaTVi Corp." />
```

This value is automatically inserted into the element if the attribute is not already present.

As with element content, the data type assigned to the attribute may be significant. For example, if the data type is 'integer', then a value of '01' will be considered to be a match for the fixed value '1', but the processor would raise an error if the data type was 'string'.

An attribute can be both fixed and required so that the attribute must both be present in every document instance and have the same value every time.

Confined set of possible values (enumeration)

The legal text content of an attribute can be constrained in various ways. One of the most popular requirements is to limit the value to one of a predefined set of possible options. The means by which this can be done is identical to the use of this mechanism to control the values of elements (this feature is fully explained in Section 14.5):

```
<attribute name="Country">
  <simpleType>
    <restriction base="string">
      <enumeration value="uk" />
      <enumeration value="us" />
      <enumeration value="fr" />
      ...
    </restriction>
  </simpleType>
</attribute>
```

Namespace issues

An attribute created within an element declaration is known as a **local attribute** because it applies only to that element. A namespace prefix is not usually added to an attribute name unless the attribute has been borrowed from another namespace. The **form** attribute can be added to the `attribute` element to override this behaviour. When set to '**qualified**' (in place of the default value of '**unqualified**'), the namespace prefix must be added to the name when it is used in a document instance. Alternatively, when many attributes are involved, it is easier to set the **attributeFormDefault** attribute on the **schema** element to the same value. However, many authorities on good document model design frown on this technique because it contradicts both tradition and the intent of the namespaces feature. Qualified attributes should be reserved for global attributes that belong to other namespaces (see Chapter 10).

When a schema document is included in another schema document (see Chapter 13), the setting of the `attributeFormDefault` attribute is not overriden and therefore continues to apply to all of the components in the included document, even when this attribute has a different setting in the including document.

6. Defining Document Structures

One of the most powerful features of XML is its ability to create significant relationships between elements through their arrangement into sequential and hierarchical structures. The XML Schema standard applies appropriate constraints on these relationships by specifying exactly what is allowed within each element type.

6.1 Document Structures

It has been seen that an element can hold text that conforms to the 'string' data type or allows text content because the `mixed` attribute value is set to 'true'. But these features alone are not sufficient to create useful XML documents. With nothing but simple text strings, the only XML document possible would be one that involves a single element. XML documents typically contain additional elements that divide the document into distinct and individually meaningful components. Frequently, these documents have a simple two-level structure in which the root element contains a straightforward sequence of child elements:

```
<EMail>
   <From>...</From>
   <To>...</To>
   <Title>...</Title>
   <Date>...</Date>
   <Message>...</Message>
</EMail>
```

At the other extreme, XML documents that represent narrative works, such as reference books, tend to have deep and complex structures, often involving a choice of elements at various points (this paragraph is the second paragraph of the first section of the sixth chapter of this book and is mixed with examples and other paragraphs).

The main concern of most XML modeling languages is to place sensible constraints on such structures. All of these modeling languages, including the XML Schema standard, adopt a top-down approach by specifying the allowed content of each element that contributes to the document structure.

6.2 Child Element References

A declaration of an element includes a specification of its allowed content, which could include child elements. When an element allowed as a child has previously been declared elsewhere in the schema definition, it is necessary to include a reference to that declaration. The **element** element references an element declaration (as well as creates one). In this case, however, the **ref** attribute replaces the name attribute. The value of this attribute must match the value of the name attribute of the other element declaration (essential markup around the reference is omitted from the example below and is discussed later):

```
<element name="From">...</element>

<element name="EMail">
   ...
     <element ref="From" />
   ...
</element>
```

Note that a reference can even be made to the enclosing element declaration, thus creating a potentially infinite loop (a recursive model). For example, a model that represents a computer disk directory structure could include a Folder element that can contain any number of child Folder elements:

```
<element name="Folder">
   ...
     <element ref="Folder"/>
   ...
</element>


   <Folder>
     <Folder>
       <Folder>...</Folder>
     </Folder>
   </Folder>
```

The element that is referenced can be declared in a different schema definition. For this reason, even when a foreign element declaration is not referenced, a namespace prefix is required in the reference when the current schema definition targets a namespace and the namespace declaration includes a prefix:

```
<schema xmlns="http://www.w3.org/2001/XMLSchema"
        xmlns:E="http://MegaTVi.com/NS/EMAIL"
        targetNamespace="http://MegaTVi.com/NS/EMAIL">
  <element name="From">...</element>
  <element name="EMail">
     ...
       <element ref="E:From" />
     ...
  </element>
</schema>
```

The `name` attribute value must not include the 'E:' prefix in the declaration of the `From` element, even though the reference to it does contain this prefix. It is absent because it is not needed. The schema processor already knows which target namespace to assign the element declaration to.

Note that the prefix 'DOC:' is used throughout this book for miscellaneous examples, and 'E:' is used for email examples, 'PB:' for program broadcast examples, and 'B:' for book examples.

The prefix is not needed when there is no target namespace and also when there *is* a target namespace but no prefix in the namespace declaration. In the latter case, the schema definition elements and data types must have a prefix:

```
<xsd:schema
        xmlns:xsd="http://www.w3.org/2001/XMLSchema"
        xmlns="http://MegaTVi.com/NS/EMAIL"
        targetNamespace="http://MegaTVi.com/NS/EMAIL">

    <xsd:element name="From">...</element>

    <xsd:element name="EMail">
       ...
        <xsd:element ref="From" />
       ...
    </xsd:element>

</xsd:schema>
```

But this approach is not recommended if some references are to elements in other schema definitions that also have a target namespace. The reason is that there will then be a mixture of references that do include prefixes and references that do not, and it may then be difficult to remember when to add one.

6.3   Complex Type Elements

When an element declaration is required to specify that child elements are allowed, it directly contains the **complexType** element:

```
<element name="EMail">
  <complexType>
     ...
  </complexType>
</element>
```

Note that in this location, the `complexType` element defines an **anonymous complex type**. It is anonymous because it has no name (see Section 16.2 for details on complex type definitions that are named and can therefore be referenced for reuse).

Within this element, it is possible to reference child elements (and also declare them). First, however, it is necessary to specify how these elements will be organized. They may have to appear in a predefined order, they may have no order constraint at all, or they consist of a set of alternatives from which a document instance author can choose only one.

6.4 Sequence of Elements

Child elements often need to occur in a specific order. The **sequence** element specifies that instances of the enclosed list of declared elements must appear within a document instance and in the same order as the references (or declarations) within this element:

```
<element name="EMail">
  <complexType>
    <sequence>
      <!-- SEQUENCE OF ELEMENTS -->
      ...
    </sequence>
  </complexType>
</element>
```

For example:

```
<schema xmlns:E="...">

  <element name="From">...</element>
  <element name="To">...</element>
  <element name="Title">...</element>
  <element name="Date">...</element>
  <element name="Message">...</element>

  <element name="EMail">
    <complexType>
      <sequence>
        <element ref="E:From" />
        <element ref="E:To" />
        <element ref="E:Title" />
        <element ref="E:Date" />
        <element ref="E:Message" />
      </sequence>
    </complexType>
  </element>

</schema>
```

The following document instance is valid according to this model of the EMail element:

```
<EMail xmlns="...">
  <From>...</From>
  <To>...</To>
  <Title>...</Title>
  <Date>...</Date>
  <Message>......</Message>
</EMail>
```

However, the following document instance is not valid. The `Title` element is in the wrong location, though this might actually be seen by a schema processor as two distinct errors:

```
<EMail xmlns="...">
  <!-- ERROR - TITLE MUST NOT APPEAR HERE -->
  <Title>...</Title>
  <From>...</From>
  <To>...</To>
  <!-- ERROR - TITLE IS MISSING HERE -->
  <Date>...</Date>
  <Message>......</Message>
</EMail>
```

Note that element references cannot appear directly within the `complexType` element. The `sequence` element, or one of the alternatives to this element introduced later, therefore needs to be employed even when there is only one element reference (but see Section 18.5 for reasons why a single child element is rarely a good idea unless it it allowed to repeat):

```
<sequence>
  <element ref="DOC:OnlyChild" />
</sequence>
```

Sequence constraints will often appear to be unnecessary. While it might, for example, be desirable for authors to create email that includes the title before the message, no information would be lost if this order were reversed. Yet it can be useful to employ a sequence even when, as in this example, there is no compelling reason to enforce this constraint on document instance authors, because it facilitates precise control over complex combinations of elements. For example, it will be shown that with this approach it is easy to specify that there can be only one `From` element, that the `Title` element is optional, and that the `To` element can be repeated. Alternatives to the `sequence` element do not share this capability.

6.5   Optional and Repeating Elements

By default, a reference to an element indicates that this element *must* be present in the document instance. The `EMail` element declaration above therefore stipulates that the `From`, `To`, `Title`, `Date`, and `Message` elements are all mandatory. The following document instance is therefore incorrect:

```
<EMail xmlns="...">
  <From>...</From>
  <To>...</To>
  <!-- ERROR - TITLE IS MISSING-->
  <Date>...</Date>
  <Message>......</Message>
</EMail>
```

Optional elements

If the information that an element is designed to contain is simply not available, then there is no need for the element itself to be present. The presence of the following element adds no value to the document:

```
<Title></Title>
```

It is certainly possible for an email author not to supply a title. In the case above, it would be better for the Title element to be absent rather than just empty (but see also the xsi:nil attribute, which is discussed in Section 7.7).

So that an element can be omitted without causing an error, the **minOccurs** attribute is added to the element reference and given the value '0', meaning that it can be absent:

```
<element ref="E:Title" minOccurs="0" />
```

It is important to recognize that it is the reference that is given this occurrence indicator rather than the declaration of the element. The same element could be referenced elsewhere and not be optional at that location. For example, consider a document that must have at least one title but may have two. In this case, two references could be used as follows (though this is not the most efficient way to achieve this effect):

```
<element ref="DOC:Title" />
<element ref="DOC:Title" minOccurs="0" />
```

The default value of the minOccurs attribute is '1', meaning that the referenced element must occur at least once. The following two examples are therefore equivalent:

```
<element ref="E:Title" />
```

```
<element ref="E:Title" minOccurs="1" />
```

Repeatable elements

As shown above, an element can be made to occur twice, or more often, simply by repetition of the element reference within a sequence model. But it is also possible to state that an element is repeatable many times, using a single reference. This feature has a number of subtle variants, but for now the possibility that any number of further occurrences would be legal can be explored. For example, email is often sent to more than one person, and an email system may have no limit on how many people an email can be sent to. The **maxOccurs** attribute can be added to a reference and given the value '**unbounded**' (there is no upper bound on the number of occurrences allowed):

```
<element ref="E:To" maxOccurs="unbounded" />
```

The following example is now valid:

```
<EMail xmlns="...">
  <From>...</From>
  <To>J_Smith@MegaTVi.com</To>
  <To>P_Jones@MegaTVi.com</To>
  <To>M_Wilkins@MegaTVi.com</To>
  <Title>...</Title>
  <Date>...</Date>
  <Message>...</Message>
</EMail>
```

Again, the default value of this attribute is '1', and the following two examples are therefore equivalent:

```
<element ref="E:Title" />
```

```
<element ref="E:Title" maxOccurs="1" />
```

Optional and repeatable elements

Because two attributes control the number of occurrences allowed, there is the potential for them to be used together to cater to additional possibilities. For example, an element can be both optional and infinitely repeatable:

```
<element ... minOccurs="0" maxOccurs="unbounded" />
```

If a `BlindCarbonCopy` element were added to the email example, it would be a good candidate for this feature. Email is typically sent without any blind carbon copy recipients (people whose names are not seen by other recipients) but is occasionally sent to one or more people in this way. The two attributes introduced above can be used together to achieve this requirement:

```
<element ref="BlindCarbonCopy"
         minOccurs="0" maxOccurs="unbounded" />
```

Range of occurrences

The mimimum number of permitted elements can be larger than '1' and the maximum does not have to be '0', '1', or 'unbounded'. Any number can be used in both the `minOccurs` and `maxOccurs` attributes. For example, it is possible to state that a book must contain at least five chapters and at most fifteen chapters:

```
<element ref="B:Chapter" minOccurs="5"
                          maxOccurs="15" />
```

It is even possible to stipulate that the element must occur an exact number of times. However, in the following example, in which both attributes are set to the value '1', this simply makes the default settings explicit:

```
<element ref="B:From" minOccurs="1"
                       maxOccurs="1" />
```

The maximum value must be at least as large as the minimum value. A minimum value of '10' and a maximum value of '5' would certainly be senseless but, more importantly, such an illogical constraint could never be fulfilled.

Unusable elements

It is not illegal to set the maximum occurrence setting to zero, provided that the minimum is also set to zero. Of course, these settings imply that the element cannot be used at all:

```
<element ref="E:BlindCarbonCopy" minOccurs="0"
                                 maxOccurs="0" />
```

There seems to be little point in referencing an element, then stating that it cannot be used after all. Yet this happens to be a convenient way to, perhaps temporarily, 'comment out' a reference. But the main use of this feature is to support the use of complex data types that are derived by restriction from other data types, because it allows an element to be disallowed in the derived type (see Section 16.6 for more details).

6.6 Choice of Elements

The optional occurrence feature gives the document instance author a choice of actions, albeit in a crude and inadequate fashion. Two elements can both be made optional, and authors can be instructed to insert only one of them into a document. But this technique would not physically prevent the author from inserting both or neither of these elements:

```
<sequence>
  <element ref="B:Parts" minOccurs="0" />
  <element ref="B:Chapters" minOccurs="0" />
</sequence>
```

A required and exclusive choice can be specified by use of the **choice** element in place of the sequence element. In the following example, both the Parts element and the Chapters element have default minimum occurrence values of '1', so they both appear to be required, but the surrounding choice element stipulates that only one of these elements can actually be selected:

```
<element name="Book">
  <complexType>
    <choice>
      <element ref="B:Parts" />
      <element ref="B:Chapters" />
    </choice>
  </complexType>
</element>
```

The two examples below are legal:

```
<Book><Parts>...</Parts></Book>

<Book><Chapters>...</Chapters></Book>
```

But the following examples are not legal:

```
<Book><!-- ERROR - MISSING ELEMENT --></Book>

<Book>
  <!-- ERROR - BOTH ELEMENTS PRESENT -->
  <Parts>...</Parts>
  <Chapters>...</Chapters>
</Book>
```

However, authors can avoid the first error above if the containing Book element can be empty, simply by specifying a minimum occurrence value of '0' on at least one of the element references. When the container is empty in a document instance, it is assumed that the optional element would have been selected, but happened not to be (as odd as this might sound):

```
<choice>
  <complexType>
    <element ref="B:Parts" minOccurs="0" />
    <element ref="B:Chapters" />
  </complexType>
</choice>
```

6.7 Complex Models

The sequence and choice elements can be embedded within each other any number of times and to any number of levels. Each of these elements can also be embedded within another instance of the same element. Such combinations can be used to create sophisticated models.

Sequences within choices

A sequence element can be placed within a choice element so that a sequence of elements can be included as one of the options. In the program broadcast example, an author should be able to include either the ProgramTitle element or the SeriesTitle, EpisodeTitle and EpisodeNumber elements:

```
<choice>
  <element ref="PB:ProgramTitle" />
  <sequence>
    <element ref="PB:SeriesTitle" />
    <element ref="PB:EpisodeTitle" />
    <element ref="PB:EpisodeNumber" />
  </sequence>
</choice>
```

Choices within sequences

A choice element can be placed within a sequence element so that a choice of elements can be made available at a specific point in a sequence. In the program broadcast example, the choice shown above needs to be included in a larger sequence:

```
<sequence>
  <element ref="PB:Ratings />
  <choice>
    <element ref="PB:ProgramTitle" />
    <sequence>
      <element ref="PB:SeriesTitle" />
      <element ref="PB:EpisodeTitle" />
      <element ref="PB:EpisodeNumber" />
    </sequence>
  </choice>
  <element ref="PB:BroadcastDetails" />
  <element ref="PB:Description" />
</sequence>
```

The example above actually demonstrates a three-level model because it involves a sequence within a choice within a sequence. It permits both of the following document instance fragments:

```
<ProgramDetails>
  <Ratings>...</Ratings>

  <ProgramTitle>A Brief History of XML</ProgramTitle>

  <BroadcastDetails>...</BroadcastDetails>
  <Description>...</Description>
</ProgramDetails>

<ProgramDetails>
  <Ratings>...</Ratings>

  <SeriesTitle>The XML Saga</SeriesTitle>
  <EpisodeTitle>Schema Wars</EpisodeTitle>
  <EpisodeNumber>5</EpisodeNumber>

  <BroadcastDetails>...</BroadcastDetails>
  <Description>...</Description>
</ProgramDetails>
```

Occurrence rules on groups

The **minOccurs** attribute and the **maxOccurs** attribute can be used on the **sequence** and **choice** elements to make these groups optional and repeatable. These attributes reveal a sensible reason for creating a sequence group within a sequence group: a series of elements in the middle of a larger sequence may be optional, repeatable, or both. The following variant of the program broadcast example includes optional elements that are to be included only if the program is part of a series:

```
<sequence>
  <element ref="PB:ProgramTitle" />
  <sequence minOccurs="0">
    <element ref="PB:EpisodeTitle" />
    <element ref="PB:EpisodeNumber" />
  </sequence>
  <element ref="PB:Copyright" />
</sequence>
```

The model above is not equivalent to the following simpler model because both the EpisodeTitle and EpisodeNumber elements must be present or both must be absent; the following example also allows one to be present without the other:

```
<sequence>
  <element ref="PB:ProgramTitle" />
  <element ref="PB:EpisodeTitle" minOccurs="0" />
  <element ref="PB:EpisodeNumber" minOccurs="0" />
  <element ref="PB:Copyright" />
</sequence>
```

Note that there are no equivalent reasons for embedding a choice element directly within another choice element.

Each sequence or choice element must by default reference at least one element because the minOccurs attribute has a default value of '1' and it would not be possible to fulfill this condition if there were no elements for a document instance author to select from. Setting the minOccurs value to '0' overcomes this limitation (and this may be a sensible precaution to take if all the elements have a minOccurs value of '0' and may later be suppressed in a derived data type).

6.8 All Elements Required in Any Sequence

One possibility that is not supported by the choice element is the need to specify that all of the referenced elements must occur. While the sequence element could be employed, it would by its nature also specify the order in which the elements can occur, and this may not be acceptable.

For example, the three elements that identify a program that is part of a series in the program broadcast example could be wrapped in a ProgramIdentifier element, but the following sequence model might be deemed too restrictive to author freedom:

```
<element name="ProgramIdentifier">
  <complexType>
    <sequence>
      <element ref="PB:SeriesTitle" />
      <element ref="PB:EpisodeTitle" />
      <element ref="PB:EpisodeNumber" />
    </sequence>
  </complexType>
</element>
```

Allowing these elements to appear in any order can be achieved with multiple embedded sequence elements within a choice element. But, as the following example demonstrates, even for three elements the model needs to be very large. In fact, this model is also ambiguous (see Chapter 8), and avoiding such ambiguity would make it even larger:

```
<choice>
  <sequence>
    <element ref="PB:SeriesTitle" />
    <element ref="PB:EpisodeTitle" />
    <element ref="PB:EpisodeNumber" />
  </sequence>
  <sequence>
    <element ref="PB:SeriesTitle" />
    <element ref="PB:EpisodeNumber" />
    <element ref="PB:EpisodeTitle" />
  </sequence>
  <sequence>
    <element ref="PB:EpisodeTitle" />
    <element ref="PB:SeriesTitle" />
    <element ref="PB:EpisodeNumber" />
  </sequence>
  <sequence>
    <element ref="PB:EpisodeTitle" />
    <element ref="PB:EpisodeNumber" />
    <element ref="PB:SeriesTitle" />
  </sequence>
  <sequence>
    <element ref="PB:EpisodeNumber" />
    <element ref="PB:SeriesTitle" />
    <element ref="PB:EpisodeTitle" />
  </sequence>
  <sequence>
    <element ref="PB:EpisodeNumber" />
    <element ref="PB:EpisodeTitle" />
    <element ref="PB:SeriesTitle" />
  </sequence>
</choice>
```

Fortunately, a more efficient technique is supported by the **all** element. In the following example, all three elements must be present, but not necessarily in the same order as they are referenced:

```
<all>
  <element ref="PB:SeriesTitle" />
  <element ref="PB:EpisodeTitle" />
  <element ref="PB:EpisodeNumber" />
</all>
```

By default, each element is required but not repeatable (as usual). Although the **minOccurs** and **maxOccurs** attributes can be added to the all element, they must be set to the default value '1' or to the value '0'.

The **minOccurs** attribute can also be used on the contained references to make some or all of the elements they reference optional, but it cannot be set to any value other than '0' or '1'; and the **maxOccurs** attribute must not be used (except possibly to make the default value explicit, or to suppress the element entirely in a restricted data type):

```
<all>
  <element ref="PB:SeriesTitle" />
  <element ref="PB:EpisodeTitle" />
  <element ref="PB:EpisodeNumber" minOccurs="0" />
</all>
```

This kind of group cannot be employed within another grouping element and, in turn, must not contain groupings of any kind.

The sequence element must be used instead of the all element if some of the elements must be able to occur more than once, even though this approach creates an otherwise unnecessary and annoying ordering constraint.

6.9   The any Element

Content models do not always have to be strictly controlled. At times, document instance authors require a lot more freedom. An option to allow *any* element to occur at a specific point in the document model is therefore provided.

Traditionally, this option has been discouraged because its disavowal of constraints subverts the whole purpose of document models. However, at least two circumstances warrant its use. One use of this technique is to define the content model of a Comment or Scratchpad element. These elements would be used to hold material that is not formally part of the document, but in the latter case may become so in future. The other use of this feature involves the unconstrained inclusion of elements from other namespaces.

Sequence or choice of any element

The **any** element can be placed within the sequence or choice element:

```
<element name="Container">
  <complexType>
    <sequence><any/></sequence>
  </complexType>
</element>
```

If the schema definition concerned also declares the elements A and B, then the two examples below are valid:

```
<Container><B>...</B></Container>
```

```
<Container><A>...</A></Container>
```

The any element can be part of a longer sequence but rarely without causing ambiguities (see Chapter 8 for more details on ambiguities in general, and Section 8.4 in particular for more on issues concerning the any element).

Namespaces

The any element has a **namespace** attribute that identifies permitted elements by naming the namespace (or namespaces) that they must belong to. This is clearly a good mechanism for supporting documents that include elements from multiple namespaces (as discussed in more detail in Chapter 12), but the use of this attribute to restrict the scope to the current namespace is discussed here. Restricting the scope is done by inclusion of the '**##targetNamespace**' keyword or the '**##local**' keyword, depending on whether or not the schema definition has a target namespace (the term 'local' in this context means that any element that is local to the document instance can be used, thereby excluding any element that is defined in a namespace):

```
<any namespace="##targetNamespace" />
```

```
<any namespace="##local" />
```

Occurrences

By default, the any element stands in for a single element, but the **minOccurs** and **maxOccurs** attributes can be used to make this 'wildcard' feature optional or repeatable:

```
<any minOccurs="0" maxOccurs="unbounded" />
```

When a choice element is used, these attributes can be used just as effectively on the choice element instead:

```
<complexType>
  <choice minOccurs="0" maxOccurs="unbounded">
    <any/>
  </choice>
</complexType>
```

There is no constraint on ordering when more than one element can occur:

```
<Container>
  <B>...</B>
  <A>...</A>
  <A>...</A>
</Container>
```

DTD feature emulation

For reproduction of the capability of the 'ANY' keyword in a DTD element declaration so that any number of elements from the current document model can appear, the following schema definition is needed:

```
<element name="Scratchpad">
  <complexType>
    <sequence>
      <any minOccurs="0"
           maxOccurs="unbounded"
           namespace="##local" />
    </sequence>
  </complexType>
</element>
```

But note that '##targetNamespace' is required in place of the '##local' keyword if the schema definition targets a namespace.

6.10   Shared Groups

When two or more element content models have identical content structures the relevant components need not be replicated. The **group** element creates a reusable component that contains a complete or partial content model. The **name** attribute gives the group an appropriate name:

```
<schema ...>
  ...
  <group name="TextComponents">...</group>
  ...
</schema>
```

The group element, in this context, must contain a single all, choice, or sequence element (although an all group is only allowed when it will become the topmost group in all element content models whose declarations include the named group):

```
<schema ...>
  ...
  <group name="TextComponents">
    <choice>
      <element ref="B:Para" />
      <element ref="B:List" />
      <element ref="B:Table" />
    </choice>
  </group>
</schema>
```

The defined group is referenced, wherever it is neeeded, by means of another group element that is empty but includes the **ref** attribute. In this guise, the group element can occur wherever an element reference or declaration can occur within a content model:

```
<element name="Chapter">
  <complexType>
    <sequence>
      <element ref="B:Title" />
      <group ref="B:TextComponents"
            minOccurs="0" maxOccurs="unbounded"/>
    </sequence>
  </complexType>
</element>

<element name="Cell">
  <complexType>
    <sequence>
      <group ref="B:TextComponents" />
    </sequence>
  </complexType>
</element>
```

The **minOccurs** and **maxOccurs** attributes must not be added to the group defini- tion itself and also should not be added to the outermost grouping elements within the definition. Occurrence rules are specified in each reference to the group, thus providing the flexibility for these rules to vary, depending on the context (as seen above).

A single group reference may be the only content of a complexType element if its definition comprises the entire allowed content of the element being declared (and in this case only, the definition of the group may contain the all element).

Apart from saving effort, this technique provides the benefit that a change to the components within a group are automatically reflected in all content models that refer to that group. In addition, named references clarify the document model because they draw attention and give meaningful names to common structures. They also make an unambiguous statement that these duplicate structures are intended to be the same and should probably retain this conformity when future modifications are made to the document model.

Indirectly, a group can contain one or more further groups, but circular references are disallowed in order to prevent a deliberate or inadvertent attempt to create an infinitely deep content model.

Groups are added to the target namespace, so a group in one schema definition can be referenced from a content model in another schema definition when using the import feature (which is discussed in Section 13.4).

Note that the `group` element can also be used to duplicate local elements (see Section 9.5) and can even contain a mixture of global element references and local element declarations.

7. Text and Simple Data Types

It is almost inevitably necesssary for XML documents to include text, as element content, attribute values, or both. This text may need to conform to the constraints of a chosen data type, and complications may arise when creating models that allow a mixture of text and elements. A 'nil' value can also be specified when a value is unknown.

7.1 Text

XML documents generally contain text, and the XML standard specifies that text can appear either as an attribute value or between the start tag and end tag of an element:

```
<AnElement AnAttribute="Text in the form of
                         an attribute value"/>

<AnElement>Text as element content.</AnElement>
```

Document model designers often have the freedom to choose either element content or an attribute to hold a value, but sometimes one is preferable over the other (Section 18.4 includes a detailed discussion on choosing which to use in various circumstances).

Attribute values

It is possible to create useful XML documents that rely exclusively upon the use of attributes to hold all of the text. This is a practical approach when the text represents atomic values with meanings that are not affected either by the existence of other values or by the relative location of other values within the XML document instance. The following XML document instance reworks the email example, using attributes to hold all of the data:

```
<EMail Title="you have been promoted!"
       Date="2002-12-05"
       Importance="urgent">
  <From Address="j.smith@MyCorp.org" />
  <To Address="p.jones@MyCorp.org" />
  <Message Text="when is the party?" />
</EMail>
```

Using attributes to hold values was particularly popular when the DTD feature of the XML standard was the only way to model XML documents, because DTDs are only able to specify constraints on attribute values. For example, a DTD can specify that an Importance attribute must contain either the value 'normal' or the value 'urgent'. It cannot constrain element content in this way.

Element content

The second option for placement of text in an XML document is to insert it between the start tag and end tag of an element. Informally, such an element is said to have **text content**. Formally, however, it is deemed to have **mixed content** (for reasons discussed later). This approach must be used when the value contains sub-structures, in the form of child elements, because attribute values cannot include elements:

```
<Para>This text contains a <Emph>child</Emph> element,
so must be element content.</Para>
```

This approach is now becoming more popular for small, atomic values because a schema definition can validate this text in the same way that it can validate an attribute value. In the following example, the value could be verified as conforming to one of the list of possible email type options suggested above:

```
<Importance>urgent</Importance>
```

There are two ways to create an element declaration that allows text to appear within the element. One method is usually simpler (but only when attributes are not wanted too) and allows validation of the text against a data type. The other method is complex but enables the mixing of elements with the text.

String data type

If an element type cannot contain child elements and attributes, then a simple approach that uses the **type** attribute (as first seen in Chapter 5) to reference the data type allows a data type to be specified. For unconstrained text, the **'string'** data type is the most suitable data type to reference:

```
<element name="Para" type="string" />
```

Such an element is considered to be a **simple element** because it exists only as a container for a single unit of information of a given type. If attributes or element content are also needed, then a more complex approach is used to create a **complex element**.

Attribute declarations may also include the type attribute to identify a simple data type that a value must conform to.

Recall that a data type name is often associated with a namespace. When no prefix is used, the data type is assumed to be part of the default namespace (often the XML Schema standard namespace). But it is often convenient, and sometimes even necessary, to use an explicit prefix for the XML Schema definition namespace. When this is the case, the prefix needs to be added to the name of a data type from this namespace:

```
<xsd:schema xmlns:xsd="...">
  <xsd:element name="Para" type="xsd:string" />
</xsd:schema>
```

Complex Type: no subelements

The alternative technique, for element content only (and again first seen in Chapter 5), involves the use of the **complexType** element. At this point, it is only necessary to focus on the use of the **mixed** attribute when it has the value '**true**':

```
<element name="Para">
  <complexType mixed="true" />
</element>
```

Note that although the complexType element is an empty element tag in the example above, it is just as valid to use a start tag and end tag, and many extensions of this general approach involve further structures within this element.

This alternative technique does not appear to be very attractive. It takes more work to construct, and the ability to specify a data type is lost without any apparent compensating gains. However, more complex scenarios (to be discussed later) actually require this second approach, and it *is* possible to regain the ability to reference a data type, albeit at the cost of still more complex markup within the complexType element.

7.2   **Text and Attributes**

Two approaches can be taken if attributes are needed on an element in addition to text content, depending on whether or not the element content should also conform to the constraints of a simple data type.

Attributes and simple text content

The following approach is relevant when attributes are needed and the content of the element does not need to conform to a data type. Again, note the use of the complexType element and the **mixed** attribute (with a value of '**true**'). However, the new ingredient here is the presence of the **attribute** elements within the complexType element:

```
<element name="Para">
  <complexType mixed="true">
    <attribute name="Date" type="string" />
    <attribute name="Security" type="string" />
  </complexType>
</element>
```

This definition allows the following paragraph to contain both attributes and text content:

```
<Para Date="3/5/2001" security="normal">This is an old,
nonsensitive paragraph.</Para>
```

Attributes and constrained content

An extension of the technique just described covers the need to have both attributes and constrained content. Essentially, the element must reference a data type (as in the first method), but this time use it to create a new data type that includes attributes that can be attached to the element. The **simpleContent** element indicates that the content will be simple (it will conform to a simple data type and will therefore not contain elements), even though the element as a whole cannot be considered to be simple, because it will be able to hold attributes.

The **extension** element encloses the attribute definitions that are to be added to this data type, and its **base** attribute specifies the simple data type that the content will be based on (the principles of extending data types for other purposes are discussed in later chapters). In this example, the '**integer**' data type is needed, so the value must be a valid integer, such as '45':

```
<element name="Age">
  <complexType>
    <simpleContent>
      <extension base="integer">
        <attribute name="Retired" type="string" />
      </extension>
    </simpleContent>
  </complexType>
</element>
```

The following element instance is valid:

```
<Age Retired="no">45</Age>
```

The following example includes element content that does not conform to the 'integer' data type, so an error will be raised by a schema processor:

```
<Age Retired="no">XYZ</Age>
```

7.3 **Mixed Content**

The term **mixed content** implies a mixture of elements and text, though this term is also officially considered to be relevant to element content that does not include child elements.

Mixed content hierarchies

Mixed content is often visualized, incorrectly, as text that may have elements embedded within it, as if these embedded elements were down at a further level in the document structure hierarchy. In fact, the text is split into separate pieces that are pulled apart to make room for the elements. Each chunk of text is an untagged **pseudo-element** in the sequence. In the following example, two pseudo-elements, the text 'An ' and the text ' word', surround one genuine element:

```
<para>An <emph>emphasized</emph> word</para>
```

Nothing prevents an element between two pseudo-elements from also containing a mixture of text and elements. Text then occurs at multiple levels in the document hierarchy:

```
<Desc>The <Stress>Schema wars</Stess>
that followed the release of XML led to numerous
candidate modeling languages <Stress>including
<Name>XML Schemas</Name></Stress>.</Desc>
```

The following Document Object Model (DOM) structure illustrates the XML fragment above:

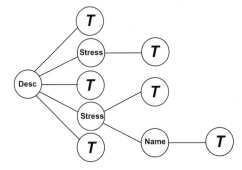

In this example, the Desc element contains text and two Stress elements, one of the Stress elements contains both text and a Name element, and all of these elements contain text.

Possible requirement constraints

Models that include a mixure of text and child elements need to be designed very carefully. The first attempt at a suitable model might allow too much freedom in the placement of text. Maybe there should be no text after the final element, or perhaps the elements need to be constrained to occur in a specific order.

For example, a program description might require a character name to always appear before the name of the actor playing that character:

```
<Desc>
  Captain <CharacterName>Korby</CharacterName>
  (<ActorName>James Jones</ActorName>) is missing,
  presumed eaten.
</Desc>
```

Schema definitions can specify both an element order and occurrence rules for the elements. The **sequence** element is permitted in this scenario:

```
<complexType mixed="true">
  <sequence>
    <element ref="CharacterName" />
    <element ref="ActorName" />
  </sequence>
</complexType>
```

However, it is not possible to limit where text is allowed to occur between the elements. For example, the schema definition cannot state that text must not appear between a character name and the associated actor name.

7.4 Any Element Mixed with Text

A model that includes the any element can also contain text:

```
<complexType mixed="true">
  <sequence>
    <any/>
  </sequence>
</complexType>
```

This remains true even when other elements are referenced explicitly:

```
<complexType mixed="true">
  <sequence>
    <element ref="..." />
    <element ref="..." />
    <any/>
  </sequence>
</complexType>
```

An element in the document instance that is validated against the any element in the document model may belong to another document model (another namespace), but any text before or after the element belongs to the target namespace (by its association with its container element), as much as it can be said to belong to any namespace at all.

7.5 Simple Data Types

The XML Schema standard includes a variety of simple data types, including the 'string' and 'integer' data types seen in prior examples. Note that it is also possible to create additional simple data types (see Chapter 14).

Type hierarchy

Data types are generally based on other, similar but less restrictive, data types, thus forming a hierarchy of types. At the top of this tree is the '**anyType**' data type.

All simple data types are directly or indirectly based on this data type (as are complex types, which involve attributes and child elements):

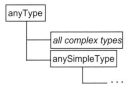

Primitive data types

The built-in simple data types that are directly based on the '**anySimpleType**' data type are called **primitive data types**. They represent dates and times, binary formats, different kinds of numbers, and other miscellaneous types (such as URLs, boolean switches and notation names).

All other simple types, including both built-in simple types and any simple types created by a schema definition author, are ultimately derived from one (or several) of the primitive data types.

Other built-in data types

The remaining built-in data types are all derived, directly or indirectly, from either the 'string' or the 'decimal' primitive data types and are usually more restrictive forms of these types.

Numeric types

All remaining built-in numeric data types are derived from the '**decimal**' type, and involve restrictions on the size of values. In many cases fractions are not allowed:

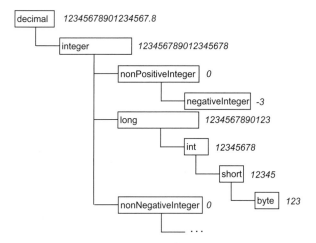

Nonnegative integers are derived a number of times to obtain various positive non-fraction types:

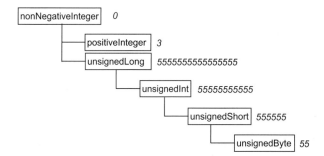

String types

All derivatives of the '**string**' data type normalize the string by removing or replacing whitespace characters. There are two levels of normalization:

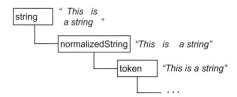

The following types are all special kinds of tokenized string:

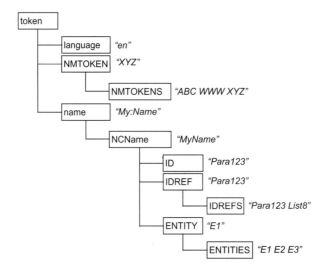

Minimum and maximum values

The following table shows all the **ordered data types** from the charts above. These are data types that have a series of possible values and a minimum and maximum allowed value (independent of the characterisics of specific central processors or operating systems). The following table shows a range of values in each case, including the upper and lower limits:

Simple type	Min and max values
byte	-128 -127 ... -1 0 1 ... 126 127
unsignedByte	0 1 ... 254 255
integer	-999999999999999999.... -2 -1 0 1 2 ... 999999999999999999
positiveInteger	1 2 3 ... 999999999999999999
negativeInteger	-999999999999999999 ... -3 -2 -1
nonNegativeInteger	0 1 2 ... 999999999999999999
nonPositiveInteger	-999999999999999999 ... -2 -1 0
int	-2147483648 ... -1 0 1 ... 2147483647
unsignedInt	0 1 2 ... 4294967295
long	-9223372036854775808 ... -1 0 1 ... 9223372036854775807
unsignedLong	0 1 2 ... 18446744073709551615
short	-32768 ... -1 0 1 ... 32767

Simple type	Min and max values
unsignedShort	0 1 2 ... 65534 65535
decimal	-999999999999999999 ... -0.00000000000000001 0 0.00000000000000001 ... +999999999999999999 *(at least 18 significant digits)*
float	99.9E 2^{24} $^{-149}$ ... ^{104} *(IEEE 754-1985) (single precision 32-bit)*
double	99.9e 2^{53} $^{-1075}$ ... ^{970} *(IEEE 754-1985) (double precision 64-bit)*
boolean	false .. true *or* 0 ... 1
time	00:00:00.000 ... 23:59:59.999 *with possible suffix offset from UTC of* -01:00 ... -12:00 *or* 01:00 ... 12:00 *(ISO 8601)*
dateTime	0001-01-01T00:00:00.000 ... 2999-12-31T23:59:59.999 ... *with possible '-' prefix offset from UTC of 'Z' (UTC) or* -01:00 ... -12:00 *or* 01:00 ... 12:00 *(ISO 8601)*
duration	PnYnMnDTnHnM (Y=Years/M=Months/D=Days/T=Time/ H=Hours/M=Minutes)
date	0001-01-01 ... 2000-01-01 ... 2999-12-31 ... *with possible '-' prefix offset from UTC of 'Z' (UTC) or* -01:00 ... -12:00 *or* 01:00 ... 12:00 *(ISO 8601)*
gMonth	--01-- ... --12--
gYear	0001 ... 2000 ...
gYearMonth	0001-01 ... 2000-12 ...
gDay	---01 ... ---31
gMonthDay	--01-01 ... --12-31
Name	*pattern (see Chapter 15):* \i\c*
QName	
NCName	*pattern (see Chapter 15):* [\i-[:]][\c-[:]]*
anyURI	
language	*pattern (see Chapter 15):* ([a-zA-Z]{2}|[iI]-[a-zA-Z]+|[xX]-[a-zA-Z]{1,8})(-[a-zA-Z]{1,8})* *(must conform to RFC 1766, as xml:lang does)*
Legacy Types	
ID	*same as NCName*
IDREF	*same as NCName*
IDREFS	*list of IDREF*
ENTITY	*same as NCName*
ENTITIES	*list of ENTITY*
NOTATION	

Simple type	Min and max values
NMTOKEN	*pattern (see Chapter 15):* \c+
NMTOKENS	*list of NMTOKEN*

7.6 Special Data Type Features

Some of the data types listed above need a little more explanation because their purpose or scope is not immediately obvious or is, in a few cases, actually misleading.

String normalization and token types

The '**normalizedString**' and '**token**' data types are not as useful as they might first appear. They cannot be used to detect unwanted whitespace, and they cannot modify the text before forwarding it to an application that is receiving the parsed data (see Section 14.13 for more details).

Their main value is that values belonging to data types derived from them will successfully validate even when they contain extraneous spaces and line-feed characters. They are therefore useful if this latitude is wanted.

Whitespace collapse

Many of the data types, including all of the numeric types, include the significant characteristic that whitespace characters are removed before processing. Often, this will not matter very much, precisely because such whitespace is irrelevant to values that conform to these data types. However, it has an impact on activation of a default value. An element that contains only whitespace characters becomes an empty element after being stripped of this whitespace, and an empty element is always replaced by a default value.

Gregorian dates

Five of the data types are designed to represent elements of time according to the Gregorian calendar (introduced in 1582 by Pope Gregory XIII). The '**gYear**', '**gMonth**', and '**gDay**' data types hold a simple year, month, or day, and the '**gMonthDay**' and '**gYearMonth**' data types hold a compound value of month and day, and year and month, respectively. A hyphen is used as a separator between the year, month, and day, as in the date '2002-12-13'. A hyphen is also used to represent a missing component.

The '**gMonth**' data type always includes two preceding and two following hyphens, with the first hyphen representing the missing year, and the final hyphen representing the missing day, as in the date '--12--'.

However, a '**gDay**' value is preceded by only three hyphens, such as '---12', because there is no hyphen for the missing year.

It could be argued that a single data type would cover all of these possibilities, but the selection of a specific type ensures that only components of the required type are used. The following example would be illegal if the Month element was assigned to the 'gMonth' data type:

```
<Month>---12</Month>
```

But the following example would be accepted:

```
<Month>--12--</Month>
```

The '**gYear**' data type must consist of at least four digits, and a zero digit must be used for padding for early dates, such as '0999' for the last year of the first millennium. A leading hyphen is interpreted as a minus symbol for BCE (Before Common Era) years, as in '-0123'. The '**gMonth**' data type must consist of two digits, so '03' represents the third month of the year. This is also true for the '**gDay**' data type, where '09' represents the ninth day of the month.

Any URI

The '**anyURI**' data type indicates that the value must be a Uniform Resource Identifier (URI), as defined in RFC 2396 and RFC 2732. The value can therefore be an absolute or relative Uniform Resource Locator (URL) reference or a Uniform Resource Name (URN).

Because of the many variant syntax rules for URLs and URNs, it is not expected that a value will be validated against a strict template. Yet some basic rules concerning the characters allowed in a URI can be tested. The value must be a URI reference or must result in a URI reference after an escaping procedure is applied (illegal characters are escaped by converting the character value into a two-character hexadecimal value prefixed by a '%' symbol). The following example is legal:

```
<element name="PageRef" type="anyURI" />
```

```
<PageRef>www.bradley.co.uk/index.html</PageRef>
```

Some characters are disallowed in URI references. This includes all non-ASCII characters, plus the excluded characters listed in IETF RFC 2396, except the number sign, '#', the percent sign, '%', and the square bracket characters that are permitted by IETF RFC 2732. For example, a schema processor may choose to report that a '^' character found in a URL reference is illegal, but is not required to do so. The space character should be escaped as '%20', though many processors will allow a normal space character to pass without error.

DTD emulation

The data types that have names consisting entirely of capital letters are equivalent to XML DTD attribute types with the same names. This includes the '**ID**', '**IDREF**', '**IDREFS**', '**ENTITY**', '**ENTITIES**', '**NOTATION**', '**NMTOKEN**', and '**NMTOKENS**' data types. Because the DTD feature only allows attribute values to be assigned to these data types, for backward compatibility they should only be used in this way in schema definitions (not to specify the possible content of an element).

Note that the 'NMTOKENS', 'IDREFS', and 'ENTITIES' data types are also unusual in that they are not *more* restrictive than their respective parent data types, but *less so*. In all three cases, a document instance author has the same level of freedom in respect to the characters that can be used in a token of each kind. For example, a valid token of the kind 'IDREF' will always be a valid token of the kind 'IDREFS'. But, in the latter case, the author can also add a space, then another token, and repeat this any number of times. This can be seen as an extension rather than a restriction of a parent data type, and it will be shown (in Section 14.9) that new data types can be created that work in the same way.

Notations

Elements can contain text that conforms to another computer language, though this is limited to text-based languages (binary formats can be handled internally by the 'hexBinary' data type, as explained below). For example, T_EX data could be embedded in a `Formula` element,

```
<Formula>-$${ \Gamma (J^\psi ...</Formula>
```

but a schema processor would not recognize the nature and significance of the embedded data and would therefore be unable to pass the data to a suitable software application that would understand how to validate, interpret, or present this data.

The '**NOTATION**' data type has been copied from a DTD feature of the XML standard. When an attribute is assigned to this type, the name of the notation given by the value of an attribute indicates the nature of the data contained within the element. This data type cannot be used directly. Instead, it is necessary to create a restricted subtype that uses one or more `enumeration` facet elements (see Section 14.5) to list the data formats that may be used. In the following example, two notations used to represent mathematical formulae are allowed ('T_EX' and 'L^AT_EX'):

```
<simpleType>
  <restriction base="NOTATION">
    <enumeration value="TeX" />
    <enumeration value="LaTeX" />
  </restrictions>
</simpleType>
```

If this data type is assigned to the Format attribute of the Formula element declaration, then the following instance of this element can identify the nature of the data it holds (and find a suitable application to process it):

```
<Formula Format="TeX">-$${ \Gamma (J^\psi ...</Formula>
```

The data formats listed must be defined by **notation** elements elsewhere in the schema definition that have matching **name** attribute values:

```
<notation name="TeX" ... />

<notation name="LaTeX" ... />
```

A notation defined in an imported schema definition can be referenced by addition of the namespace prefix to the notation name.

A **public** attribute is not required (despite an error in the schema for schemas that implies that it is) but if present holds a unique name for the data format that could be looked up in a catalogue to find a software application that can interpret information encoded in that format. Typically, this attribute takes a MIME type, such as 'text/tex', a URL (so that a resource can be located explicitly), or an official public identifier construction, such as '-//MyCorp//NOTATION TEX Docs//EN':

```
<notation name="TeX" public="text/tex" />
```

Also present may be a **system** attribute, which is interpreted as a URL reference that directly targets a software application that can interpret the data. Often, this will be a rendering application, such as a T_EX viewer, that allows the information to be seen:

```
<notation name="TeX" public="text/tex"
                system="TEXviewer.exe" />
```

Although neither the public attribute nor the system attribute is individually required, at least one of them must be present (note that such attribute presence dependencies cannot be specified in a schema definition, which is partly why the schema for schemas makes the mistake of insisting that the public attribute must always be present).

Binary data

Binary data can be included within an XML document by conversion of each byte into a two-character representation of its value. The hexadecimal system uses 16 characters to represent a value between 0 and 15, by employing the letter 'A' to represent the value 10, 'B' to represent 11, 'C' to represent 12, 'D' to represent 13, 'E' to represent 14, and 'F' to represent 15. Two such characters are sufficient to represent any value from 0 to 255 (8 bits, 1 byte), with a leading '0' character for values smaller than 16. For example, 'FF' represents 255 and '0F' represents 15.

When an attribute value or element content is constrained to conform to the '**hex-Binary**' data type, it is checked to ensure that no other characters are present and to ensure that there are an even number of characters:

```
<Image>55FD030541DEDD04</Image>
```

It is expected that a software application that understands the purpose of a particular element of this type will be able to convert the hexadecimal representations back into the true binary version, as a precursor to passing this data to a subroutine or separate application that can process it in this form. For example, image data might be presented to the reader of the document.

The alternative, '**base64Binary**', works in a similar way but has a different encoding mechanism (see RFC 2045).

Entity references

An attribute can include a reference to an entity. The '**ENTITY**' data type gives the value this meaning. However, it is not possible to define entities within a schema definition, so if this feature is used, then entity declarations must be present in the document instance or in a separate file that is referenced from another entity declaration. Entities typically represent extended characters (those not found in the ASCII character set), reusable text strings, large fragments of XML data held in separate files, and data conforming to other notations which, in some cases (such as most image data formats), are usually held externally to the XML document instance:

```
<!DOCTYPE Book [

  <!ENTITY eacute    "&#233;">
  <!ENTITY XML       "eXtensible Markup Language">
  <!ENTITY appendix  SYSTEM "appendix.xml">
  <!ENTITY myFormula SYSTEM "myformula.tex"  NDATA TeX>
  <!ENTITY boat      SYSTEM "boat.gif"       NDATA gif>

]>
<Book>
  ...
</Book>
```

Note that many parsers will assume that a DTD should follow as soon as the document type declaration (the DOCTYPE instruction above) is added to a document instance (and therefore complain that none of the elements in the document are declared), though some parsers may have the option to suppress this interpretation and enforce validation against the schema definition instead.

Note that the 'NDATA' keyword in the last two examples refers to a notation, but in this case it is expected that the notation declaration will be used instead of the notation scheme definition described above. The reason is that DTD validation takes place before schema validation, so the processor will not yet have access to the schema definition:

```
<!NOTATION TeX SYSTEM "TEXviewer.exe">
```

```
<!ENTITY bigFormula SYSTEM "bigformula.gif" NDATA TeX>
```

When a single attribute value must be able to contain multiple (space-separated) entity references, the '**ENTITIES**' data type is used instead of the 'ENTITY' data type.

7.7   Nil Values

Many of the simple data types listed above require that a value of some kind be present. For example, consider an `Age` element that is required to carry the age of a person in years:

```
<Age>7</Age>
```

A good data type to select for this purpose is the 'nonNegativeInteger' type.

Now suppose that the age of a person happens to be unknown. In database terms, this would be a field that has a 'null' value. One possibility would seem to be to leave the element empty:

```
<Age></Age>
```

But the 'nonNegativeInteger' data type does not allow for an absent value. The value in this case must be either '0' or a positive integer value.

The element could be omitted entirely, and this would seem to be a clear indicator that the value is unknown. However, it might also mean that the author simply forgot to add the element. In addition, vital attributes attached to this element that might be lost if it was absent. Finally, this technique would not be available if the schema definition was developed elsewhere, did not allow the element to be omitted, and could not be changed.

Yet another possibility might be to use an unusual value, such as '0' or '999'. But in the first case there would be no distinction between an unknown age and a true age of '0' (a baby less than one year old). In the second case, some applications reading the XML file may not be aware of the significance of this high value and perhaps assume that it describes an extremely old person. In addition, this technique would prevent the establishment of a sensible upper limit, such as '120' (using a derived data type, as discussed in Chapter 14).

Another approach would be to define a new data type that combined an original ordered type with a special keyword, such as 'none', 'nil' or 'absent'. But this still leaves the problem of communicating the meaning of this keyword to software applications.

The final option is to use the **nil** attribute from the XMLScheme-Instance namespace. If this namespace is not already declared for other purposes, then it must be declared, and it can of course be placed directly on the element concerned. The nil attribute can then be used and given the value '**true**' (in place of the default value of '**false**'), and the element can be empty without causing a validation error (the presence of this attribute with the value 'true' also prevents a default value from being added to the empty element). Recall that this method preserves attributes, in this case, the Youngest attribute, which would be lost if the element was omitted instead:

```
<Age
  xmlns:xsi="http://www/w3/org/2001/XMLSchema-instance"
  xsi:nil="true"
  Youngest="yes"></Age>
```

This option is only available if the relevant element declaration states that it is allowed to contain this attribute. The **nillable** attribute is given the value '**true**' in place of the default value of '**false**':

```
<element name="Age" nillable="true"
         type="nonNegativeInteger" />
```

Of course, if the schema definition was developed elsewhere and could not be modified in this way, then the document instance author cannot use this technique, and must therefore rely on one of the other options discussed above.

It remains to be seen whether this technique becomes a *de facto* way to communicate the absence of values.

8. Ambiguities

Unfortunately, it is all too easy to create a content model that will not be reliably interpreted by a schema processor or that will confuse the processor, causing it to raise an error and refuse to validate a document instance. However, there are rules that can be learned to avoid the traps that lead to such problems.

8.1 Unequivocal Determination

Unconstrained use of the techniques introduced in the previous two chapters can cause problems. It is possible to create a content model that a schema processor will be unable to interpret or that will confuse the processor and trick it into producing false error reports. An **ambiguous content model** may fall into this category, though some forms of ambiguity are not as dangerous as others.

The best way to explore this issue is to first consider a content model that is unambiguous and then discuss the reasons why this is the case. Here, the ProgramIdentity element has been added to the program broadcast example, and this element contains the title or titles needed to identify the program:

```
<element name="ProgramIdentity">
  <complexType>
    <choice>
      <sequence>
        <element ref="PB:ProgramTitle" />
      </sequence>
      <sequence>
        <element ref="PB:SeriesTitle" />
        <element ref="PB:EpisodeTitle" />
        <element ref="PB:EpisodeNumber" />
      </sequence>
    </choice>
  </complexType>
</element>
```

In this model, the ProgramIdentity element can contain either the ProgramTitle element or the SeriesTitle, EpisodeTitle and EpisodeNumber elements. A schema processor has no problem validating a document instance that includes the ProgramIdentity element. When this element is encountered, the processor looks at the first child element it finds and checks whether it is a ProgramTitle element or a SeriesTitle element, reporting an error if it is neither. Assuming that the processor finds a SeriesTitle element, it then knows which model sequence is being followed in the document instance and compares the next ele-

ment to the requirement for an `EpisodeTitle` element. At no point does the processor have to **look ahead** in order to determine which part of the model is
applicable. This is properly called **unequivocal determination** because there is no
equivocation (lack of committment) about which model applies to the document
fragment being validated.

8.2   Serious Ambiguities

Contrast the example above with the following model:

```
<element name="ProgramIdentity">
  <complexType>
    <choice>
      <sequence>
        <element ref="PB:ProgramTitle" />
        <element ref="PB:StandaloneProgram" />
      </sequence>
      <sequence>
        <element ref="PB:ProgramTitle" />
        <element ref="PB:EpisodeTitle" />
        <element ref="PB:EpisodeNumber" />
      </sequence>
    </choice>
  </complexType>
</element>
```

In this example, both sequences begin with the `ProgramTitle` element, and stand-
alone programs and episodes of a series are distinguished from each other by the
presence of different subsequent elements. When the processor encounters the
`ProgramIdentity` element, it then expects to find a `ProgramTitle` element as its
first child. Of course, if the `ProgramTitle` element is absent, an error is reported
as is normal. But a problem arises even when this element is found, because the
processor does not then know which of the sequences the document fragment is
claiming to conform to.

Now consider an even simpler example. The following model is not ambiguous
even though the `Item` element occurs twice. If only one instance of the `Item` element occurs, then the second occurrence is missing, and this error is easily
detected:

```
<sequence>
  <element ref="DOC:Item" />
  <element ref="DOC:Item" />
</sequence>
```

However, the model shown below *is* ambiguous because the processor cannot tell,
when it first encounters an `Item` element, whether it is the optional first `Item` element or the required `Item` element:

```
<sequence>
  <element ref="DOC:Item" minOccurs="0" />
  <element ref="DOC:Item" />
</sequence>
```

Some processors can cope with this issue. For example, a processor could look ahead to see which elements occur later. Alternatively, it could keep both options open, creating two interpretation branches and eventually pruning the irrelevant branch when the processor later discovers which one is relevant. This does not sound too onerous. Certainly, it is technically possible to do either. In the example above, the processor would only need to look ahead one element to discover which Item element it has encountered or to create two very temporary branches. But other examples of this problem may require the parser to manage many branches or to look ahead a long way, perhaps even to the end of a very large document.

For this reason, the XML Schema standard does not assume the use of processors with these capabilities. If there is the slightest possibility that documents belonging to the document class being defined will *ever* be validated by a processor that cannot cope with such models, then it is crucial to avoid them.

8.3   Common Solutions

In the following case, the schema definition author has attempted to specify that a list must include at least two items:

```
<sequence>
  <element ref="DOC:Item" minOccurs="1"
                          maxOccurs="unbounded" />
  <element ref="DOC:Item" minOccurs="1"
                          maxOccurs="1" />
</sequence>
```

This model is ambiguous, but the author can fix it by switching the references around:

```
<sequence>
  <element ref="DOC:Item" minOccurs="1"
                          maxOccurs="1" />
  <element ref="DOC:Item" minOccurs="1"
                          maxOccurs="unbounded" />
</sequence>
```

Alternatively, and more simply, the author can combine them into a single reference:

```
<sequence>
  <element ref="DOC:Item" minOccurs="2"
                          maxOccurs="unbounded" />
</sequence>
```

The solution to the email example is to rationalize the model as follows:

```
<element name="ProgramIdentity">
  <complexType>
    <sequence>
      <element ref="PB:ProgramTitle" />
      <choice>
        <element ref="PB:StandaloneProgram" />
        <sequence>
          <element ref="PB:EpisodeTitle" />
          <element ref="PB:EpisodeNumber" />
        </sequence>
      </choice>
    </sequence>
  </complexType>
</element>
```

8.4 any Element Ambiguities

Use of the **any** element often leads to fatal ambiguities when the minOccurs attribute has the value '0' or the maxOccurs attribute has a value that is greater than '1'. This is true both when the **namespace** attribute is set to '##targetNamespace' and when the default value ('##any') is implicitly or explicitly selected. Giving this attribute the value '##other' usually avoids the problem because the inserted elements must then be from another namespace (as explained in Section 12.4). However, even this will not work if the next element reference in the sequence is imported from another schema definition:

```
<sequence>
  <any namespace="##other" minOccurs="0" />
  <element ref="OTHER_NS:RemoteElement />
</sequence>
```

This problem arises because an instance of the OTHER_NS:remoteElement element could be matched either to the optional any element or to the explicit reference. It is similar to the earlier problem of an optional Item element followed by a required Item element.

The problem can be avoided if the any element either specifies a fixed number of element occurrences or is the last component in the sequence.

8.5 Theoretically Trivial Ambiguities

Any content model that can be interpreted in more than one way is considered to be an **ambiguous content model**. This includes models in which unequivocal determination is maintained. These models are therefore theoretically safe to use. For example:

```
<sequence maxOccurs="unbounded">
  <element ref="DOC:Item" maxOccurs="unbounded" />
</sequence>
```

In this case, the Item element can occur any number of times within the sequence, and the sequence itself can also occur any number of times. A processor cannot know if the presence of three Item elements in a document is from the same sequence, if two Item elements are from a second sequence, or indeed if three single instances of the Item element from three sequences is the case. But the processor should realize that any interpretation it chooses to make will be equally as valid as the other two interpretations. Unequivocal determination is not put at risk. However, processors vary in their ability to detect this scenario, and some raise spurious errors with certain combinations of an ambiguous model and a particular usage of the elements it permits in a document instance. For example:

```
<sequence minOccurs="2" maxOccurs="unbounded">
  <element ref="DOC:Item" minOccurs="1"
                          maxOccurs="unbounded" />
</sequence>


  <Item>...</Item>
  <Item>...</Item>
  <Item>...</Item>
```

A processor may report an error in this case if it fails to realize that the last Item element needs to be matched to the second occurrence of the sequence (and this would be true even if the minOccurs attribute had been omitted, because the default value is also '1').

9. Local Elements

Several elements can be declared with the same name but different content models, attributes, default or fixed values, provided they are used in different parts of the document model. The element type that an element instance belongs to is then determined by its name *and* its location in the document structure. This is a flexible, but sometimes complex and confusing, option that among other things, gives schema definition authors control over the scope of document instances.

9.1 Global Element Limitations

It was shown earlier that declared elements can be referenced from the content model of another element declaration. This approach is simple, allows the same element to be referenced from multiple declarations, and even allows it to be referenced from content models in other schema definitions. These elements are said to have a **global scope**, and this approach is often desirable. For example, a Title element that holds the title of each chapter and section might reasonably have the same attributes and content options in each of these locations:

```
<Chapter>
  <Title>Chapter <Emph>One</Emph></Title>
  <Section>
    <Title>Section <Emph>One</Emph></Title>
    ...
  </Section>
  ...
</Chapter>
```

A significant benefit is that when the content model or attributes are modified in the schema definition, these changes are automatically applied, without possibility of error, wherever the element can be used. But this tight linking of the element name to the element model can also be a hindrance in some circumstances. If the author title should be restricted to containing only 'Mr', 'Mrs', 'Miss' or 'Ms', then another element type is needed, with a different name (such as 'AuthorTitle'):

```
<Chapter>
  <Author>
    <AuthorTitle>Mr</AuthorTitle>
    <FirstName>John</FirstName>
    <LastName>Smith</LastName>
  </Author>
  <Title>Chapter <Emph>One</Emph></Title>
  ...
</Chapter>
```

The name 'AuthorTitle' might seem reasonable, and indeed it is more descriptive than the name 'Title', which is no bad thing in itself. But there are at least two problems with this name. First, the parent element name already provides sufficient context to identify the meaning of the title, and for this reason it is generally considered bad practice to repeat an element name within the names of its children (just as it is more natural to say 'the author has a title' than to say 'the author has an author title'). Second, document authors should not have to learn numerous element names for similar concepts that are distinguished only by context.

The XML Schema standard includes the concept of **local scope**. A declared element of this type is allowed to be used only within the confines of another specified element (such as the `Author` element in the example above), but it is free to have the same name as another local or global declaration while having a different content model, a different set of attributes, or just a different default or fixed value.

9.2 Local Element Declarations

The structure of a local element declaration is the same as the structure of a global declaration, in that the **element** element declares the element and the `name` attribute still gives the new element type its name. The declaration can be inserted wherever it is possible to insert a reference to a global declaration. In this scenario, the `ref` attribute is not used, but the **name** attribute is still needed to give the element a name. In the following example, the `Title` element is defined within the `Author` element:

```
<element name="Author">
  <complexType>
    <sequence>
      <element name="Title">...</element>
    </sequence>
  </complexType>
</element>
```

There is another obvious benefit of this approach. When an element is only used in a single context, local elements are often declared for no other purpose than to avoid having to create a declaration and then having to create a separate reference to this declaration. It is much easier to declare the child element directly within the declaration of its parent.

The `Title` element above can only be used within the `Author` element. If other `Title` elements are present elsewhere, then they must conform to other declarations that happen to have the same names; if no such declarations are to be found, then an error should be raised.

A local element declaration may contain further declarations. In this case, the local `Title` element declaration contains another local declaration, this time for the `Emph` element:

```
<element name="Author">
  <complexType>
    <sequence>
      <element name="Title">
        <complexType mixed="true">
          <sequence>
            <element name="Emph" type="string" />
          </sequence>
        </complexType>
      </element>
    </sequence>
  </complexType>
</element>
```

Taking this concept to its extreme, a schema definition may contain a single global declaration that contains local definitions for all the other elements used in the document model. This approach may not be particularly legible, but it is very compact when elements are generally only allowed in a single location in the document structure, and (for reasons explained later) it forces document instance authors to always create complete documents.

The minOccurs, maxOccurs, and default attributes are all available in local declarations. Indeed, in this scenario there is no ambiguity about where these attributes can be used, because there is no shared global declaration upon which they could be incorrectly used.

Multiple local element declarations within the same element content model may even have the same name, provided that they all adopt the same data type (though occurrence rules and default values can differ between the declarations):

```
<sequence>
  <element name="To" type="string" />
  <choice minOccurs="0" maxOccurs="unbounded">
    <element name="To" type="string" />
    <element name="Cc" ... />
  </choice>
</sequence>
```

9.3 Context Element Requirement

A locally declared element cannot be the root element of a document instance, because an enclosing, globally declared element is needed to unambiguously identify it. Recall that the name alone is not sufficient, especially when the document model includes several local elements with the same name but different content models or attributes. Consider the following two element declarations, both of which create a local Title element:

```
<element name="Chapter">
  <complexType>
    <sequence>
      <element name="Title"> ... </element>
      ...
    </sequence>
  </complexType>
</element>

<element name="Author">
  <complexType>
    <sequence>
      <element name="Title"> ... </element>
      ...
    </sequence>
  </complexType>
</element>
```

The following example would be ambiguous. The schema processor could not know which Title element was intended:

```
<?xml ... ?>
<Title>...</Title>
```

The following two examples are unambiguous. In these cases, the surrounding elements provide the required context:

```
<?xml ... ?>
<Chapter><Title>...</Title>...</Chapter>
```

```
<?xml ... ?>
<Author><Title>...</Title>...</Author>
```

Schema definition authors can exploit this limitation of local elements and use it to restrict document instance authors to a small number of possible document root elements. In the most extreme case, document instance authors can be limited to a single root element to ensure that they always create a complete document (in the past, using DTDs, document instance authors were allowed to create XML documents that were arbitrarily small fragments of the complete document model).

9.4   Sharing Local Elements

If several elements require the same local element declaration, the declaration need not be repeated in each context. Of course, a global declaration cannot be referenced to facilitate such sharing (by definition, a global element is not a local element), but other, similar techniques can be used.

A global complexType element can contain local element declarations, and this complexType element can be referenced by each element declaration that requires the model it contains (see Chapter 16 for more details).

Alternatively, the **group** element can be used to enclose a set of local element declarations, but there must be a surrounding sequence or choice element, so this technique cannot be used to provide a fragment of a single group. Yet the following example is legal because a sequence element can contain another sequence element:

```
<group name="localElementsGroup">
  <sequence>
    <element name="Author">...</element>
    <element name="Title">...</element>
  </sequence>
</group>

<element name="Chapter>
  <complexType>
    <sequence>
      <group ref="B:localElementsGroup" />
      <choice>
        <!-- paras/lists/tables/examples -->
      </choice>
    </sequence>
  </complexType>
</element>
```

When only one element declaration needs to be shared, it can be surrounded by either a sequence element or a choice element without any possibility of creating problems in the document models it will be referenced from:

```
<group name="sharedAuthorElementGroup">
  <sequence>
    <element name="Author">...</element>
  </sequence>
</group>

<element name="Chapter>
  <complexType>
    <choice>
      <!-- paras/lists -->
      <group ref="B:sharedAuthorElementGroup" />
      <!-- tables/examples -->
    </choice>
  </complexType>
</element>

<element name="Section>
  <complexType>
    <choice>
      <!-- paras/lists -->
      <group ref="B:sharedAuthorElementGroup" />
      <!-- tables/examples -->
    </choice>
  </complexType>
</element>
```

9.5   **Namespace Complications**

The technique described above works perfectly for documents that do not use namespaces. But namespaces cause a few issues to arise and force decisions to be made by the schema definition author.

Conditions on usage

Local element declarations do not belong to the target namespace. This fact introduces a number of constraints. First, local element declarations cannot be referenced from other element declarations or be involved in substitution groups (see Section 17.8). Second, they cannot be the outer element of a document instance fragment belonging to a different namespace (for the same reason that they cannot be the root element of the entire document). Although there are limitations, the following technique allows local elements to be namespace qualified, but it does not override the limitations described here.

Unqualified local definitions

By default, local element declarations are not qualified, even when a namespace is targeted. Consider the following definitions:

```
<schema ...
        targetNamespace="http://MegaTVi.com/NS/EMAIL"
        xmlns:E="http://MegaTVi.com/NS/EMAIL">
  ...
  <element name="EMail">
    <complexType>
      <sequence>
         ...
         <element name="Message" type="string" />
      </sequence>
    </complexTyp>
  </element>
  ...
</schema>
```

A valid document instance would appear as follows; note the absence of a prefix on the embedded `Message` element:

```
<E:EMail xmlns:E="http://MegaTVi.com/NS/EMAIL">
  ...
  <Message>...</Message>
</E:EMail>
```

This scenario can cause confusion in documents that happen to also employ a default namespace. The Namespaces standard states that "*A default namespace is considered to apply to the element where it is declared (if that element has no namespace prefix), and to* all elements *with no prefix within the content of that element.*" This means that elements belonging to no namespace cannot be present within the scope of a document fragment that has a default namespace associated with it. For example:

```
<Book xmlns="http://MegaTVi.com/NS/BOOK">
  <Para>This email was received on the 12th:</Para>

  <E:EMail xmlns:E="http://MegaTVi.com/NS/EMAIL">
    <Title>...</Title>
    <From>...</From>
    <To>...</To>
    <Date>...</Date>
    <Message>...</Message>
  </E:EMail>

  <Para>The implications of its message are
  clear.</Para>
</Book>
```

In this example, the `Title`, `From`, `To`, `Date` and `Message` elements have been locally declared within the `EMail` element declaration, and a processor is expected to recognize them. Yet, according to the Namespaces standard, they must be associated with the default namespace, 'http://MegaTVI.com/NS/BOOK', which includes the `Book` and `Para` elements (but not these email-related elements). It might be expected that this confusion would be easy to resolve because the processor can simply look in both schemas for the element declarations, but if the book namespace happened to contain a conflicting declaration (such as its own `Title` element), then the problem could not be resolved.

However, a default namespace can be overriden. As the Namespaces standard states, *"The default namespace can be set to the empty string. This has the same effect, within the scope of the declaration, of there being no default namespace."* The example above can be modified as follows to avoid the confusion:

```
<Book xmlns="http://MegaTVi.com/NS/BOOK">
  <Para>This email was received on the 12th:</Para>
  <E:EMail xmlns:E="http://MegaTVi.com/NS/EMAIL"
           xmlns="">
    <Title>...</Title>
    <From>...</From>
    <To>...</To>
    <Date>...</Date>
    <Message>...</Message>
  </E:EMail>
  <Para>The implications of its message are
  clear.</Para>
</Book>
```

In this version, the embedded, unqualified elements are unambiguously not part of any namespace. But the processor will then not recognize them as belonging to the email schema definition.

Not adding a prefix to the local elements should therefore be avoided unless it can be guaranteed that document authors will never use a default namespace in an enclosing document (and not use an editing tool that will automaticaly add an empty namespace declaration).

Another, slightly less dangerous, scenario remains. The enclosing document may not use a namespace at all. In the following example, two unqualified Date elements with different date formatting rules are defined in the two schema definitions concerned:

```
<Book>
  <Para>This email was received on the 12th:</Para>
  <Date>12/5/2002</Date>
  <E:EMail xmlns:E="http://MegaTVi.com/NS/EMAIL">
    <From>...</From>
    <To>...</To>
    <Title>...</Title>
    <Date>12052002</Date>
    <Message>...</Message>
  </E:EMail>
  <Para>The implications of its message are
  clear.</Para>
</Book>
```

The question that arises is what the parser should do when it encounters the inner Date element. The Namespaces standard does not say anything about unqualified elements from multiple domains. The following explanation therefore applies only to the XML Schema standard.

A schema processor looks for a relevant element declaration in the currently active schema definition, rather than in the schema definition for non-namespace documents (it only switches that schema definition back in if there is an any element in the current definition with a namespace attribute value of '##local').

But confusion remains a possibility if the document is ever likely to be processed by a parser that does not include a schema processor. There is no mention of unqualified elements that override a default namespace in the Namespaces standard itself, and the XML application that ultimately receives the document has no clues to enable it to distinguish among elements that belong to the default namespace and those that, contrary to appearances, actually do not.

Qualified local definitions

The **elementFormDefault** attribute on the **schema** element can be given the value 'qualified', overriding the default value of 'unqualified' for all local elements. Alternatively, the **form** attribute on the **element** element can be given the same value to selectively activate this feature.

This action could be interpreted as adding the local declarations to the target name-space. But according to the Namespaces standard, "*The combination of the universally managed URI namespace and the document's own namespace produces identifiers that are universally unique.*" Identifiers cannot be guaranteed to be unique when local element declarations are added to a namespace, except within the context of a surrounding element. Indeed, the main reason for this feature is to overcome the need for global uniqueness. However, this does not have to be a practical obstacle. Processors actually use namespaces to detect boundaries between document fragments that belong to different domains, and only globally declared (guaranteed to be unique) elements are allowed at such locations.

Whatever the interpretation, these elements must then be qualified when used in a document instance, meaning that they must either be given an explicit namespace prefix or still not be given a prefix if a default namespace happens to be used.

Note that when a schema document is included in another schema document, the setting of the `elementFormDefault` attribute is not overridden, and therefore continues to apply to all of the components declared in the included document, even when this attribute has a different setting in the including document.

Default namespace complication

Errors will certainly arise if the default namespace is used for global elements, and local elements are unqualified. Consider the following cut-down version of the email model seen earlier, and note that the `To` element is referenced, and thus is a global element, whereas the `Message` element is declared locally:

```
<element name="EMail">
  <complexType>
    <sequence>
      <element ref="E:To" />
      <element name="Message" type="string" />
    </sequence>
  </complexType>
</element>
```

In addition, assume for this scenario that the `schema` element does not include the `elementFormDefault` attribute to override the default setting of 'unqualified', so local elements should not be qualified.

Now consider an email document for which the document instance author has chosen to use the default namespace:

```
<EMail xmlns="http://MegaTVi.com/NS/EMAIL">
  <To>...</To>
  <Message>...</Message>
</EMail>
```

At first sight it appears that this should work. The To element has no prefix because the default namespace is in use, and the Message element has no prefix because it is a local element. Yet this document is not valid. This is because a default namespace applies to *all* elements that have no prefix within the scope of the declaration, so the schema processor considers the Message element to belong to this namespace, but it does not (because it is an unqualified local element). This problem can be solved by any of three different means.

The document instance author could avoid using the default namespace. It is now clear that the Message element does not belong to the namespace, and the schema processor is free to match it with a local element declaration:

```
<EMail xmlns:E="http://MegaTVi.com/NS/EMAIL">
  <E:To>...</E:To>
  <Message>...</Message>
</E:EMail>
```

Alternatively, the Message element could be made a global element, just as the To element is in the example above, and then given the explicit prefix (or no prefix if the default namespace is used).

Finally, the **elementFormDefault** attribute on the schema element could be set to 'qualified'. The schema processor will then expect local elements to be qualified (explicitly or implicitly) along with the rest of the document, so will not simply look for a global declaration (and will indeed look for a local declaration first):

```
<schema ... elementFormDefault="qualified">
  ...
  <element name="EMail">
    ...
      <element name="Message" ... />
    ...
  </element>
  ...
</schema>

<E:EMail xmlns:E="http://MegaTVi.com/NS/EMAIL">
  <E:To>...</E:To>
  <E:Message>...</E:Message>
</E:EMail>
```

The third solution is the best, in the sense that local declarations are still allowed. The only cost of this approach is the seemingly unnecessary presence of prefixes on the local elements, but even this has at least one positive repercussion (which is covered next).

Missing prefix confuses authors

Another problem with avoiding prefixes on local elements is that a document instance author has to know which elements are global and which are local, in order to add prefixes only to the global elements (though an intelligent, schema-sensitive XML editing tool could handle this on the author's behalf).

So that document instance authors are not confused, the value of the **element-FormDefault** attribute should be set to '**qualified**', despite this having no effect on the fact that only global elements can be root elements (because the context these elements give is still essential to distinguishing one local element from another one with the same name). The only disadvantages of this approach are that it increases the keystrokes needed to create tags when a simple text editor is used as an XML editing application, and that the size of the XML document increases slightly.

Note that a similar issue arises for global attribute declarations (as discussed in Chapter 10).

9.6 SGML Exclusions and Inclusions

Some DTD authors will be familiar with the SGML inclusions/exclusions feature. More than any other feature, its absence from the XML specification has fueled the claim that SGML is still needed for serious document modeling tasks. This feature allows the content model of an element in an SGML DTD to be overridden, with elements added to or removed from the model, depending on the context within which an instance of the element happens to occur. The local element declaration feature is not quite the same as the inclusions/exclusions feature, though it can emulate some of its characteristics.

SGML exclusions

The real purpose of the SGML exclusions feature is to prevent an element from occurring within a given context, despite the fact that some other elements, which continue to be allowed, name this element as a legal child element.

A classic example of the need for this feature concerns the inability of many rendering and publishing tools to format tables that occur within another table cell. In the following example from an SGML DTD, the Table element is normally allowed within the Text element, but not when the Text element descends from the table element (the '-(...)' part of the table element declaration lists the element to be excluded (in this case itself)):

```
<!ELEMENT Chapter (Title, Text)

<!ELEMENT Text     (Para|List|Table)*>

<!ELEMENT Table    (Row+)   -(Table)>
<!ELEMENT Row      (Cell+)>
<!ELEMENT Cell     (Text)>
```

Using a schema definition, a document author could emulate this feature by declaring the Text element twice; the first time perhaps globally, and the second time locally within the Cell element. The second declaration would not include the Table element as a possible child element.

SGML inclusions

The main purpose of the SGML inclusions feature is to add an element reference simultaneously to the declaration of every element that occurs within a given fragment of the model structure. It is simply the reverse of the exclusions feature.

Authors misuse this feature as a lazy way to add a reference to every other element declaration, often simply by adding an inclusion to the root element declaration. In this case, the Rev element can be used anywhere in a book:

```
<!ELEMENT Book    (Title, Chapter)* +(Rev)>
```

Unfortunately, the local declaration feature does not help replicate this capability. However, a classic example of this feature in action would add a TableFooter element only to elements that happen to occur within a Table element. In this case, local element declarations are again able to emulate the need.

10. Global and Shared Attributes

Attribute declarations can be shared across several element declarations, and can even be made accessible to element declarations in other schema definitions, but namespace qualification is a complication that schema definition authors must consider before deciding whether to use the features that support these concepts.

10.1 Global Declarations

An attribute declaration can appear directly within the schema element. It takes the same form as it would take within a complexType element, but in this case it is not directly associated with any specific element declaration. An element can reference such a **global attribute** with the **attribute** element, but this time must reference the name (rather than specify the name and data type) with the **ref** attribute:

```
<schema...>
  ...
  <attribute name="Version" ... />
  <element name="Book">
    <complexType>
      ...
      <attribute ref="B:Version" />
    </complexType>
  </element>
</schema>
```

This technique should look familiar because it is identical to the way that global element declarations are referenced.

One immediate benefit of this approach is that a single change to the attribute declaration automatically updates all the elements that refer to it.

The **use**, **default**, and **fixed** attributes are used in the reference, rather than the declaration (though a default can be set in the declaration and then overridden in some of the references). This allows multiple references to have different requirement constraints from each other, and different default or fixed values.

A global attribute is added to the target namespace and can therefore be referenced from another schema definition (just as a global element can). A reference to a global attribute must therefore include the namespace prefix of the namespace containing the declaration.

10.2 **Namespace Complications**

The preceding description of the declaration of global attribute declarations applies to schema definitions that do not target a namespace. But namespace complications make its use in schema definitions that target a namespace impractical (except in one special circumstance described in the next section).

A global attribute is always added to the target namespace:

```
<schema ...
        targetNamespace="http://MegaTVi.com/NS/BOOK">
   ...
   <attribute name="Version" ... />
```

It should be recalled at this point that attributes do not normally carry an explicit qualification. The problem here is that because the attribute is added to the namespace, it becomes essential to qualify the attribute whenever it is used:

```
<B:Book xmlns:B="http://MegaTVi.com/NS/BOOK"
        B:Version="2.2">
   ...
</B:Book>
```

This approach is clearly not desirable because it runs contrary to the conventional use of attributes in XML documents that use namespaces. Normally, attributes that belong to the element they are on are not qualified, even when the element itself is qualified and has a prefix.

Note that the `attributeFormDefault` and `form` attributes are of no help in this circumstance. They apply only to local declarations. Global attributes must always be qualified.

But there is one circumstance under which prefixing of attributes is not only desirable but essential. An attribute from one document model may be attached to an element from another document model. A good example is the `schemaLocation` attribute:

```
<Book xmlns:xsi="..." xsi:schemaLocation="...">
   ...
</Book>
```

This attribute is used in documents that belong to a variety of different namespaces. The only documents in which it is not usually found are schema definition documents (though the schema for schemas might be referenced in this way to validate a schema).

10.3   **Attribute Groups**

If the global attributes feature is not a suitable mechanism for simply sharing attribute declarations within the same schema definition (perhaps because a namespace is targeted), then another feature is available for just this purpose. The **attributeGroup** element holds a group of attribute references or declarations. It is placed directly within the schema element and contains a **name** attribute to give the group an identity that can be used to reference and employ it whenever it is needed:

```
<attributeGroup name="commonAttributes">
  <attribute ... />
  <attribute ... />
  <attribute ... />
</attributeGroup>
```

Note that the name of the attribute*Group* element is perhaps a little misleading because it can also be used to hold a *single* attribute reference or declaration.

Also note that an attribute group may contain an attribute wildcard, using the anyAttribute element (see Section 12.6), but this should probably be avoided. The reason is that there are complex rules for resolving conflicts when several referenced attribute groups all contain this element or when there is also one in the complexType element.

A group is referenced from within a complexType element in exactly the same way that a global attribute is, except that the attributeGroup element is used instead of the attribute element. The **ref** attribute serves the same purpose:

```
<schema...>
  ...
  <attributeGroup name="versionAttrGroup">
    <attribute name="Version" ... />
  </attributeGroup>
  ...
  <element name="book">
    <complexType>
      ...
      <attributeGroup ref="B:versionAttrGroup" />
    </complexType>
  </element>
</schema>
```

Several attributeGroup and attribute elements can appear in any order at the end of the complexType element, and the order is not significant.

With this technique, the attributes are not added to the target namespace and are therefore not prefixed in the document instance:

```
<B:Book xmlns:B="http://MegaTVi.com/NS/BOOK"
        Version="2.2">
  ...
</B:Book>
```

But note the loss of ability to specify different use constraints, default values, and fixed values, depending on which element the attributes in the group are assigned to. When such variance is required, it is necessary to either use a global attribute declaration (and accept the namespace issues) or resort to separate local attribute declarations.

Attribute groups are assigned to the target namespace. A reference must therefore include a namespace prefix when a prefix has been assigned to the target namespace within the schema definition. In the following example, the grouped Version attribute is used in three element declarations, and in the third case is added to a simple data type (see Chapter 14):

```
<element name="Para">
    <complexType mixed="true">
       ...
       <attributeGroup ref="B:versionAttrGroup" />
    </complexType>
</element>

<element name="Image">
  <complexType>
    <attribute name="Format" type="token" />
    <attributeGroup ref="B:versionAttrGroup" />
  </complexType>
</element>

<element name="Age">
  <complexType>
    <simpleContent>
      <extension base="integer">
        <attributeGroup ref="B:versionAttrGroup" />
      </extension>
    </simpleContent>
  </complexType>
</element>
```

Grouping benefits

When the same set of attributes is needed in several elements, the attributeGroup element should always be used, even in schema definitions that do not target a namespace (when global definitions could easily be used instead). This is good practice because it reduces the size of the schema definition, prevents the schema definition author from accidentally forgetting to reference an attribute in one of the locations where they should all appear, and allows a group of related attributes to be given a meaningful name that clarifies the purpose of the attributes (thereby improving the legibility of the schema definition as a whole).

Groups referencing groups

An attribute group can reference other attribute groups to build larger groupings of attributes:

```
<attributeGroup name="allCommonAttributes">
  <attributeGroup ref="B:adminAttributes" />
  <attributeGroup ref="B:statusAttributes" />
</attribute>
```

However, an attribute group must not directly reference itself, because this would create an infinite loop that may crash a schema processor. This rule also applies to indirect referencing for the same reason:

```
<!-- INVALID CIRCULAR REFERENCE -->

<attributeGroup name="adminAttributes">
  <attributeGroup ref="B:allCommonAttributes" />
  <attributeGroup ref="B:statusAttributes" />
</attribute>

<attributeGroup name="allCommonAttributes">
  <attributeGroup ref="B:commonAttributes" />
  <attributeGroup ref="B:adminAttributes" />
</attribute>
```

An attribute group can include a mixture of attribute group references and single attribute declaration references.

11. Unique and Referenced Elements

It is possible to validate that each occurrence of a specified element type within a document instance contains a different value than the others and check that an element that claims to contain a reference to another element in the same document really does contain a valid reference.

11.1 Unique Fragments and References

A document instance may contain many related values, and it is often the case that there should be no duplicates among such a set. For example, it would be reasonable to insist that all the chapters of a book should have different titles. The following would then be invalid because there is a duplicate chapter title:

```
<Book>
  ...
  <Chapter>
    <Title>The Trouble With DTDs</Title>
    ...
  </Chapter>
  <Chapter>
    <Title>Schema Wars</Title>
    ...
  </Chapter>
  <Chapter>
    <Title>Schema Wars</Title>
    ...
  </Chapter>
</Book>
```

Unique fragments

The term **unique fragment** is used here to describe any element within a document instance that has a potentially meaningful existence in its own right and that contains all the information needed for it to be identified and located for selection or extraction.

Such a fragment could be any size and may be an empty element or an element that contains text or other elements. In the example above, each chapter should be a unique fragment.

Every unique fragment must have a single 'root' element that defines the boundary of the fragment, and this element can be any element in a document instance except the root element of the document itself. In the example above, the Chapter elements are the fragment root elements.

Database-derived terminology

Many XML documents are created by extraction of information from a database or are destined to populate a database with values. The features described below are particularly suited to validating the highly structured information associated with databases, and some of the terminology used in describing these features has been borrowed from database concepts.

Keys

Every row in a relational database table consists of multiple fields and must be uniquely identifiable either from the value of a single field or from a combination of values from several fields. The values of these fields form the **key** to the entire row (one candidate key is chosen to be the 'primary' key when several combinations of different fields can be used as alternative 'candidate' keys). In XML terms, a fragment is loosely equivalent to a row, and attributes or elements within the fragment are equivalent to fields. The key might therefore be the content of a single element (such as the Title element in the example above) or perhaps the combined values of several attributes.

References

A row in one database table is often involved in a one-to-many relationship with rows in another table. This concept is similar to the idea of hypertext links by which one Web page, or fragment thereof, is the target of many references from other Web pages.

In an XML document, a reference is made by placing a copy of the key in a referencing element (the ChapterRef elements below) or attribute, and it can be useful to check that such references are valid. The third reference in the example below is not valid because there is no chapter title 'Schema Quibbles' in the document:

```
<Chapter>
  <!-- OTHER CHAPTERS REFERENCE THIS TITLE -->
  <Title>Schema Wars</Title>
  ...
</Chapter>
```

```
<Chapter>
  <Title>W3C XML Schema Standard</Title>
    . . .
    ...see <ChapterRef>Schema Wars</ChapterRef>...
    . . .
    ...see <ChapterRef>Schema Wars</ChapterRef>...
    . . .
    . . .                    <!-- ERROR -->
    ...see <ChapterRef>Schema Quibbles</ChapterRef>...
    . . .
</Chapter>
```

11.2   Simple DTD-Based Identifiers

The XML standard includes a feature for ensuring that values are unique within a document instance. When a DTD is employed to create a document model, any number of attributes can be assigned to the '**ID**' attribute type and the values of these attributes in a compliant document instance must then be unique in order to avoid a parsing error. This attribute type is also supported by the XML Schema language, which includes it as one of the built-in simple data types (see Section 7.5 and Section 7.6):

```
<attribute name="Id" type="ID" />
```

This concept was originally introduced to support a hypertext linking feature, but nothing prevents the use of the 'ID' attribute type to simply validate that a set of values includes no duplicates. For example, the third paragraph below has an identifier that has already been used:

```
<Para Id="P123">This is paragraph 123</Para>
<Para Id="P124">This is paragraph 124</Para>
<Para Id="P124">This is paragraph 124</Para>
```

The identifier value is constrained to a strict set of allowed characters. The first character can be a letter, a '_' symbol, or a colon, and the remaining characters can also include digits, '.', and '-' symbols. For example, 'P123' and '_X-1.2' are valid identifier values.

References to these attributes elsewhere in the document can be validated by a DTD too. The value of an attribute that is assigned to the '**IDREF**' attribute type must match the value of an identifier in the same document. Again, this attribute type is available in schema definitions as a built-in simple data type:

```
<attribute name="Ref" type="IDREF" />


  ... see <Link Ref="P123">paragraph 123</Link> ...
```

Note that in the DTD feature, only attributes can be assigned to the 'ID' and 'IDREF' types. Neither the target element nor the referencing element can hold the key value as element content instead of as attribute values. The equivalent data types in schema definitions should also only be used to define attributes, if only to retain backward compatibility with documents originally designed to be validated against a DTD.

11.3 Advanced Requirements

The DTD-based feature described above is limited in a number of ways:

- The key must be a single-word value ('Schema Wars' would not be allowed, though 'Schema_Wars' would).
- The key must be a single value, not a combination of values.
- The key is limited to a small number of valid characters, both for the first character and for remaining characters ('1para' would not be valid because the identifier cannot start with a number, and neither would 'para*1', because the '*' symbol is not allowed anywhere in an identifier).
- The key must be an attribute value, not element content.
- The identified fragment must be an element that directly contains the attribute that holds the key value; the attribute cannot be on an embedded element.
- Only one set of unique values is allowed in a document instance because of the danger of unexpected duplication of keys when separate uniqueness validation is needed in various unrelated sections of the document.

These limitations can be overcome by use of a more sophisticated feature that is provided by the XML Schema standard. But before discussing this feature, it is worthwhile exploring just how serious some of these limitations are and introducing some relevant techniques for solving them.

Key values

If unnecessary limitations are placed on the characters that may make up a key value, this almost inevitably means that key values must be invented and added to the document for just this purpose. It is clearly better if existing, meaningful values can be exploited whenever possible. In particular, the presence of spaces and symbols should not be a barrier to using a unique value as a key. Phrases, dates, times, and existing codes of any kind should all be allowed to be used as the key value:

```
<Title>Schema Wars</Title>

<Publisher ISBN="1-304-99865" />

<StartTime>19:00</StartTime>
```

Flexible key location

The key should not have to be the direct content of the fragment root element or of an attribute on this element. A key could be anywhere within a fragment (and an XPath expression could be used to find it). In the following example, the key happens to be the ISBN attribute, but this attribute is on a descendent element of the Book fragment root element:

```
<Books>

  <!-- FRAGMENT -->
  <Book>
    <Details>            <!-- KEY -->
      <Publisher ISBN="1-304-99865" ... />
      ...
    </Details>
    ...
  </Book>
</Books>
```

Similarly, in earlier examples the content of the Title element could be the identifier of the enclosing chapter.

Context-specific sets of keys

Context can be very important within an XML document: two forms of context are considered here.

First, there may be multiple categories of fragments. Typically, different element types, such as Chapter and Section elements, denote each category. Although chapter titles should be unique, there may be no reason why a section title should not be the same as a chapter title:

```
<Chapter>
  <Title>Schema Wars</Title>
  <Section>
    <Title>Historical Perspective</Title>
    ...
  </Section>
  <Section>
    <Title>Schema Wars</Title>
    ...
  </Section>
</Chapter>
```

A different **set** of keys could apply to each category, and duplicate key values would then be allowed, provided that they were in different sets. A set of keys may be given a name, such as 'UniqueChapters' or 'UniqueSections'. A fragment is then identified by a combination of this name and the key value (the fragments '*UniqueChapters*/Schema Wars' and '*UniqueSections*/Schema Wars' can be clearly distinguished).

The fact that fragments of one type are nested within fragments of another in the example above is not particularly significant; it is just interesting to note that distinct sets do not in principle have to be in separate parts of the document. However, the second kind of context to consider relates to the distribution of fragments throughout the document. Fragments of the same kind may form subgroups in which duplication is allowed, provided that the fragments concerned are in different subgroups. For example, there may be no reason why two Section elements could not have the same title, provided that these sections were in different chapters. In this scenario, a different set of keys is needed for each bunch of Section elements:

```
<Chapter>
  . . .
  <Section>
    <Title>Schema Wars</Title>
    . . .
  </Section>
  . . .
</Chapter>
<Chapter>
  . . .
  <Section>
    <Title>Schema Wars</Title>
    . . .
  </Section>
  . . .
</Chapter>
```

This second definition of context reveals that an earlier assumption was false. The name of the set ('UniqueSections') and the key to the fragment ('Schema Wars') are no longer sufficient to unambiguously identify a fragment in the document. It is now also necessary to know which context element (in this case, which Chapter element) is wanted too. 'UniqueSections/*Chapter3*/Schema Wars' would then be distinguishable from 'UniqueSections/*Chapter4*/Schema Wars'.

Unique compound values

Sometimes a single value that uniquely identifies a fragment cannot be found. For example, while the starting time alone can differentiate the following two fragments, there may be many other broadcasts starting at 7:00 PM or 8:00 PM (on other channels and on other days):

```
<Broadcasts>
  <Broadcast>
    <Channel>BBC 2</Channel>
    <Sate>2002-07-21</Date>
    <StartTime>19:00</StartTime>
    . . .
  </Broadcast>
```

```
  <Broadcast>
    <Channel>BBC 2</Channel>
    <Date>2002-07-21</Date>
    <StartTime>20:00</StartTime>
    ...
  </Broadcast>
</Broadcasts>
```

In the following case, it is the channel name that differs, rather than the date or time:

```
<Broadcasts>
  <Broadcast>
    <Channel>BBC 2</Channel>
    <Date>2002-07-21</Date>
    <StartTime>20:00</StartTime>
    ...
  </Broadcast>
  <Broadcast>
    <Channel>BBC 1</Channel>
    <Date>2002-07-21</Date>
    <StartTime>20:00</StartTime>
    ...
  </Broadcast>
</Broadcasts>
```

But even when a fragment does not have a single value that is guaranteed to be unique, a unique identifier might still be constructed from a combination of several values. In this case, the channel name, date, and start time together fulfill this requirement because it is not possible for a broadcaster to broadcast two programs simultaneously on the same channel.

11.4   Unique Fragment Identification

A schema definition can contain information that identifies fragments which must have unique values contained within them. The **unique** element is inserted into the element declaration for an element that is certain to enclose the fragments. In simple cases, this will typically be the declaration of the root element. In any case, the element chosen must be a complex element, because no possible identifiable fragments in a value conform to a simple data type. The declaration must either refer to a complex data type from its type attribute or contain a complexType element. In the latter case, the unique element is placed after the complexType element:

```
<element name="Book" type="bookType">
  <unique>...</unique>
</element>

<element name="Book">
  <complexType>...</complexType>
  <unique>...</unique>
</element>
```

Named sets

The unique fragments are given an identifier by the **name** attribute:

```
<element name="Book">
  <complexType>...</complexType>
  <unique name="UniqueChapters">...</unique>
</element>
```

One reason why this name is required is to ensure that meaningful error messages can be presented when nonunique values are found. The name must therefore be unique:

```
ERROR: "Schema Wars" not unique in "UniqueChapters"
```

Missing values and key elements

An empty value is treated like any other in a unique set, which means that two empty values would raise a duplication error:

```
<Chapter>
  <Title></Title>
  ...
</Chapter>
<Chapter>
  <Title></Title> <!-- DUPLICATION ERROR -->
  ...
</Chapter>
```

But if the element (or attribute) is absent or several are absent, this is not deemed to be significant. For example, a chapter not containing a `Title` element would be considered to be valid (assuming, of course, that the `Title` element is optional). But this interpretation of uniqueness may not be sufficiently stringent for a given purpose. For this reason, an alternative element to the `unique` element can be used. The **key** element is almost identical to the `unique` element. It has the same content options and attributes, including the **name** attribute, but now the identifier must always be present (even if the `Title` element remains optional):

```
<key name="UniqueChapters>
  ...
</key>


  <Chapter>
    <!-- ERROR - MISSING TITLE -->
    ...
  </Chapter>
```

Again, the `name` attribute value must be unique and, indeed, must not even be found in the name of a `unique` element.

Multiple definitions

A number of `unique` and `key` elements may appear within a single element declaration, and the order in which they appear is not significant, but note that the names
are particularly significant here because an error message must be easily traced
back to a particular set of keys:

```
<element name="Book">
  <complexType>...</complexType>

  <key name="key1">...</key>
  <unique name="unique1">...</unique>
  <key name="key2">...</key>
  <unique name="unique2">...</unique>
</element>
```

Finding fragments and keys

Regardless of whether a `unique` element or `key` element is used, two tasks need to
be performed. First, the fragments must be identified (maybe they are the chapters
of a book). Second, the value or values within these fragments that will serve as
keys must be isolated (such as the title of each chapter). The same two elements,
(which are introduced below) appear in both the `unique` element and the `key` element to perform these tasks. The next three sections cover these topics.

11.5   Fragment Selectors

The **selector** element performs the task of finding fragments. It may be preceded
by an `annotation` element but must otherwise be the first element within the
`unique` or `key` element. It must be present and may not repeat:

```
<key>
  <annotation>...</annotation>
  <selector ... />
  ...
</key>

<unique>
  <selector ...>...</selector>
  ...
</unique>
```

The `selector` element may also contain an `annotation` element but is otherwise
empty. It holds a required **xpath** attribute that identifies the fragments by their
locations. As its name suggests, this attribute holds an XPath expression (for
details see http://www.w3.org/TR/xpath):

```
<element name="Book">
   ...
  <key name="...">
    <selector xpath="Chapter">
      <annotation>
        <documentation>Chapter titles must not be
        missing,
        even if the document model allows them to
        be absent.</documentation>
      </annotation>
    </selector>
     ...
  </key>
  <unique>
    <selector xpath="Chapter/Section">
      <annotation>
        <documentation>Section titles must be
        unique, but can be absent.</documentation>
      </annotation>
    </selector>
     ...
  </unique>
</element>
```

Note that the selector does not necessarily identify the element that directly contains the key. In the examples above, the fragments of interest are the chapters and
sections of a book, but the key in both cases is the content of an embedded Title
element. The means by which the actual key is targeted is discussed later.

The xpath attribute value must conform to the constraints of a subset of the pattern
language part of the XPath standard that allows for the following kinds of path to
be specified:

```
*            (all child elements)
A            (child A elements)
child::A     (child A elements)
A/B          (B element children of A children)
A | B        (child A elements and child B elements)
A/B | C/D    (B children of A children and
              D children of C children)
.//*         (all descendent elements)
.//B         (all descendent B elements)
A//B         (all descendent B elements within
              all A child elements)
```

Only the child axis ('**child::**') and descendent axis ('**//**') are permitted, so the target
must be an element, not an attribute or other XML component, and this element
must be within the element whose declaration contains the unique or key definition. Those familiar with the XPath language will be aware of the concept of absolute paths, which clearly cannot be used here, because the path must not begin with
a '/' symbol.

Child target fragments

In the simplest case, the fragments are children of the element whose declaration contains the `unique` or `key` element. Consider the schema definition for a book, and a rule that all chapters must be unique. In this case, it is only necessary to include the name of the child element in the `xpath` attribute:

```
<element name="Book">
  <complexType>...</complexType>

  <unique name="UniqueChapters">
    <locator xpath="Chapter" />
    ...
  </unique>
</element>
```

However, the meaning can be made clearer by inclusion of the optional 'child::' axis keyword:

```
<locator xpath="child::Chapter" />
```

Descendent target fragments

Now consider a rule that all sections must be unique. In this case, the target element is not the child of the root element; it is a child element of these children. Both of these element names are included in the path, separated by a '/' character:

```
<locator xpath="Chapter/Section" />
```

Again, the meaning is clearer when the more verbose method is used:

```
<locator xpath="child::Chapter/child::Section" />
```

Multilevel descendents

All fragments of a particular kind need not have the same fragment 'root' element. For example, a book might contain both chapters and appendices, and the titles may need to be unique across both. Uniqueness can be ensured by inclusion of two expressions within the `xpath` attribute, separated by a '|' symbol:

```
<locator xpath="Chapter | Appendix" />
```

As another example, an email should not be sent twice to the same person, so the name should not be repeated in a `To`, `CarbonCopy`, or `BlindCarbonCopy` element. Note that whitespace may surround the '|' separator, including line-feed characters:

```
<locator xpath="To | CarbonCopy | BlindCarbonCopy" />
```

Wildcards

The '*' symbol is a wildcard that stands in for any element. In the following modified version of the email example, all elements directly within a `Recipients` element are supposed to be unique fragments:

```
<locator xpath="Recipients/*" />
```

```
<Recipients>
  <To>...</To>
  <To>...</To>
  <CarbonCopy>...</CarbonCopy>
  <BlindCarbonCopy>...</BlindCarbonCopy>
</Recipients>
```

When every descendent occurrence of a specified element type is to be included, all the elements can be targeted by inclusion of an empty step, '//', which stands in for any number of intermediate elements (including none). A book might include unique definitions that are sprinkled throughout the text and identified by `Definition` elements. The example below finds all such definitions that are within chapters, even if they are actually embedded with a section or subsection:

```
<locator xpath="Chapter//Definition" />
```

```
<Book>
  <Chapter>
    <Para>...<Definition>XML</Definition> ...</Para>
    <Section>
      <Para>...<Definition>XSLT</Definition>
      ...</Para>
      <SubSection> <!-- DUPLICATION ERROR -->
        <Para>...<definition>XSLT</definition>
        ...</Para>
      </SubSection>
      ...
    </Section>
    ...
  </Chapter>
  ...
</Book>
```

Current element

The '.' symbol represents the current element. In this case, it stands for an instance of the element whose declaration includes the `unique` or `key` element. Its use here is really restricted to a single scenario (but is seen later in a more significant role). When an empty step is needed to search all descendents, including children of the current element, then the path must begin with './/'. In the following example, `Definition` elements that occur directly within the `book` element are treated as fragments (as well as those in lower-level structures, as shown above):

```
<locator xpath=".//Definition" />
```

Namespace qualifications

Namespace prefixes must be included in paths that navigate into documents that contain elements from at least one namespace. The prefixes used are matched to prefix definitions in the schema definition, rather than to those in a document instance (document instance authors are free to choose any prefix, and this choice cannot be known in advance by the schema definition author). In the following example, the document instance happens to use the default namespace for one of the namespaces, but this is also not an issue, because it is the namespace names that are really compared:

```
<schema xmlns:TN="TargetNamespace"
        xmlns:ON="OtherNamespace">
  ...
  <Locator
   xpath="TN:LocalElem/ON:ForeignFrag/ON:ForeignElem"/>
   ...
</schema>


  <Doc>
    <LocalElem xmlns="TargetNamespace"
               xmlns:F="OtherNamespace">
       <F:ForeignFrag>
          <F:ForeignElem>...</F:ForeignElem>
       </F:ForeignFrag>
    </LocalElem>
  </Doc>
```

11.6   Scope of Uniqueness

The unique and key elements do not have to be placed in the declaration of the root element. There are two reasons why some or all of them could or should be inserted into a different element declaration.

First, a document instance might not include the root element (a document that contains a single chapter does not include the Book element). When the element whose declaration includes the unique or key element is not present in the document instance, uniqueness validation is not performed. For this reason, the definition should be placed as deeply into the document model hierarchy as is possible without its inadvertently falling into the scenario to be discussed next.

Second, uniqueness across the entire document is not always desirable, and an earlier example showed how sections within a chapter should be unique (have different titles), but two or more sections may be allowed to have the same titles when the sections concerned are in different chapters. This local-scoping concept is enabled by a careful choice of where to place the unique or key element. Uniqueness is asserted specifically within the content of each instance of the element chosen. A key element in the declaration of the Chapter element instead of the Book element creates separate section key sets for each chapter. As another example, the EMail element may contain several To elements, but an email should not be sent to the same person twice, yet other email stored in the same XML document may have to be sent to some of the same people. In this case, the appropriate place to put the unique or key element is within the EMail element declaration:

```
<element name="EMail">
  <complexType>...</complexType>
  <unique>
    <locator xpath="To" />
    ...
  </unique>
</element>
```

The duplication error in the first entry would be reported, but the same email address appearing in another entry would not count as a duplicate:

```
<EMails>
  <EMail>
    ...
    <!-- DUPLICATION ERROR -->
    <To>p.jones@MegaTVi.com</To>
    <To>p.jones@MegaTVi.com</To>
    ...
  </EMail>
  <EMail>
    ...
    <!-- NOT ANOTHER DUPLICATE -->
    <To>p.jones@MegaTVi.com</To>
    ...
  </EMail>
</EMails>
```

Note that these subgroups do not have distinct names. A set called 'UniqueSections' or 'UniqueRecipients' would apply to all the relevant subgroups. This fact has implications for referencing a specific fragment (as will be seen later).

11.7 Identifier Fields

So far, although fragments have been identified, their keys have not. In the case of the To element, the key is simply the content of this element, but in the case of the Chapter element, it is the content of the child Title element. In other cases, it might be an attribute value or even a combination of values from several elements and attributes. The **field** element is used in the unique and key elements to find the key within the fragment. At least one field element must be present, following the selector element, but there may be more than one field element:

```
<key>
  <annotation>...</annotation>
  <selector ... />
  <field ... />
</key>

<unique>
  <selector ...>...</selector>
  <field ... />
  <field ... >...</field>
  <field ... >...</field>
</unique>
```

The `field` element is similar to the `locator` element in that it is also empty, apart from an optional `annotation` element, and again contains an **xpath** attribute. The value of this attribute must follow the same constraints as before, except that in this case it can target an attribute value. The '**attribute::**' axis keyword or the '**@**' symbol before a name indicates an attribute name, rather than an element name. When the path consists of just an attribute name, it is assumed that this attribute is attached to the element that represents the entire fragment:

```
<unique ...>
  <selector xpath=".//Para" />
  <field xpath="@Id" />
</unique>


  <Para Id="X123">...</Para>
  <Para Id="X124">...</Para>
  <Para Id="X125">...</Para>
```

The field could just as easily be the text content of the fragment's root element, in which case the current element identifier, '.', is used:

```
<unique name="UniqueDefinitions">
  <selector xpath=".//Definition" />
  <field xpath="." />
</unique>


  ... <Definition>XML</Definition> ...
  ... ... <Definition>XSLT</Definition> ...
  ... ... ... <Definition>XML Schemas</Definition> ...
```

It could also be the content of an enclosed element or an attribute attached to such an element, in which case the '/' step separator is used to separate the names of descendent elements:

```
<unique ...>
  <selector xpath="ProgramBroadcast" />
  <field xpath="BroadcastDetails/Channel" />
  <field xpath="BroadcastDetails/Date" />
  <field xpath="BroadcastDetails/StartTime" />
</unique>


  <ProgramBroadcasts>

    <!-- FRAGMENT -->
    <ProgramBroadcast>
      <ProgramDetails>
        ...
      </ProgramDetails>
      <BroadcastDetails>
        <Channel>BBC 2</Channel>
        <Date>2002-07-21</Date>
        <StartTime>19:00</StartTime>
        ...
      </BroadcastDetails>
    </ProgramBroadcast>

    ...

  </ProgramBroadcasts>
```

This example also shows how multiple `field` elements identify each component of a multipart key value.

11.8 Key References

The techniques described above are suitable for identifying keys and checking that they are indeed unique. In particular, the `key` element is aptly named (in the sense that it is, as a dictionary would define this word, '*something that provides a means of gaining access to something*') and is slightly more suitable for identifying keys than is the `unique` element. But if a key provides access to information, it must then be asked who is holding the key and whether this holder has a genuine key that opens the door to a real fragment of the document. A document instance may include a set of references (key holders) to fragments that contain keys; it can be useful to validate each **key reference** because a reference may be correct but the fragment it refers to may be missing, or the reference may be correct but the fragment it refers to has an incorrect key, or the reference may simply not include an accurate copy of the key to the fragment it is supposed to target.

Reference identification

The means by which references in an XML document are identified is identical to the way in which keys are identified. The location of a fragment containing a reference and then the location of the field or fields that constitute the reference value are again found with the **selector** and **field** elements, respectively. This time, however, these elements are placed within the **keyref** element (instead of the unique or key elements). Once again, a single selector element is allowed and required, and at least one field element is required (and an annotation element may precede them). For example, imagine that a reference to a chapter takes the form of an attribute called ChapterTitle in an element called ChapterReference:

```
<keyref ...>
  <selector xpath="./ChapterReference" />
  <field xpath="@ChapterTitle" />
</keyref>
```

```
... as discussed in
<ChapterReference ChapterTitle="Schema Wars" />.
```

Note that any number of references may be made to the same key fragment (there may be many holders of duplicate keys) because there is no uniqueness requirement. For example, there may be many references to the chapter entitled 'Schema Wars'.

Reference to key in specified set

While the ability to create multiple sets of keys is valuable, it also raises a significant problem. Some or all of the keys may be duplicated elsewhere in the document. Authors can solve this problem by giving each set of unique values a distinct name, thus revealing the second purpose of the **name** attribute on the **unique** and **key** elements. The relevant name can be added to the unique values within the set it defines to make every key totally unique. For example, 'UniqueChapters/ Schema Wars' and 'UniqueSections/Schema Wars' both refer to a fragment with the identifier 'Schema Wars', but in the first case from the set of fragments identified as chapters, and in the second case from the set of fragments identified as sections. A reference must therefore identify a specific set of keys, as represented by a single unique or key element. The **refer** attribute value must match the value of the name attribute of the relevant key set:

```
<keyref ... refer="UniqueChapters">
  <selector xpath="./ChapterReference" />
  <field xpath="@ChapterTitle" />
</keyref>
```

Note that when there is a target namespace and a prefix is assigned to this namespace within the schema definition, then the reference must include the prefix (the key definitions can be considered to be part of the namespace, along with element groups, attribute groups, data types, attributes, and elements, but in yet another partition):

```
<schema targetNamespace="http://MegaTVi.com/NS/BOOK"
        xmlns:B="http://MegaTVi.com/NS/BOOK" ... >
  ...
    <key name="UniqueChapters">...</key>
    <keyref name="ChapterRefs"
            refer="B:UniqueChapters">
    ...
    </keyref>
  ...
</schema>
```

Subgroups create an additional complication. The keyref element need not appear in the same element declaration as the unique or key element that it refers to, though it should probably do so when all of the references are in the same section of the document as the keys:

```
<element name="Book" type="bookType">
  <key name="UniqueChapters">
    <locator xpath="Chapter" />
    <field xpath="Title" />
  </key>
  <keyref name="ChapterRefs"
          refer="B:UniqueChapters">
    <locator xpath=".//ChapterReference" />
    <field xpath="@ChapterTitle" />
  </keyref>
</element>
```

When references can occur in various locations within a document instance, the reference definition needs to be placed in the declaration of an element that will certainly encompass all of these references. Yet, at the same time, only ancestor elements of the element declaration that contains the relevant key definition can be considered, because the actual keys must be within the scope of this definition too. The reason is that multiple sets of fragments may have the same identifiers, in different sections of the document, and there must be no ambiguity about which of these sets the references are targeting.

But moving a reference definition up the document model hierarchy also carries risks. A reference must not be added to the declaration of an element that will enclose multiple subgroups. Suppose, for example, that section titles need not be unique across the whole book so that keys for sections are defined within the Chapter element declaration. The key reference should not then be defined in the declaration of the parent Book element, because it would encompass sections in multiple chapters. This would not be a sensible thing to attempt in any case, because a key reference set should be associated with a single key set to avoid ambiguity when two keys (in different subgroups) have the same value.

Reference names

The **name** attribute must be added to the keyref element to name the reference:

```
<keyref ... name="ChapterRefs">
  <selector xpath=".//ChapterReference" />
  <field xpath="@ChapterTitle" />
</keyref>
```

This name should appear in error messages that are generated when one or more of the references are not valid. For example, a reference to the 'Schema Quibbles' chapter is incorrect because the chapter is actually called 'Schema Wars':

```
ERROR: bad key ref "Schema Quibbles" in "ChapterRefs"
```

There may also be multiple `keyref` elements, which must have different names, that refer to the same set of keys.

Data type matching

A reference field must conform to the same data type as the field it targets in a unique fragment. A reference will not work, even if there is an exact match of characters, when the data types differ. For example, the reference value '13' will not match the target field value '13' if the reference is a string type and the target is an integer. On the other hand, if there are multiple ways of representing the same value when adopting a given data type, a match will work even if different representations are used (see Section 14.6 for details on value spaces and lexical spaces). For example, '19' will match '019' if both data types are integers, and will also match '19.0' if both data types are decimals.

Multiple-field references

When a reference to a set of fragments in which each key comprises multiple fields is created, the reference must also contain multiple fields. In fact, the same number of fields must be present, with a one-to-one match of values and data types. However, the names of the fields can differ, and there is no need for attributes to match attributes and element content to match element content. For example, a program broadcast could be referenced by three attributes, despite the the key being derived from the content of three elements.

Because the names of elements and attributes may differ from those in the target fragment, the only way for a schema processor to determine which field in the reference matches a specific field in the target fragment is by comparing the order in which the `field` elements occur. The order must be the same.

Supporting hypertext linking

Keys and references can form the basis of a hypertext linking mechanism, just as the 'ID'/'IDREF' feature of the DTD modeling language has been used for many years. One good reason why the `selector` element is employed by the `keyref` element (apart from using its ability to group several fields into a single reference)

is that it identifies the 'hot text' area of the document that a user can select to follow the link. Apart from this, the distinction between referencing and linking is too
subtle to be of much relevance here. But it remains to be seen whether schema-sensitive browser applications will build hypertext links from information contained
in schema definitions, as many have done (using the ID and IDREF attribute types)
in the past when this information has been contained in a DTD.

Note that the XLink standard provides a more appropriate mechanism for creating
links when they are made across document instances, or have multiple end points
(see http://www.w3.org/TR/xlink/).

11.9 Complete Book Example

The following example combines previous snippets to show how an XML Schema
definition specifies the following unique and referenced elements. First, the book
must have unique chapters: established by comparison of the content of the chapter
titles. Second, each chapter must have unqiue sections: established by comparison
of the content of section titles within the same chapter. Third, references to chapters must refer to chapter titles that actually exist within the document instance:

```
<element name="Book">
  <complexType>...</complexType>
  <!-- UNIQUE CHAPTERS -->
  <key name="UniqueChapters">
    <locator xpath="Chapter" />
    <field xpath="Title" />
  </key>
  <!-- REFERENCES TO CHAPTERS -->
  <keyref name="ChapterRefs">
    <locator xpath=".//ChapterReference" />
    <field xpath="@ChapterTitle" />
  </keyref>
</element>

<element name="Chapter">
  <complexType>...</complexType>
  <!-- UNIQUE SECTIONS (within each chapter) -->
  <key name="UniqueSections">
    <locator xpath="Section" />
    <field xpath="Title" />
  </key>
</element>
```

12. Namespace Switching

Locations in a document model where it is allowable for document instance authors to insert document fragments that belong to other namespaces can be specified in the schema definition. The schema processor can also be instructed to validate these foreign fragments against other schema definitions less stringently than it validates the rest of the document.

See Chapter 21 for a comprehensive explanation of the Namespaces standard.

12.1 Namespace and Schema Relationship

A document model described by a schema definition is often associated with a namespace. There is usually a one-to-one relationship between the schema definition and the namespace. Indeed, a schema definition can even be viewed as a way to create a namespace for the document model, using the targetNamespace attribute to assign the name to the namespace (in contrast to the idea that this attribute is used to refer to a namespace that already exists).

Namespace markup in a document instance tells the schema processor which namespace an element belongs to and therefore which schema definition should be used to validate it. Typically, a document that belongs to one namespace or to no namespace will contain local (native) elements and one or more fragments that belong to other (foreign) namespaces. At the boundary point before such a fragment, the schema processor needs to 'switch out' the current schema definition, and temporarily 'switch in' the other:

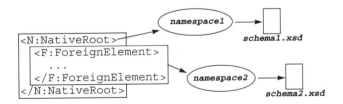

The original schema definition is recalled when the processor reaches the end of the element at the root of the fragment. Note that for this reason the first schema definition, called in to process the document root element, will always be back in control at the end of the document. Also note that foreign fragments may themselves contain fragments belonging to other namespaces and even to the namespace of the surrounding document.

Neither the schema processor nor the document instance actually controls the switching of schema definitions. Instead, the currently active schema definition decides when and whether to allow another schema definition to temporarily replace it. It specifies exactly where foreign elements are allowed to occur and raises an error if the document instance contains an element from another namespace in an unexpected location. The same principles apply to attributes, except that the fragments are, of course, much smaller.

12.2 Element Importing

If a specific element from another namespace should be allowed to occur at a given location in the document structure, it is possible to directly reference the foreign element declaration. First, it is necessary to 'import' the other schema definition (see Section 13.4). Once this is done, any element can be referenced from that schema definition by inclusion of the relevant namespace prefix in the element reference:

```
<schema ... targetnamespace="ForeignNamespace">
  ...
  <element name="ForeignElement" ... />
  ...
</schema>


<schema xmlns:X="ForeignNamespace" ...>
  <import namespace="ForeignNamespace" />
  ...
    <element ref="X:ForeignElement" ... />
  ...
</schema>
```

The acts of importing the schema definition and referencing an element from it do not change the namespace that the element belongs to. When added to a document instance, the relevant prefix must be added:

```
<RootNativeElement xmlns:X="ForeignNamespace" ...>
  <NativeElement>
    <X:ForeignElement>...</X:ForeignElement>
  </NativeElement>
</RootNativeElement>
```

When the processor detects the presence of this element in a document instance, it needs to refer to the declaration of that element in the foreign schema definition.

A Broadcast element could be added to the possible content of the email Message element in order to allow the message to hold a broadcast description from the broadcast namespace.

There is more on this topic in Section 13.4.

12.3   Attribute Importing

During validation of an attribute value, there may be a need to switch to another schema definition that defines the data type the value should conform to. Again, an imported definition is referenced:

```
<schema xmlns:X="ForeignNamespace" ...>
  <import namespace="ForeignNamespace" ... />
  ...
  <element name="NativeElement">
    <complexType>
      ...
      <attribute ref="X:AnAttribute" ... />
    </complexType>
  </element>
  ...
</schema>
```

It does not matter if an existing attribute on the same element has the same name, because the imported attribute must always be prefixed in a document instance:

```
<NativeElement AnAttribute="..."
               X:AnAttribute="..." />
```

12.4   Any Element from Other Namespace

The **any** element by default allows for the insertion of elements from any namespace and also from no namespace. This can be made explicit by giving the **namespace** attribute the value '**##any**'. The following two examples are therefore equivalent:

```
<any/>
```

```
<any namespace="##any" />
```

However, the namespace attribute can specify that only elements from other namespaces are allowed when it is given the value '**##other**'. Alternatively, only elements from a specific namespace are allowed by inclusion of the namespace name in this attribute:

```
<any namespace="http://MegaTVi.com/NS/PB" />
```

Recall that the any element can be inserted directly into the choice and sequence elements, at the same locations at which a normal element declaration or reference can appear. In the following example, any element from the schema definition that models the program broadcast namespace is allowed to appear within the Broadcast element:

```
<element name="Broadcast">
  <complexType>
    <sequence>
      <any namespace="http://MegaTVi.com/NS/PB" />
    </sequence>
  </complexType>
</element>
```

```
http://MegaTVi.com/NS/PB
<ProgramBroadcast>
  <StartTime>
    <Description>
```

The following inclusion of the `Description` element from the program broadcast namespace is therefore legal:

```
<E:EMail xmlns:E="http://MegaTVi.com/NS/EMAIL"
         xmlns:PB="http://MegaTVi.com/NS/PB">
  ...
  <E:Title>Please check this description!</E:Title>
  ...
  <E:Message>
    <E:Broadcast>
      <PB:Description>...</PB:Description>
    </E:Broadcast>
  </E:Message>
</E:eMail>
```

But note that this mechanism cannot constrain the content of the container element to a particular foreign element. The example above would be just as valid if it contained the `StartTime` element instead of the `Description` element. If such precision is required, the import-and-reference technique discussed earlier must be used.

By default, the `any` element stands in for only one required element. The **minOccurs** and **maxOccurs** attributes need to be added in order to make the embedded fragment optional or to allow several 'root' elements to occur:

```
<any namespace="http://MegaTVi.com/NS/PB"
     minOccurs="0" maxOccurs="unbounded" />
```

The following two fragments are now valid:

```
<E:Broadcast>
  <PB:Description>...</PB:Description>
  <PB:StartTime>...</PB:StartTime>
</E:Broadcast>
```

```
<E:Broadcast><!-- EMPTY --></E:Broadcast>
```

Text can be placed around elements from the other namespace:

```
<element name="Broadcast">
  <complexType mixed="true">
    <sequence>
      <any namespace="http://MegaTVi.com/NS/PB"
           minOccurs="0" maxOccurs="unbounded" />
    </sequence>
  </complexType>
</element>
```

The following fragment conforms to this model:

```
<E:Broadcast>the time
  <PB:StartTime>...</PB:StartTime> and the
  description <PB:Description>...</PB:Description>.
</E:Broadcast>
```

The text surrounding embedded elements is, for all practical purposes, deemed to belong to the namespace of the enclosing element. This distinction is significant when several applications process different fragments of the document because there must be no ambiguity about which application will process this text.

Specific namespaces allowed

More than one namespace can be referenced in the **namespace** attribute, but there must be at least one whitespace character between each namespace URL:

```
<any namespace="http://MegaTVi.com/NS/PB
                http://MegaTVi.com/NS/BOOK" />
```

The processor is expected to access all the relevant schema definitions and use whichever is most appropriate at any given moment to validate the content of embedded elements. Namespace markup supplies the necessary context to match each element to the correct namespace.

The namespace of the current schema definition can be added to the list, with the keyword '**##targetNamespace**', thus allowing any element from the current model. Alternatively, this might even be the only value of the attribute:

```
<any namespace="##targetNamespace" />

<any namespace="##targetNamespace
                http://MegaTVi.com/NS/PB" />
```

This approach is only relevant when the current schema definition targets a namespace. It is not usable in schema definitions aimed at modeling basic XML documents.

No qualified elements allowed

Elements from a schema definition that does not target a namespace are permitted by inclusion of the '**##local**' keyword in the namespace attribute. The name 'local' reflects the nature of the elements in the document instance, in that they are local to the (unqualified) document instance, rather than being from a fragment that belongs to a foreign namespace.

This keyword is also used when the current schema definition does not target a namespace and when any element from the current model model must be allowed to occur. In this case, it serves the equivalent role to the '##targetNamespace' keyword in an any element within a schema definition that *does* target a namespace.

Choices

Subtle combinations of allowed elements can be constructed by means of a choice group. For example, any element from a specified namespace, or one of a few specific elements from the current namespace, can be combined in this way:

```
<choice>
  <any namespace="otherNamespace" />
  <element ref="DOC:Element1" />
  <element ref="DOC:Element2" />
  <element ref="DOC:Element3" />
</choice>
```

12.5   Validation Options

By default, a schema processor is expected to validate elements from other schema definitions just as diligently as it validates locally declared elements, but other options are available. It is possible to avoid validating unrecognized elements, or even *all* elements, though well-formed conformance remains an essential requirement in all XML documents.

The default value of the **processContents** attribute is '**strict**', meaning that the processor should validate the content of foreign elements against the relevant schema or schemas. Because this is the default option, the following two instructions are equivalent:

```
<any/>

<any processContents="strict" />
```

The '**lax**' option forces the schema definition to accept elements that belong to any namespace referenced from the document instance (possibly including namespaces that are not even acknowledged by the schema definition). In the following example, the AnyContainer element can contain both text and any number of elements. The processor will not validate the content of any element that it does not recognize, though the parser will still check it for well-formed conformance:

```
<element name="AnyContainer">
  <complexType mixed="true">
    <sequence>
      <any minOccurs="0"
           maxOccurs="unbounded"
           processContents="lax" />
    </sequence>
  </complexType>
</element>
```

Even if the Unknown element in the following example is not declared in any recognized schema definition, no errors are raised when this element is encountered. However, an error *is* raised when the StartTime element is validated because it is a recognized element that is known to have required content:

```
<AnyContainer>Some text and a
new <Unknown><!--UNRECOGNIZED - OK--></Unknown>
element, and a
<E:StartTime><!--RECOGNIZED, BUT WRONG--></E:StartTime>
element.</AnyContainer>
```

No schema validation takes place at all when the processContents attribute is given the value 'skip'. The example above becomes valid, and so does the following example:

```
<AnyContainer>Some text and a
<E:StartTime><!--OK (well-formed)--></E:StartTime>
element.</AnyContainer>
```

12.6   Any Attribute from Other Namespace

Just as the any element allow elements from other namespaces to occur in a document instance, the **anyAttribute** element can allow attributes from other namespaces to occur.

Attributes on this element for specifying one or more namespaces and for controlling the strictness of validation are identical to the attributes that have these roles on the any element. Again, the **namespace** attribute has a default value of '**##any**', but may also contain one or more namespace names, plus the keywords '**##other**', '**##local**', and '**##targetNamespace**'; the **processContents** attribute still has the default value '**strict**' but may also be set to '**lax**' or '**skip**'. The following two definitions are equivalent:

```
<anyAttribute/>

<anyAttribute namespace="##any"
              processContents="strict" />
```

The occurrence attributes found on the any element are not available here. The definition automatically stands in for any number of attributes, including none.

This element appears in the same location as attribute references, but always immediately following any such references. Only one anyAttribute element can appear in any of these locations. In the following example, any attributes from any number of namespaces or from no namespace can appear on the Book element:

```
<element name="Book">
  <complexType>
    <!-- CONTENT MODEL -->
    ...
    <!-- ATTRIBUTES -->
    <attribute name="ISBN" ... />
    <attribute name="AuthorName" ... />
    <attribute name="Price" ... />
    <anyAttribute/>
  </complexType>
</element>
```

This element can be used directly within the attributeGroup element:

```
<attributeGroup name="BookAttributes">
  <attribute name="ISBN" ... />
  <attribute name="AuthorName" ... />
  <attribute name="Price" ... />
  <anyAttribute/>
</attributeGroup>
```

It can also be used in the restriction and extension elements. Note that when a complex data type is restricted, normal attribute declarations can be automatically carried forward to the new definition (see Section 16.6), but this is not the case for the anyAttribute element. Its absence implies that the option to include any attribute is not wanted in the derived data type (the anyAttribute element is always optional). So, if it is still wanted, this element must be repeated in the re-defined data type. It is then possible to limit the options, perhaps by replacing an original '##any' keyword with the name of a single namespace.

13. Including External Components

Schema definitions can be spread across multiple files, exploit declarations and definitions that already exist in common 'libraries,' and selectively override external declarations and definitions (keeping the same name, but modifying the declaration or definition itself). As briefly discussed in Section 12.2, a schema definition can even incorporate references to components declared in other schema definitions that target different namespaces.

13.1 Definitions and Documents

While it has already been seen that one schema definition can utilize declarations in another, it has perhaps been implied that the components that constitute a single schema definition are all to be found within a single document file. This is not necessarily the case. A single schema definition can be constructed from a number of **schema document** files. Indeed, files can incorporate files that incorporate further files, to any number of levels.

However, there must always be a **head schema document** at the top level. This is the document that is selected by a user or by reference from a document instance. Other schema documents are 'merged in' before any attempt is made to interpret the instructions that they and the head document contain (just as if there had only been a single document to start with).

All schema document files include the **schema** element, so can also be treated as a complete schema definition or as the head of a set of schema documents.

There are actually three mechanisms to consider for incorporating components from subsidiary schema documents. A schema document can include, redefine, or import other schema documents. Note that although including and importing might sound similar they are not the same and are used in very different circumstances.

13.2 **Including a Schema Document**

Schema definition authors sometimes have difficulty handling and updating large schema definitions and therefore prefer to move related groups of definitions into separate data files. Typically, the 'main' definition file is reduced to little more than a skeleton consisting of references that **include** a number of subsiduary files. The **include** element is used for this purpose, and its required **schemaLocation** attribute contains a URL that locates the schema document to be included:

```
<include schemaLocation="OtherSchemaDocument.xsd" />
```

Any number of include elements may be present, though each one must target a schema document different from the others. Circular references are also not allowed. This applies both to direct reverse references, as well as to indirect closing of a circle that involves multiple schema documents.

An included file must be a complete schema document in its own right and must therefore contain the root schema element. The settings of the attributeForm-Default, elementFormDefault, blockDefault, and finalDefault attributes will continue to apply to all relevant components defined in that schema. They are not overridden by settings in the including schema document.

A component of an included document can refer to a component of the including document or to a component of another included document because interpretation of components does not take place until all the inclusions have occurred. In this sense, inclusion is much like the act of physically copying and pasting components into a single document before processing the document. Unlike that more primitive approach, however, the include feature is namespace sensitive. The including process also happens every time the head schema document is processed, which means that later modifications to a document are guaranteed not to be overlooked the next time that document is included.

A schema document can be incorporated into any number of schema definitions if it does not target a namespace, including into those that do target a namespace. This is convenient because it removes the need for duplication when two or more schema definitions, targeting different namespaces, require some of the same components. When the including document targets a namespace, the included components are dynamically assigned to this namespace. For this reason, this technique should not be used when the shared components need to retain their own group identity. For example, it is common in publishing applications to include the same table-building elements in many document models (see Section 18.9 for more on common table models), but rendering technologies need to be able to recognize them, so they should always belong either to a dedicated namespace or to no namespace at all (the importing technique described later is more appropriate in this scenario).

When the including document targets a namespace, any reference to a component from the included document should include a namespace prefix (assuming that prefixes are used for the target namespace in the schema document) because by the time the reference is actually followed by the schema processor, the component has become part of the current namespace. However, it should not be necessary to remember to include the prefix. Both references in the following example should work, though only the second one works reliably in tested processors:

```
<!-- (OtherSchemaDoc.xsd) NO TARGET NAMESPACE -->
<xsd:schema ...>
  <xsd:element name="NonNamespaceElement"
               type="xsd:string">
  ...
</xsd:schema>

<!-- NAMESPACE IS TARGETED -->
<schema targetNamespace="DocNS"
        xmlns:DOC="DocNS" ...>
  <include schemaLocation="OtherSchemaDoc.xsd" />
  ...
  <element name="NamespaceElement" type="string" />
    ...
    <!-- WORKS,
         BECAUSE ORIGINAL IS IN NO NAMESPACE -->
    <element ref="NonNamespaceElement" />
    <!-- ALSO WORKS,
         BECAUSE IT IS NOW IN TARGET NAMESPACE -->
    <element ref="DOC:NonNamespaceElement" />
    ...
  ...
</schema>
```

13.3   Redefining a Schema Document

A variant on the include feature allows components to be modified as they are included, but only within strict limits. Mainly, this variant permits an included data type to be derived by restriction or extension without the need to give the new data type a different name. The new document type thereby replaces the original definition. This feature can also be used to override element group and attribute group definitions.

Limitations of include feature

As previously described, the include element can be used to 'pull in' and use declarations and definitions from other schema documents, provided that they target the same namespace or do not target a namespace at all. This is an important feature that nevertheless suffers from one significant weakness: the declarations and definitions must either be used without modification or, if a derived component is needed, then this component must have a different name than the original. For example, an included file called 'myTVDataTypeLibrary' may contain a definition for a simple data type called 'copyrightYear' which contains a year value that must take the form 'YYYY' and includes a restriction that the smallest possible value is '1936' (the year that television broadcasts began). In the following example, this data type is assigned to the Copyright element:

```
<schema ...>
  <include schemaLocation="myTVDataTypeLibrary" />
  ...
  <element name="Copyright" type="copyrightYear" />
  ...
</schema>
```

But the current need might actually be for the copyright year to be at least '1978' (perhaps the earliest year for which programs were catalogued and described by the MegaTVi Corporation). Assuming that the original definition cannot be altered because other schema definitions that include the library still require the earliest date to be '1936', two obvious approaches can be taken.

First, the current schema definition could create a new data type that restricts the original. This approach requires a new data type name and modified references:

```
<schema ...>
  <include location="myTVDataTypeLibrary.xsd" />
  ...
  <simpleType name="NEWcopyrightYear">
    <restriction base="DOC:copyrightYear">
      <minInclusive value="1978" />
    </restriction>
  </simpleType>
  ...
  <element name="Copyright" type="NEWcopyrightYear" />
  ...
</schema>
```

Alternatively, the original could be ignored entirely, although this leads to duplication of effort, still requires a different name to be used, and also introduces the possibility of errors being introduced:

```
<schema ...>
  <include location="myTVDataTypeLibrary" />
  ...
  <simpleType name="NEWcopyrightYear">
    <restriction base="integer">
      <minInclusive value="1978" />
      <pattern value="\d\d\d\d" />
    </restriction>
  </simpleType>
  ...
  <element name="Copyright" type="NEWcopyrightYear" />
  ...
</schema>
```

Neither technique is particularly satisfactory. It would be useful to be able to employ a technique that allows the data type to be modified in the head schema document without an author having to assign a new name to it while simultaneously the update is also applied to all included components that use this data type.

Redefinitions

It is possible to override, or **redefine**, a simple type, complex type, element group, or attribute group definition. The **redefine** element is used in place the `include` element. Again, the **schemaLocation** attribute contains a URL that locates the schema document, and the referenced schema document must either target the same namespace or must not target a namespace at all. Any number of `redefine` elements may be present, provided that each one references a different schema document.

The `redefine` element can be empty, although the `include` element might as well be used in this case. The following two inclusions are therefore interchangeable:

```
<redefine schemaLocation="myTVDataTypeLibrary.xsd" />

<include schemaLocation="myTVDataTypeLibrary.xsd" />
```

The `redefine` element actually contains the definitions for the data types, element groups, and attribute groups that need to be redefined. All other component definitions and declarations are also included, but without modification (except for possible assignment to the target namespace), just as they are when using the `include` element. The **redefine** element may therefore contain any number of `simpleType`, `complexType`, `group`, and `attributeGroup` elements, in any combination. In the following example, a single `simpleType` element redefines a simple data type definition:

```
<schema xmlns:DOC="..." ...>
  <redefine schemaLocation="myTVDataTypeLibrary">
    <simpleType name="copyrightYear">
      <restriction base="DOC:copyrightYear">
        <minInclusive value="1978" />
      </restriction>
    </simpleType>
  </redefine>
  ...
  <element name="Copyright" type="copyrightYear" />
  ...
</schema>
```

In this case, the 'copyrightYear' data type is modified to restrict the dates to '1978' or later (without creating a new name for the data type).

In earlier chapters it was stated that named components are placed directly within the schema element. This is the one exception to that rule.

No backward references

All definition references are considered to be references to the redefined versions of the components concerned. It is not possible to reference the original definitions. Even references from other components that are defined in the included document are updated.

Data type redefinitions

Redefined simple type and complex type definitions must be based on their original definitions (they must reference themselves). A complexType element must therefore contain a complexContent or simpleContent element. When redefining a simple data type, however, the schema author cannot extend the type by using the union or list elements. In this context, only the restriction element may be used. This avoids confusing a processor that expects the original data type (see Chapter 17 for advanced inheritance concepts).

The redefine feature does not offer any protection from unintended conflicts between definitions. For example, a redefined data type could add an element with the same name as an added element in a derived version of the same base data type. In the following example, the change to 'eMailType' adds a reference to the Date element, but because this change applies to definitions made in the included file, the derived data type there called 'eMailWithDateType' is now picking up the new version, yet also tries to add the same element, thus stating that there must be two Date elements:

```
<schema ...>
  <complexType name="eMailType">
    <sequence>
      <element ref="E:From" />
      <element ref="E:To" />
      <element ref="E:Title" />
      <element ref="E:Message" />
    </sequence>
  </complexType>

  <complexType name="eMailWithDateType">
    <extension base="E:eMailType">
      <sequence>
        <element ref="E:Date" />
      <sequence>
    </extension>
  </complexType>
  ...
</schema>
```

```
<schema ...>
  <redefine schemaLocation="eMailTypeLibary.xsd">
    <complexType name="eMailType">
      <extension base="E:eMailType">
        <sequence>
              <!-- WARNING: TWO DATES NOW -->
          <element ref="E:Date" />
        <sequence>
      </extension>
    </complexType>
  </redefine>
  ...
</schema>
```

This could even cause a conflict that leads to errors, such as setting a minimum value that is higher than the redefined minimum value.

Group redefinitions

A redefined element or attribute group definition must closely resemble the original definition. The principle is almost identical to restrictions or derivations of data types, in that the replacement group must be a restricted or extended version of the original group.

In the simplest case, the group can just include a single reference to itself (recall that this is not normally allowed), although the following example is redundant, since it would do nothing more than bring the group into the target namespace and this would happen in any case. The reference below already assumes it is in the namespace because it includes the prefix:

```
<group name="originalGroup">
  <sequence>
    <group ref="DOC:originalGroup" />
  </sequence>
</group>
```

The group can instead be an exact copy of the original, but again this would be pointless:

```
<group name="originalGroup">
  <sequence>
    <element ref="DOC:OriginalElement1"
             maxOccurs="20" />
    <element ref="DOC:OriginalElement2"
             maxOccurs="20" />
  </sequence>
</group>
```

A restriction works similarly to complex data type restrictions. The original model is first replicated, then any allowed constraints, such as narrowing the number of permitted occurrences, is added:

```
<group name="originalGroup">
  <sequence>     <!-- FEWER OCCURRENCES -->
    <element ref="DOC:OriginalElement1"
             maxOccurs="10" />
    <element ref="DOC:OriginalElement2"
             maxOccurs="10" />
  </sequence>
</group>
```

An extension works by first referencing the original group, then adding further definitions or references. However, unlike complex type extensions, the new definitions do not have to be added after the original ones, as the following example demonstrates:

```
<group name="originalGroup">
  <sequence>
    <element ref="DOC:NewElement" />
    <group ref="DOC:originalGroup" />
  </sequence>
</group>
```

In the case of attribute groups, optional attributes can be suppressed entirely or made to be required, or a default or fixed value can be added or overridden. All the original attribute declarations must be repeated in the redefinition.

13.4 Importing a Schema Document

The include and redefine elements cannot be used when the required schema document targets a namespace different from the current schema definition. If, for example, a schema definition needs to access XHTML elements, which belong to the XHTML namespace, then a third method of incorporating components must be used. The definitions from the foreign namespace must be imported into the current schema definition. The **import** feature allows schema definition authors to reference particular elements and attributes from a foreign namespace and to specify the precise points in the current document model where they will be allowed to occur (rather than just letting the schema processor switch to other schema definitions at predefined points, using the any element, as discussed in Section 12.4). For example, the linking attribute from the XLink namespace might be allowed only on the Link element of the current document model.

There must be a separate **import** element for each namespace from which elements or attributes are needed. These elements, if present, must be the first children of the schema element (they should even precede any include or redefine elements), and, just like include elements, they are either empty or contain an annotation element:

```
<schema ... >
  <import ... />
  <import><annotation>...</annotation></import>
  <import ... />
  <!-- OTHER INSTRUCTIONS -->
  ...
</schema>
```

Finding the document to import

The `import` element may optionally hold the **schemaLocation** attribute to find the schema document (recall that this attribute is not optional on the `include` and `redefine` elements):

```
<!-- ON.XSD -->
<schema ... targetNamespace="OtherNamespace">
  ...
</schema>


<schema ... targetNamespace="LocalNamespace">
  <import schemaLocation="ON.xsd">
    <annotation>
      <documentation>
        IMPORT OTHER NAMESPACE
      </documentation>
    </annotation>
  </import>
  ...
</schema>
```

Note that circular references *are* legal. The imported schema could include an `import` element that references the importing schema, without tying the processor up in knots. This is because importing, unlike including, does not actually involve the copying of definitions into the main schema. In fact, this feature really behaves more like a referencing technique than an importing mechanism.

The `schemaLocation` attribute is optional because an alternative approach to finding the schema document is available. The **namespace** attribute can be used to simply refer to the target namespace of the other schema document. In this case, it is assumed that the schema document targeting this namespace can be found from a catalogue that maps namespace names to files:

```
<import namespace="OtherNamespace" />
```

Local namespace declaration

The namespace targeted by the remote schema definition must be declared in the importing schema definition too, so that the prefix it is mapped to here can be included in references to its components (see Section 12.2 for more details on such references):

```
<schema ... xmlns:ON="OtherNamespace">
  <import namespace="OtherNamespace" />
  ...
    <element ref="ON:RemoteElement"/>
  ...
</schema>
```

The way in which imported elements and attributes are referenced is discussed in depth in Chapter 12.

Local element prefix retention

The namespace of a complex data type is retained when that data type is referenced from the head schema definition. All elements declared within an imported schema definition retain their identity, including local elements. This is significant when local elements are required to include prefixes, as in the following example:

```
<schema xmlns="..."
        xmlns:N1="N1"
        targetNamespace="N1"
        elementFormDefault="qualified">

  <complexType name="CT">
    <sequence>
      <element name="E2" type="string" />
    </sequence>
  </complexType>

  <element name="E1" type="N1:CT" />

</schema>
```

Direct use of this schema document would require a document instance such as:

```
<X:E1 xmlns:X="N1">
  <X:E2>original local element</X:E2>
</X:E1>
```

There is nothing new here. But now the schema document above is imported into another schema definition, and the data type is extended:

```
<schema xmlns="..." xmlns:X="N1" xmlns:N2="N2"
        targetNamespace="N2"
        elementFormDefault="qualified">

  <import namespace="N1" />

  <complexType name="extendedCT">
    <extension base="X:CT">
      <sequence>
        <element name="E3" type="string" />
      </sequence>
    </extension>
  </complexType>
```

```
    <element name="docN2" type="N2:extendedCT" />

</schema>
```

The document instance below includes the new element, which is in the new namespace, but an instance of the original element still belongs to the original namespace:

```
<N2:docN2 xmlns:X="N1"
          xmlns:N2="N2">
  <X:E2>original local element</X:E2>
  <N2:E3>additional local element</N2:E3>
</N2:docN2>
```

Import or copy

Instead of importing components that belong to another namespace, schema definition authors can simply 'copy and paste' the definitions and declarations into the current schema definition. This makes the components an integral part of the current schema definition and part of the same namespace. The benefit of this approach is that document instance authors do not have to be aware of the other namespace (and do not have to include the appropriate namespace declaration in their documents). But one disadvantage of this approach is that this work must be repeated if the pasted-in schema components are ever updated. Also, software that supports the other namespace will no longer recognize the elements copied from that namespace when a document instance containing them is processed. The decision on whether to copy-and-paste or to import is ultimately a judgement call that must take these factors into consideration.

14. Creation of New Simple Types

New simple data types can be created by deriving characteristics from existing, built-in simple data types, and then either restricting or expanding the scope of values allowed. Simple data types can be anonymously created to constrain the content of a specific element or attribute, or they can be named, shared, and added to the target namespace so that they can be used in many element and attribute declarations.

14.1 Simple Type Definitions

It is not strictly necessary to create simple data types, because it is entirely possible to build useful schema definitions using only the simple data types that are built in to the language. However, there are many specialist needs that a standard list of data types, no matter how extensive or carefully chosen, cannot adequately cover. A new simple data type can therefore be created with the **simpleType** element:

```
<simpleType>...</simpleType>
```

Elements with custom simple data types

Just as a complexType element can be used within an element element, the simpleType element can also be placed here, and, as before, the element declaration in this case does not include either the ref attribute or the type attribute:

```
<element name="MySimpleElement">
  <simpleType>...</simpleType>
</element>
```

In this scenario, the element cannot contain child elements and also cannot have attributes (except for the XML Schema Instance attributes, such as xsi:type and xsi:nil).

Attributes with custom simple data types

The simpleType element can also be used within the **attribute** element, unlike the complexType element, because an attribute can hold a simple value. In this case, the attribute element does not include either the ref attribute or the type attribute because the definition is embedded:

```
<attribute name="MyAttribute">
  <simpleType>...</simpleType>
</attribute>
```

Named simple types

A simple data type can be shared and added to the target namespace if the definition is placed directly within the schema element and given a name by the **name** attribute. Element and attribute declarations can then adopt the new data type by reference to its name, just as they can refer to the built-in simple data types:

```
<schema ...>
  <simpleType name="mySimpleType">
    ...
  </simpleType>

  <element name="MySimpleElement"
           type="DOC:mySimpleType" />

  <element name="MyElement">
    ...
    <attribute name="MyAttribute"
               type="DOC:mySimpleType" />
  </element>

</schema>
```

Elements and attributes refer to a data type, whether it is simple or complex, by using the same type attribute. For this reason, all data type names must be unique. There cannot be a simple type with the same name as a complex type. However, there is no such conflict between data type names and the names of other constructs. A data type name can be the same as an element name or an element group name.

14.2   Derivations

While complex data types can be created 'from scratch' within a schema definition, a new simple data type must be **derived** from an existing simple data type, either directly or indirectly from one of the simple data types built in to the XML Schema standard (as listed in Section 7.5).

A new simple data type is derived from another simple data type first by a reference to the existing data type, and then by creation of the new one as either a restricted version or an extended version of that type. For example, it is possible to create a new numeric type that is based on the 'integer' type but is constrained to values between '5' and '50' (complex types can also be derived in similar ways, as discussed in Chapter 16).

This feature is not limited to the creation of custom types from built-in data types. It is also possible to create new types from other custom types, and there are also ways to prevent this from happening, either at all or in specific ways (using techniques described in Chapter 17).

The `simpleType` element can contain an initial `annotation` element, then can either create an extended version of the base type (a list type or a combination of two or more existing types (a 'union')), or create a restricted version of an existing data type:

```
<simpleType><list>...</list></simpleType>

<simpleType><union>...</union></simpleType>

<simpleType>
  <annotation>...</annotation>
  <restriction>...</restriction>
</simpleType>
```

14.3   Restrictions

A new data type can be a restricted version of an existing type. In the following example, the **restriction** element first identifies, in its **base** attribute, the existing data type that is to be the basis of the new, more restrictive data type (in this case, 'NMTOKEN'), then holds various elements that define the nature of the restriction:

```
<attribute name="Security">
  <simpleType>
    <restriction base="NMTOKEN">
      <enumeration value="normal" />
      <enumeration value="secret" />
      <enumeration value="topSecret" />
    </restriction>
  </simpleType>
</attribute>
```

Facets

As shown above, a restricted data type is defined by specifying the constraints to be applied to an existing data type. These constraints are known as **facets**.

The facets available vary somewhat depending on the base data type that is being restricted. For example, the 'NMTOKEN' type has an 'enumeration' facet, and indeed this facet applies to all data types except for the 'boolean' type. But other facets are less ubiquitous. For example, the 'length' facet cannot be used with any of the number-based types, including the 'integer' data type.

The fundamental facet types are shown in the table below:

- length (the L column)
- minimum length (the MINL column)
- maximum length (the MAXL column)
- pattern (the P column)
- enumeration (the E column)
- whitespace (the W column)

Simple type	L	MINL	MAXL	P	E	W
string	Y	Y	Y	Y	Y	Y
normalizedString	Y	Y	Y	Y	Y	Y
token	Y	Y	Y	Y	Y	Y
base64Binary	Y	Y	Y	Y	Y	Y
hexBinary	Y	Y	Y	Y	Y	Y
byte				Y	Y	Y
unsignedByte				Y	Y	Y
integer				Y	Y	Y
positiveInteger				Y	Y	Y
negativeInteger				Y	Y	Y
nonNegativeInteger				Y	Y	Y
nonPositiveInteger				Y	Y	Y
int				Y	Y	Y
unsignedInt				Y	Y	Y
long				Y	Y	Y
unsignedLong				Y	Y	Y
short				Y	Y	Y
unsignedShort				Y	Y	Y
decimal				Y	Y	Y
float				Y	Y	Y
double				Y	Y	Y
boolean				Y		Y
time				Y	Y	Y
dateTime				Y	Y	Y
duration				Y	Y	Y

Simple type	L	MINL	MAXL	P	E	W
date				Y	Y	Y
gMonth				Y	Y	Y
gYear				Y	Y	Y
gYearMonth				Y	Y	Y
gDay				Y	Y	Y
gMonthDay				Y	Y	Y
Name	Y	Y	Y	Y	Y	Y
QName	Y	Y	Y	Y	Y	Y
NCName	Y	Y	Y	Y	Y	Y
anyURI	Y	Y	Y	Y	Y	Y
language	Y	Y	Y	Y	Y	Y
ID	Y	Y	Y	Y	Y	Y
IDREF	Y	Y	Y	Y	Y	Y
IDREFS	Y	Y	Y	Y	Y	Y
ENTITY	Y	Y	Y	Y	Y	Y
ENTITIES	Y	Y	Y	Y	Y	Y
NOTATION	Y	Y	Y	Y	Y	Y
NMTOKEN	Y	Y	Y	Y	Y	Y
NMTOKENS	Y	Y	Y	Y	Y	Y

Enumerated type facets

Enumerated types have additional facets. These types can be constrained to a specific range of values by a minimum and maximum setting. There may also be a maximum total number of digits in the value or in just the fractional part of the value.

The following table shows the enumerated types that can have some or all of these facets applied to them. Note that many of these data types have a fixed fractional digit setting of '0' digits:

- maximum inclusive (the MAXI column)
- maximum exclusive (the MAXX column)
- minimum inclusive (the MINI column)
- minimum exclusive (the MINX column)
- total digits (the TD column)
- fractional digits (the FD column)

Simple type	MAXI	MAXX	MINI	MINX	TD	FD
byte	Y	Y	Y	Y	Y	Y
unsignedByte	Y	Y	Y	Y	Y	Y
integer	Y	Y	Y	Y	Y	Y
positiveInteger	Y	Y	Y	Y	Y	Y
negativeInteger	Y	Y	Y	Y	Y	Y
nonNegativeInteger	Y	Y	Y	Y	Y	Y
nonPositiveInteger	Y	Y	Y	Y	Y	Y
int	Y	Y	Y	Y	Y	Y
unsignedInt	Y	Y	Y	Y	Y	Y
long	Y	Y	Y	Y	Y	Y
unsignedLong	Y	Y	Y	Y	Y	Y
short	Y	Y	Y	Y	Y	Y
unsignedShort	Y	Y	Y	Y	Y	Y
decimal	Y	Y	Y	Y	Y	Y
float	Y	Y	Y	Y		
double	Y	Y	Y	Y		
time	Y	Y	Y	Y		
dateTime	Y	Y	Y	Y		
duration	Y	Y	Y	Y		
date	Y	Y	Y	Y		
gMonth	Y	Y	Y	Y		
gYear	Y	Y	Y	Y		
gYearMonth	Y	Y	Y	Y		
gDay	Y	Y	Y	Y		
gMonthDay	Y	Y	Y	Y		

Many combinations of facets are meaningless or contradictory and are therefore mutually exclusive. For example, it is not possible (or sensible) to set a minimum inclusive value while also setting a minimum exclusive value.

14.4   Facet Elements

A distinct element type is used to represent each kind of facet. These are the `length`, `minLength`, `maxLength`, `pattern`, `enumeration`, `whiteSpace`, `maxInclusive`, `maxExclusive`, `minInclusive`, `maxInclusive`, `totalDigits`, and `fractionDigits` elements. All of these elements are empty, apart from an optional `annotation` element, and all have a **value** attribute to specify a constraint for that particular facet type. For example, the 'length' facet can constrain a value to 13 characters:

```
<length value="13" />

<length value="13">
  <annotation>...</annotation>
</length>
```

The **fixed** attribute can be added to any of the facet elements and set to 'true' to ensure that any other data type that uses this data type as its base type cannot override the facet value (see Section 17.4).

14.5   Enumeration Facet

An attribute value is often used to specify the status of the element it belongs to. For example, a document that contains sensitive material may need to include paragraphs that are 'secret' or 'top-secret', while all others are by default considered to be 'normal' paragraphs. In this example are three possible values, and all three values consist of characters that would be legal in an attribute that conforms to the 'NMTOKEN' data type. Of course, this data type could be used in the attribute definition, as in the following example:

```
<attribute name="Level" type="NMTOKEN"
                        default="normal" />
```

With this approach, a missing value implies the 'normal' status, as desired, and a a document instance author can certainly enter either of the other two values. However, the author has to remember the options and then enter the value required. The author may make a mistake, typing 'top_secret' or 'TopSecret' instead of 'top-secret' or forgetting the keyword entirely and typing 'very-sensitive' instead. Clearly, it would be better if the schema definition could be told which values are legal. This information could then be used to validate the attribute, and authors would see a list of options to select from when using a schema-sensitive XML editing tool:

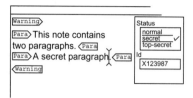

The **enumeration facet** defines a single possible legal value. Typically, there will be several **enumeration** elements, between them defining a range of options:

```
<restriction base="NMTOKEN">
  <enumeration value="normal" />
  <enumeration value="secret" />
  <enumeration value="top-secret" />
</restriction>
```

```
<Para Security="secret">...</Para>
<Para Security="normal">...</Para>
<Para Security="unimportant">..</Para><!-- ERROR -->
```

Although the `enumeration` element can repeat here, this is not typical of the facet elements (only the `pattern` element shares this capability).

When restricting a numeric type, this element does not specify an exact string format to represent the number, so a specified value of '4.4' actually permits the text string '4.4000' or '+04.4' to occur.

Note that an enumeration value can have a space in it (unlike a DTD enumerated type), but this is not advisable if there is a possibility that a new list type will be derived from this type (as discussed later), because spaces are used in list types to separate the items.

Note also that this technique *must* be used when the 'NOTATION' base data type is selected (see Section 7.6).

14.6 Whitespace and Pattern Facets

The following two facets differ from the other facets, and between them they reveal a chain of events in the validation of a value.

Whitespace facet

The **whitespace facet** affects the whitespace characters in a value and can be used to '**replace**' line-feed, carriage return, and tab characters with space characters, or go further and '**collapse**' such a value by then also removing leading and trailing spaces, while collapsing a series of embedded spaces down to a single space. The value 'collapse' is assumed and fixed for data types that are not string based. The same is true for all list types. At the other extreme, the value '**preserve**' is applied to the 'string' data type. The **whiteSpace** element can be used to set any of the three options for all types derived from 'string' (the default setting is 'preserve').

Note that, uniquely, this facet type modifies the value for further validation (though it cannot modify the value that is passed to an application afterwards):

```
<!-- ORIGINAL -->
<Para> This is a
    paragraph.   </Para>


<restriction base="string">
  <whiteSpace value="replace" />
</restriction>

  <!-- REPLACED -->
  <Para> This is a    paragraph.   </Para>


<restriction base="string">
  <whiteSpace value="collapse" />
</restriction>

  <!-- COLLAPSED -->
  <Para>This is a paragraph.</Para>
```

The built-in 'integer' data type has an implied 'collapse' setting. The example below is valid because whitespace collapsing is performed before other checks are made. In this case, there must be no spaces in an integer value, but the leading and trailing spaces in the example will be removed before this test is made:

```
<Int>   123   </Int>
```

Pattern facet

The **pattern facet** defines a template against which a value must be compared. For example, a pattern can specify that a value must begin with three letters followed by four digits. A value of 'abc1234' would match this template and so would 'xyz9876', but 'ab12345' would fail to match because it has too few letters and too many digits. Patterns can be very complex (see Chapter 15). For example, 'ab?c(x\^x|[d-w-[m]]|zz\p{IsGothic})+' is a valid pattern:

```
<pattern
      value="ab?c(x\^x|[d-w-[m]]|zz\p{IsGothic})+" />
```

The pattern element can be used repeatedly within the same restriction of a data type. Each pattern specifies one possible template. A value is incorrect only if it fails to match all of them (it is allowed to match more than one). This is essentially the same as the use of multiple enumeration elements. The following example replaces the enumeration element with the pattern element but otherwise has structure and meaning identical to that of the earlier example:

```
<restriction base="NMTOKEN">
  <pattern value="normal" />
  <pattern value="secret" />
  <pattern value="top-secret" />
</restriction>
```

However, patterns do not respect data type characteristics, so a restriction of an integer to a single possible value of '4.4' would require this exact sequence of characters, and not such permutations as '4.40'.

This element could be used to constrain the values of the From and To elements in the email example in order to ensure that all emails are internal to the organization. In the following example, lower-case and upper-case letters are allowed to form the name of a person with a single period (.) to separate the first name from the last name (in this simple case, no accented letters are allowed). Finally, the address must be completed with the address 'MegaTVi.com':

```
<simpleType name="internalEMailAddress">
  <restriction base="anyURI">
    <pattern
         value="[a-zA-Z]+\.[a-zA-Z]+@MegaTVi.com" />
  </restriction>
</simpleType>
```

Value spaces and lexical spaces

The purpose and behavior of the whitespace and pattern facets can be better understood by distinguishing between three concepts:

- the serialization space (the parsed text with entities replaced)
- the lexical space (the characters that combine to represent the value after whitespace normalization)
- the value space (the representations allowed by the data type)

The **serialization space** is the character sequence that represents the value after it has been parsed. By this time, entities have been expanded. Consider the following examples. The first replaces the '&#20;' and 'é' entity references, and the second retains the spaces around the number:

```
<Cafe>XML&#20;Caf&eacute;</Cafe>
```

XML Café

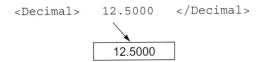

The **lexical space** is the final series of characters that together represent the value. This could be identical to the serialization space, but the **whiteSpace** element specifies how the serialization space can be transformed into the lexical space. For example, the value 'collapse' removes the leading and trailing spaces in the second of the examples above:

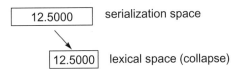

The **pattern** element validates the lexical space. For example, the pattern '\d\d\.\d{4}' specifies that the value must consist of two digits, followed by a decimal point, followed by another four digits. The example above would pass this test, because the whiteSpace element has already ensured that the surrounding spaces have been removed.

Finally, the **value space** is the allowed range of values, in some cases including various alternative representations of the same value. For example, the enumeration element can be used to specify that a decimal value must actually be '12.5', but this alone does not prevent other valid representations of the same value, including '12.5000', to be used (there are many more options in the decimal '12.5' value space than are shown below):

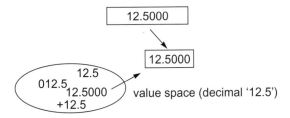

Using the pattern element, as shown above, a schema definition author is able to constrain the value to a specific representation. Indeed, both pattern and enumeration elements can be used together as a kind of 'belt-and-braces' (or 'belt-and-suspenders') technique, whereby the value must conform to at least one of the enumerations and also to at least one of the patterns (the pattern facet could be used alone but schema processors that cannot interpret patterns would then have no fallback validation method):

```
<restriction base="decimal">
  <enumeration value="12.4" />
  <enumeration value="12.5" />
  <enumeration value="12.6" />
  <pattern value="12\.4" />
  <pattern value="12\.5" />
  <pattern value="12\.6" />
</restriction>
```

14.7 Length and Numeric Facets

The remaining facets all constrain the value space in some way. This means that how they are to be interpreted depends on the nature of the selected base data type.

Length facets

The **length facet** constrains the value to a fixed number of characters, whereas the **minimum length facet** and the **maximum length facet** merely constrain the value to a minimum and maximum number of characters, respectively. The last two facets can be used together, but it would not make sense to use either of them with the length facet, which already specifies a minimum and (identical) maximum value. The **length**, **minLength**, and **maxLength** elements are used, and the following two examples are equivalent:

```
<restriction type="string>
  <length value="5" />
</restriction>

<restriction type="string>
  <minLength value="5" />
  <maxLength value="5" />
</restriction>
```

If the new data type were used to help define a FiveCharacters element, then the following example would be valid:

```
<FiveCharacters>12345</FiveCharacters>
```

But the following two examples would not be valid:

```
<FiveCharacters>1234</FiveCharacters>

<FiveCharacters>123456</FiveCharacters>
```

Number and date limiting facets

The **minimum inclusive facet** specifies a minimum allowed value. The term 'inclusive' means that the specified value is allowed. So for a number to be legal, it must be at least this high. A **minimum exclusive facet**, on the other hand, excludes the specified value, and a stated lower limit of '15' means that the actual value must be higher than '15'. How close a value can get to the limit depends on the base data type. For an integer type, the lowest possible value would be '16', but for a decimal type it could be lower than '15.0000000001'. The same considerations pertain to the **maximum inclusive facet** and the **maximum exclusive facet** except that it is the highest possible value that is limited.

The `minInclusive`, `minExclusive`, `maxInclusive`, and `maxExclusive` elements set these limits on values:

```
<!-- 1 - 99 inclusive -->
<restriction base="integer">
  <minInclusive value="1" />
  <maxInclusive value="99" />
</restriction>

<!-- 0.00001 - 0.99999 (not '0' or '1') -->
<restriction base="decimal">
  <minExclusive value="0" />
  <maxExclusive value="1" />
</restriction>
```

These facets apply to all of the built-in date-based data types, so the earliest and latest possible dates can be stipulated.

Number of digits facets

The **total digits facet** specifies the maximum number of digits allowed in a numeric value. This is not the same as the length constraint, because other symbols, such as a leading '+' or '-' sign, or a decimal point, can appear in a number. The value '6' simply states that there may be no more than six *digits* in the value, so both '+111111' and '111.111' would still be legal.

It is also possible to control the number of digits that follow a decimal point by using the **fraction digits facet**. The value of this facet type is the maximum number of digits allowed in the fractional part of a decimal number.

If both the `totalDigits` and `fractionDigits` elements are present, then an implied rule holds that there can be no more fraction digits than total digits (as makes sense):

```
<restriction base="decimal">
  <totalDigits value="4" />
  <fractionDigits value="2" />
</restriction>
```

```
<Amount>1</Amount>
<Amount>12</Amount>
<Amount>123</Amount>
<Amount>1234</Amount>
<Amount>1.2</Amount>
<Amount>12.3</Amount>
<Amount>123.4</Amount>
<Amount>12.34</Amount>

<!-- TOO MANY DIGITS -->
<Amount>123.45</Amount>

<!-- TOO MANY FRACTION DIGITS -->
<Amount>1.234</Amount>

<!-- BOTH CONSTRAINTS BROKEN -->
<Amount>12.345</Amount>
```

14.8   Derivation of Derivation Limitations

Derived data types are constrained by the facets of the data types they are derived from. When a **minInclusive**, **maxInclusive**, **minExclusive**, or **maxExclusive** element is used in a derived data type, the specified limit must be within the range of values allowed by the parent data type, regardless of which elements are used in the parent to set this scope. For example, if the minInclusive element sets a value of '0' in the original data type, this facet cannot be set to a lower value in any derived data type, using either the minInclusive or minExclusive elements (this topic is discussed in Chapter 17).

If the base data type has a **length** element, then the value of this facet cannot be modified at all in the derived type.

The **totalDigits** element must not specify more allowed digits than are allowed by the parent data type. There are no specific rules for the fractionDigits element, except that the setting must, as usual, be no greater than the total number of digits allowed in the original.

If any **enumeration** elements are present in the derived data type, then their values must be a subset of enumeration element values in the parent data type, and the missing definitions therefore determine the nature of the restriction. However, if the original data type has enumeration elements but the derivation has none, then all of the parent enumerations remain valid.

If the base data type includes the **whiteSpace** element, then it can only be set to a more normalized state than the original. This means that if the base value is already set to 'collapse', then it cannot be overridden at all. However, 'replace' can be changed to 'collapse' (but not to 'preserve'). Finally, 'preserve' can be overriden by either of the other two options.

14.9   **Lists**

One way to extend an existing simple data type is to allow multiple occurrences of any compliant value to appear. The **list** element creates lists of values of a given type. The **itemType** attribute identifies the data type that all the items in the list must conform to:

```
<simpleType name="scoresList">
  <list itemType="integer" />
</simpleType>
```

Within a document instance, spaces separate each item in the list. The following example shows multiple integer values in a Scores element that has adopted the 'scoresList' type defined above:

```
<Scores>57 123 19 87 87</Scores>
```

As an alternative to referencing an existing data type, the list element can contain a complete simple type definition, including one that creates a union or a restriction. This approach avoids the need to separately define (and name) the data type that will form the basis of the list type:

```
<simpleType name="scores">
  <list><simpleType>...</simpleType></list>
</simpleType>
```

Features of lists

Note that duplicate values are allowed; there is no assumption that each item in a list must be unique. The value '87' appears twice in the example above.

Also note that lists are not approprate for values that might contain spaces, or when each value in the list might eventually need to be enhanced by means of attributes or substructures.

It is dangerous to base a list type on the 'string' data type, because strings can contain spaces. It would not be possible to distinguish between embedded spaces and item-separating spaces. A value that includes a space would be treated as two items instead of one.

Facets in list types

The **length facet**, **minimum length facet**, and **maximum length facet** are, in this case, used to constrain the number of items in the list, rather than the length of each of these items:

```
<!-- value is either 'none', or a number and
      is repeatable -->
<simpleType name="scoreList">
  <list itemType="integer" />
</simpleType>

 <!-- no more than 10 scores in list -->
<simpleType name="scoreListLimits">
  <restriction base="DOC:scoreList">
    <length value="10" />
  </restriction>
</simpleType>
```

Alternatively:

```
 <!-- ALTERNATIVE METHOD -->
<restriction base="DOC:scoreList">
  <simpleType>
    <list itemType="integer" />
  </simpleType>
  <length value="10" />
</restriction>
```

This technique is needed to force a list to contain at least one item (that is, to not be empty).

This scenario autoamtically applies to the 'NMTOKENS', 'IDREFS', and 'ENTITIES' built-in data types, which are now revealed to be list types.

The **enumeration facet** restricts the items that can appear in the list to the given values. It does not prevent repetition of a value from the given set.

When the **pattern** element is applied to a list, the pattern is compared with the whole list, not separately with each item in the list.

14.10 Unions

It is possible to create a new data type that is an amalgamation of two or more existing types. Values are considered valid when they conform to the constraints of any of the adopted types.

Consider the need for a single attribute value to register when an event occurs. It must be able to contain either a time, such as '13:03:44.123', or a month and day, such as '--05-28'. In this example, an Event element contains a When attribute:

```
... <Event When="13:03:44.123" /> ...

... <Event When="--05-28" /> ...
```

Normally, either the 'time' or 'gMonthDay' data type would be adopted, but selecting either one rules out values of the other kind. Naturally, one way to make both of the example values above valid would be to allow the When attribute to contain any string of characters, but this would waste an opportunity to validate the values. For example, the values '88:77:66.987' and '--13-32' would both be considered correct, but so would the value 'sometime yesterday', and this is clearly not desirable. The alternative approach is to create a new data type that encompasses both of the applicable data types. The **union** element can include a list of existing data types within its **memberTypes** attribute. For example:

```
<attribute name="When">
  <simpleType>
    <union memberTypes="time gMonthDay" />
  </simpleType>
</attribute>
```

The following example creates a new data type, called 'scoreOrNoScore', from a union of the 'integer' type and the 'noScore' type:

```
<!-- value is 'none' only -->
<simpleType name="noScore">
  <restriction base="NMTOKEN">
    <enumeration value="none" />
  </restriction>
</simpleType>

<!-- value is either 'none', or a number -->
<simpleType name="scoreOrNoScore">
  <union memberTypes="integer DOC:noScore" />
</simpleType>
```

A Score element that adopts this data type can have such values as:

```
<Score>44</Score>
<Score>none</Score>
<Score>9</Score>
```

Note that it is not necessary to reference existing data types. Instead, one or more of the types to be merged can be created within the union element itself. This approach requires another, embedded **simpleType** element, usually containing a restriction element. This technique avoids the need to separately define a data type just for the purpose of using it in one union type. For example, the When attribute discussed above may need to be able to contain the value 'recurring' or 'unknown' instead of a time or a day and month:

```
<attribute name="When">
  <simpleType>
    <union memberTypes="time gMonthDay">
      <simpleType>
        <restriction base="NMTOKEN">
          <enumeration value="recurring" />
          <enumeration value="unknown" />
        </restriction>
      </simpleType>
    </union>
  </simpleType>
</attribute>
```

The `simpleType` element can repeat in this location, and the `memberTypes` attribute is therefore not essential:

```
<union>
  <simpleType>...</simpleType>
  <simpleType>...</simpleType>
  <simpleType>...</simpleType>
</union>
```

It is possible to create a restricted derivation of a union data type, but only by using the `enumeration` or `pattern` elements to constrain a value to specific examples of the values from those allowed across all of the base data types.

Note that an instance of an element that conforms to a union data type can, by means of the `xsi:type` attribute, refer directly to one of the base data types. This gives a clearer signal to the schema processor or to an application that is receiving the parsed data as to what kind of value the element contains. But this feature is really only useful when the base data types happen to have value sets that overlap, when it is not necessarily obvious which base data type a particular value is supposed to conform to. Of course, this mechanism is unavailable to values held in attribute values, because an attribute cannot contain other attributes.

14.11   Combinations of Unions and Lists

It is possible to create a list of union types and to create a union of types that includes one or more list types.

Union of types

Referring to another union type within a union definition is allowed and saves the effort of having to individually refer directly to its constituent types. But while it is possible to refer to another union in the `memberTypes` attribute of a `union` element, it is not possible to include a `simpleType` element that restricts or lists a union type.

No list of lists

It is not legal for a list to consist of items of another type of list, in part because it would not achieve anything.

List of union types

A list can be created from a union type. Any value allowed by any of the original types can occur and can be mixed with values from other allowed types. For example:

```
<!-- value is either 'none' or a number, and
     is repeatable -->
<simpleType name="scoreOrNoScoreList">
  <list itemType="DOC:scoreOrNoScore" />
</simpleType>
```

A `Scores` element that adopts this type could have a value, such as:

```
<Scores>44 none 9</Scores>
```

The union must not have a list type as one of its base types, because it is illegal for a list to be composed of sublists.

Union including list type

A union can include a list as one (or more) of its components. In the following example, the scores list type is combined with a simple boolean type:

```
<simpleType name="scoreOrGamePlayed">
  <union memberTypes="DOC:scoreOrNoScoreList
                      boolean" />
</simpleType>
```

This construct can be confusing. It it important to understand that it does not allow the two component types to be mixed within a single value just because one of the component types happens to be a list type. Instead, it is only possible to have a list of values from the list type or to have a single value from the other type. An element called `ScoresOrGamePlayed` that adopted this type could have the following values:

```
    <!-- game was played -->
<ScoresOrGamePlayed>true</ScoresOrGamePlayed>

    <!-- game was not played -->
<ScoresOrGamePlayed>false</ScoresOrGamePlayed>

    <!-- game was played, and here are the scores -->
<ScoresOrGamePlayed>44 none 9</ScoresOrGamePlayed>
```

14.12 Example Built-in Extended Data Types

The XML Schema standard includes a number of base data types and a number of built-in extensions of the 'string' and 'decimal' data types. It is instructive to see how the standard describes how some of these derived types would be created if it were necessary to use the techniques described above.

Fraction digits

```
<simpleType name="integer">
  <restriction base="decimal">
    <fractionDigits value="0" fixed="true" />
  </restriction>
</simpleType>
```

Unfortunately, this definition of the 'integer' data type is not adequate because simply removing fraction digits still allows a trailing decimal point, yet it should not be permitted for '123.' to be considered to be an integer value.

Maximum value

```
<simpleType name="nonPositiveInteger">
  <restriction base="integer">
    <maxInclusive value="0" />
  </restriction>
</simpleType>
```

The maximum value of the 'nonPositiveInteger' data type is '0'. All negative integers are allowed.

Range of values

```
<simpleType name="long">
  <restriction base="integer">
    <minInclusive value="-9223372036854775808" />
    <maxInclusive value="9223372036854775807" />
  </restriction>
</simpleType>
```

The 'long' data type has a wide, but nevertheless limited, range of possible values. If larger values are needed, the 'string' data type can be used to permit a number of any length, and a pattern facet can be used to constrain the content of the string to valid characters.

Inherited limits

```
<simpleType name="unsignedShort">
  <restriction base="unsignedInt">
    <maxInclusive value="65535" />
  </restriction>
</simpleType>
```

The value of the 'unsignedShort' data type must be at least '0' (as inherited from 'unsignedInt') and at most '65535' (a value occupies exactly 2 bytes).

Whitespace replace

```
<simpleType name="normalizedString">
  <restriction base="string">
    <whiteSpace value="replace" />
  </restriction>
</simpleType>
```

Tabs and line-feeds are replaced by spaces in 'normalizedString' data type values; derived types apply other facets *after* this has happened, as discussed in Section 14.13.

Whitespace collapse

```
<simpleType name="token">
  <restriction base="normalizedString">
    <whiteSpace value="collapse" />
  </restriction>
</simpleType>
```

Initial and final spaces are removed from 'token' data type values, and multiple spaces are reduced to a single space. Tabs, line-feeds, and carriage-return codes are also replaced; derived types apply other facets *after* all of this has happened, as discussed in Section 14.13.

Patterns

```
<simpleType name="language">
  <restriction base="token">
    <pattern value="([a-zA-Z]{2}|
                    [iI]-[a-zA-Z]+|
                    [xX]-[a-zA-Z]{1,8})
                    (-[a-zA-Z]{1,8})*" />
  </restriction>
</simpleType>
```

The 'language' data type pattern complies with the RFC 1766 standard. The value may begin with two alphabetic characters, such as 'en' or 'EN', or with the letter 'i' or 'I', then a dash, then at least one alphabetic character, or with the letter 'x' or 'X', a dash, and between one and eight alphabetic characters. Whichever option the value conforms to, it may then consist of any number of sequences comprising an initial dash, followed by between one and eight characters (see Chapter 15 for details on the expression language).

Restricted lists

```
<simpleType name="NMTOKENS">
  <restriction>
    <simpleType>
      <list itemType="NMTOKEN" />
    </simpleType>
    <minLength value="1" />
  </restriction>
</simpleType>
```

The 'NMTOKENS' data type is a list of 'NMTOKEN' values, and there must be at least one token in the list.

14.13 String Normalization and Tokens

Two built-in derivations of the 'string' data type appear to do more than they actually do.

In the case of the '**normalizedString**' type, line-feeds and tab characters in the text are replaced by space characters, but only for the purposes of further validation. Consider the following declaration for the BookTitle element:

```
<element name="BookTitle" type="normalizedString" />
```

This constraint will not raise a validation error when the following document fragment is encountered, despite the presence of a tab character and a line-feed code:

```
<BookTitle>The[TAB]XML Schema[LF]
Companion</BookTitle>
```

The '**token**' data type is similar except that leading and trailing spaces are supposed to be absent, and sequences of whitespace characters are supposed to be reduced to a single space:

```
<BookTitle>[SP][SP][SP]The[SP][SP]
XML Schema Companion[SP][SP]</BookTitle>
```

These types could be referenced as a more concise alternative to creating a new type and adding the whitespace facet, with the appropriate value attribute setting when no other constraints are required. The following two definitions are equivalent to each other, but the first is easier to implement:

```
<element name="Title" type="normalizedString" />
```

```
<element name="Title">
  <simpleType>
    <restriction base="string">
      <whiteSpace value="replace" />
    </restriction>
  </simpleType>
</element>
```

The following two definitions are also equivalent to each other:

```
<element name="Title" type="token" />

<element name="title">
  <simpleType>
    <restriction base="string">
      <whiteSpace value="collapse" />
    </restriction>
  </simpleType>
</element>
```

Still, nothing is really achieved by this. Values with additional whitespace are not rejected and are not modified as they are passed through to a software application.

Of course, these data types can be used to help create other data types, yet even here they are the best, but not the only, option. The following restrictions are equivalent, but the first example is easier to create and to read:

```
<restriction base="token">
  <length value="10" />
</restriction>

<restriction base="string">
  <whiteSpace value="collapse" />
  <length value="10" />
</restriction>
```

However, simply assigning these data types to an element or attribute could be useful to an application that can interrogate the schema definition. Such an application might then decide that it is appropriate to normalize the values before processing them.

14.14   Type Library

Many commonly required data types are predefined in the 'type library' provided with the standard, at www.w3.org/2001/03/XMLSchema. This library includes such types as:

- text (TypeLibrary-text.xsd)
- arrays (TypeLibrary-array.xsd)
- lists (TypeLibrary-list.xsd)

- mathematics (TypeLibrary-math.xsd)
- quantity test (TypeLibrary-quantity.xsd)
- binary (TypeLibrary-binary.xsd)

Schema definition authors are encouraged to explore these sets and to adopt relevant data types instead of inventing equivalent data types.

15. Patterns

The 'pattern' facet requires more explanation than the brief description given in Section 14.6 provides. This XML feature is based on the regular expression capabilities of the Perl programming language. It is therefore very powerful, but this strength comes at the cost of some complexity.

15.1 Introduction

Although the XML Schema language has a large number of built-in data types that can be used, restricted, and extended, some requirements demand much finer control over the exact structure of a value. For example, a simple code might need to consist of three lowercase letters:

```
<Code>abc</Code>     <!-- OK -->

<Code>ABC</Code>     <!-- ERROR -->

<Code>abcd</Code>    <!-- ERROR -->
```

Similarly, when an element or attribute contains an ISBN (International Standard Book Number), it should be possible to apply constraints that reflect the nature of ISBN codes. All ISBN codes are composed of three identifiers (location, publisher, and book) and a check digit, separated by hyphens (or spaces). Valid values would include '0-201-41999-8' and '963-9131-21-0'. The schema processor should detect any error in an ISBN attribute:

```
<Book ISBN="0-201-77059-8" ...>   <!-- OK -->

<Book ISBN="X-999999-"  ...>      <!-- ERRORS -->
```

Some programming languages, such as Perl, include a **regular expression** language, which defines a **pattern** against which a series of characters can be compared. Typically, this feature is used to search for fragments of a text document, but the XML Schema language has co-opted it for sophisticated validation of element content and attribute values.

15.2   **Simple Templates**

The **pattern** facet element holds a pattern in its **value** attribute. The simplest possible form of pattern involves a series of characters that must be present, in the order specified, in each element or attribute declaration that uses the data type constrained by the pattern facet.

The pattern 'abc' might be specified as the fixed value of a Code element:

```
<Code>abc</Code>
```

The pattern '0-201-41999-8' might be specified as the fixed value of an ISBN attribute:

```
<Book ISBN="0-201-41999-8" ... >
```

In this simple form, a pattern is similar to an enumeration, except that in the case of patterns the match must be exact, regardless of the data type used (recall that Section 14.6 explains how patterns differ from enumerations in this respect).

Although specifying an exact sequence of characters is among the simplest things that can be achieved with the pattern language, specifying a sequence of characters that must *not* appear in a value is much harder.

It is often a good idea to use the 'normalized' or 'token' data type as the base data type for the restriction when the presence of surrounding whitespace should not be allowed to trigger an error.

Just as a restriction element can contain multiple enumeration elements, it can also contain multiple pattern elements. The element content or attribute value is valid if it matches any of the patterns:

```
<restriction base="token">
  <pattern value="abc" />
  <pattern value="xyz" />
</restriction>
```

```
      <Code>abc</Code>          <!-- OK -->
      <Code>xyz</Code>          <!-- OK -->
      <Code>   abc   </Code>    <!-- OK -->
      <Code>acb</Code>          <!-- ERROR -->
      <Code>xzy</Code>          <!-- ERROR -->
      <Code>abcc</Code>         <!-- ERROR -->
```

Alternatively, a single pattern can contain multiple 'branches'. Each **branch** is actually a distinct, alternative expression, separated by the 'l' symbol from previous or following branches. Again, the pattern test succeeds if any one of the branches matches the pattern (the 'l' symbol is therefore performing a function similar to its use in DTD content models). The following example is equivalent to the multipattern example above:

```
<restriction base="string">
  <pattern value="abc|xyz" />
</restriction>
```

Note that, although branches are never essential at this level, because multiple pattern elements can be used instead, they are the only technique available in another circumstance discussed later (involving subexpressions).

15.3 Atoms

Each branch of an expression (or the whole expression, if it is not divided into branches) consists of a number of **atoms**. In the examples above, the letter 'a' is one atom and the letter 'b' is another.

Apart from individual characters, an atom can also be a **character class** (an escape sequence, or a selection from a predefined or user-defined group of characters) or a complete subexpression (as explained further below).

Each atom validates one portion of the value of the pattern it is being compared to, and the atoms are considered in sequential order from left to right. In the case of the pattern 'abc', the first atom, 'a', is expected to match the first character of the value. If the value does not begin with an 'a' character, then the pattern has already failed to match the value. If the value *does* begin with 'a', then the next atom, 'b', is compared with the next character in the value.

15.4 Quantifiers and Quantities

By default an atom represents a fragment of the pattern that must occur in a value and may not repeat:

```
<pattern value="a" />

  <Code>a</Code>   <!-- OK -->
  <Code></Code>    <!-- ERROR ('a' must be present) -->
  <Code>aaa</Code><!-- ERROR ('a' must not repeat) -->
```

The expression 'abc' specifies that there must be one 'a' character, followed by one 'b' character, followed by one 'c' character. The values 'ab', 'bc', and 'abcc' would not match this pattern.

But it is possible to state that an atom is optional or repeatable, or even to specify an allowed range of occurrences. The pattern language achieves this by allowing **quantifier** symbols to be placed after the atoms they relate to. The symbols '?', '+'

and '*' are used for this purpose (and have meanings that will be unsurprising to those familiar with DTD content models). Alternatively, a **quantity** allows any number of occurrences to be precisely specified.

Optional quantifier

The '**?**' quantifier indicates that the atom before it is optional. For example:

```
ab?c
```

Legal values in this case include 'abc' and 'ac'.

Note that it is possible to have two identical optional tokens in sequence, such as 'a?a?b'. This is because, unlike the case with DTD and schema element models, look-ahead parsing is permitted. This means the value 'ab' can be matched to this pattern, as can 'aab' (and just 'b'), without causing any problems for the parser. The level of violence and strength of language in a TV program could be indicated with star ratings, '*' (the minimum), '**', '***', '****' or '*****' (the five-star maximum), but perhaps using the letter 's' to represent each star (asterisks cannot be used without further complications that are explained later):

```
<pattern value="ss?s?s?s?" />
```

```
<Ratings Violence="ssss" StrongLanguage="ss" />
```

Repeatable quantifier

The '**+**' quantifier signifies that the atom is repeatable. The atom must be present, but any number of further occurences are allowed. For example:

```
ab+c
```

Legal values in this case include 'abc' and 'abbbbbbbbbbc', but 'ac' would not be valid.

It is not ambiguous to create patterns such as 'b+b+' (though it would be pointless). The parser would not need to match a particular 'b' character to one atom or the other (except for the first and last 'b' in the sequence).

Optional and repeatable quantifier

The '*****' quantifier indicates that the atom is both optional and repeatable. This could be seen to be functionaly equivalent to '?+' if such combinations were legal:

```
ab*c
```

This expression makes the 'b' atom optional and repeatable so legal values include 'ac', 'abc' and 'abbbbbbc'.

Again, it is not ambiguous to create patterns such as 'b*z?b*'. If the 'z' atom is absent, no attempt is made to decide whether a particular 'b' atom belongs to the first part of the pattern or to the last part.

Greedy quantifiers and backtracking

When a single atom can be matched to multiple characters in a value, matching patterns to values can become quite complex, including multiple interpretations where only one of the possible interpretations would successfully match. The perceived issue here is one of 'greed.' Consider the pattern 'a+b?a' (a series of 'a' characters or a series of 'a' characters followed by a single 'b' character and a single 'a' character) and an attempt to validate the value 'aaa' against it. There are two possible interpretations of the pattern, and one of them would not report a match with the value.

In the first scenario, the first atom, 'a+', could reasonably match the entire value (it could be greedy). But the remainder of the pattern, 'b?a', could not then be matched to anything, so the value would be deemed to be invalid (the missing character 'b' is not a problem here, because it is optional, but the missing additional 'a' character would trigger a failed match).

In the second scenario, the initial atom is only matched to the first two characters of the value instead of all three. The final atom of the pattern, 'a', could then be successfully matched with the final 'a' of the value.

A successful match should be reported if either of the interpretations is applicable to the value. In fact, a pattern is matched to a value first by an attempt at the greedy approach, then, if this fails to match the value, by attempts at less greedy interpretations until (hopefully) a successful match can made.

Readers familiar with the use of expression languages to find text strings should note that in XML an expression is always expected to apply to the content of an entire element or to a complete attribute value. Hence, there need be no concern that expressions could be crafted that might inadvertently (through sheer greed) find a false match spanning two real instances of a value (and everything between) within a single line of text.

Complex example

The following example includes all three quantifiers, and all the following Code elements are valid according to this pattern:

```
<pattern value="a+b?c*" />

    <Code>a</Code>
    <Code>ab</Code>
    <Code>ac</Code>
    <Code>abc</Code>
    <Code>aaa</Code>
    <Code>aaab</Code>
    <Code>aaabc</Code>
    <Code>aaabccc</Code>
```

Quantities

A **quantity** is a more finely tuned instrument for specifying occurrence options than the qualifiers described above. Instead of a single symbol, such as '+', a quantity involves either one or two integer values enclosed by curly braces ('{' and '}').

The simplest form of quantity involves a single integer value. This value specifies how many times the atom must occur. For example:

```
ab{3}c
```

This pattern specifies that the value must be 'abbbc'.

A quantity range involves two values, separated by a comma. The first value indicates the minimum number of occurrences allowed, and the second value indicates the maximum number of occurrences allowed. For example:

```
ab{3,5}c
```

This pattern specifies that the value must be 'abbbc', 'abbbbc', or 'abbbbbc'.

It is also possible to specify just a minimum number of occurrences. If the second value is absent but the comma is still present, then only a minimum is being specified. The following pattern allows for everything from 'abbc' to 'abbbbbbbbbc' and beyond:

```
ab{2,}c
```

Note that it is not possible to specify just a maximum number of repetitions in this way. It is always necessary to supply a minimum value. However, a minimum value of '0' is allowed, so '{0,55}' achieves the aim of specifying a maximum of '55'.

15.5   **Escape Characters**

A number of significant symbols have now been introduced, such as '*' and '{'. These symbols cannot be used as atoms within an expression, because they would be misinterpreted as significant pattern markup. It is therefore necessary to escape these characters when they are needed to match characters in a value (just as '&' and '<' must be escaped in XML documents when they are part of the document text).

The '\' symbol is used in a pattern to escape the character that follows it. This can be seen as similar to the function of the '&' character in XML entity references. But in this case, only the following single character is escaped, so there is no need for another symbol to end an escape sequence (as ';' is needed in the case of entity references).

Just as the sequence '&' is needed in XML documents to allow the '&' character to be included as a data character, so must the '\' symbol also be escaped in patterns. In this case, the '\' escape symbol is placed before the '\' data character, giving '\\' (this should be familiar to C and Java software developers). The following pattern matches the text 'a\b':

```
a\\b
```

The other escape sequences for single characters are: '\|', '\.', '\?', '*', '\+', '\{', '\}', '\(', '\)', '\[', and '\]':

```
\|  (not a branch separator)
\.  (not a not-a-line-end character)
\?  (not an optional indicator)
\*  (not an optional and repeatable indicator)
\+  (not a required and repeatable indicator)
\{  (not a quantity start)
\}  (not a quantity end)
\(  (not a subgroup start)
\)  (not a subgroup end)
\[  (not a character class start)
\]  (not a character class end)
```

The following pattern matches the value '{a+b}':

```
\{a\+b\}
```

In some circumstances, the '-' and '^' characters must also be escaped ('\-' and '\^'):

```
\-  (not a character class subtractor or range
     separator)
\^  (not a negative group indicator)
```

In addition, escape sequences are used to include whitespace characters that would otherwise be difficult or impossible to enter from a keyboard, including '\n', '\r', and '\t':

```
\n (newline)
\r (return)
\t (tab)
```

Note that an atom can be an escape sequence, rather than a single character, and it is possible to quantify such a sequence. For example, '\++' states that the '+' character is required and repeatable.

15.6 Character Classes

Atoms (quantified or otherwise) can be larger than a single character or escaped character sequence. An atom can also be a **character class**. This feature allows a particular atom in the pattern to be one of a number of predefined options. For example, perhaps the third character in a value is allowed to be 'a', 'b', or 'c'.

All ISBN numbers used by a particular publisher might start with '0-201-' and therefore be completed by a five-digit book identifier and a check digit, such as '77059-8'. In this case, the first part of the ISBN number can be represented by the six fixed characters, but it is clearly not practical to cater to all possible book identifier numbers, using the techniques seen so far (nor the check digit, which can also be an 'x' as well as any digit). However, a **character class** pattern, which is enclosed by square brackets ('[' and ']'), can assist in this situation. The expression '-[0123456789]' specifies that the digit '0', '1', '2', '3', '4', '5', '6', '7', '8', or '9' may appear after a hyphen character. A complete, but very verbose, pattern for the example above follows (but could not be broken over lines as shown here):

```
<pattern value="0-201-[0123456789][0123456789]
                [0123456789][0123456789]
                [0123456789]-[0123456789x]"/>
```

Negative classes

A character class becomes a **negative character class**, reversing its meaning, when the character '^' is placed immediately after the opening square bracket. This specifies that any character *except* those in the group can be matched. For example, the pattern '[^abc]' specifies that any character except 'a', 'b', or 'c' must be included.

Note that this feature must not be interpreted as matching no character in the value. The pattern 'a[^b]c' would match the value 'axc' but not 'ac'.

The '^' symbol can be used later in the group without having this significance, so '[a^b]' simply means that the character must be 'a' or '^' or 'b'. It should not be necessary to place this character first within such a group, where it would be interpreted as an indicator of a negative character class, but it can be placed there without misinterpretation if it is escaped ('[\^ab]').

Readers familiar with other expression languages should also note that '^' does not play its usual role as a line-start indicator. Similarly, the '$' symbol is not significant here (as an end-line indicator). Attribute values do not contain lines of text (a multiple-line attribute value is normalized by the parser before the point at which patterns are used to validate the value) and, while element content can contain lines of text, this concept is rarely relevant.

Quantified classes

Quantifiers can be used on character classes. The quantifier or quantity simply follows the ']' class terminator:

```
[...]?

[...]+

[...]*

[...]{5,9}
```

When the qualifier indicates that more than one occurrence is allowed, this does not mean that only a selected character can repeat. For example, '[abc]+' specifies that at least one of the letters 'a', 'b', and 'c' must appear but that additional characters from this set may also appear, so 'abcbca' would be just as valid a match as 'aa', 'bbb', or 'ccccc'.

The earlier ISBN example can now be shortened considerably:

```
<pattern
    value="0-201-[0123456789]{5}-[0123456789x]" />
```

15.7 Character Class Ranges

It is not necessary to individually specify every possible character in a large group of characters when the options form a sequence. For example, '[abcdefghijklmnopqrstuvwxyz]' is a verbose way to specify that any lowercase letter can occur. When a large set of options have sequential character code values (according to the Unicode standard, which incorporates the ASCII standard), as in the example above, then a **range** can be specified instead. A '-' separator is placed between the first character in the range and the last character in the range. For example, '[a-z]' is a more succinct method of specifying that any lowercase letter is allowed.

Multiple ranges can be given. The following expression allows digits and all non-accented letters to occur:

```
<pattern value=" [a-zA-Z0-9]+" />
```

If the '-' character is needed within a character class, it can be escaped with '\-', but it is not necessary to do this outside of a character class. Alternatively, it does not need to be escaped if it is the first or last character in the character class, so '[-abc]' and '[abc-]' both specify that the character must be 'a', 'b', 'c', or '-'.

The ISBN example can now be shortened still further:

```
<pattern value="0-201-[0-9]{5}-[0-9x]" />
```

Alternatively, here is a simplified ISBN pattern that unfortunately allows the 'x' check digit to occur anywhere in the code and does not specify exactly three hyphens, as earlier examples did:

```
<pattern value="[0-9x-]{13}" />
```

A more generalized ISBN code can also now be represented. In this case, no assumption is made as to the area or publisher, so the exact number of digits in each part of the code cannot be known:

```
<pattern value="[0-9]+-[0-9]+-[0-9]+-[0-9x]" />
```

An XML character reference such as '{' or 'ª' can be included in a range. This is particularly useful for representing characters that are difficult, or even impossible, to enter directly from a keyboard (but note that escape sequences that achieve the same purpose in similar expression languages are not supported here).

This approach can still be used even when some of the characters in the range would not be valid. Individual characters can be selectively removed from the range, by use of a **subclass** with a '-' prefix. For example:

```
<pattern value=" [a-z-[aeiou]]+" />
```

This pattern removes all vowels as valid options from the list, including the 'a' character itself, despite the fact that it actually appears in the range (where it is needed because it signifies the start of the range):

```
<Consonants>bcd</Consonants>          <!-- OK -->
<Consonants>xyz</Consonants>          <!-- OK -->
<Consonants>abcdefgh</Consonants>     <!-- ERROR -->
```

Such a subclass can be included within a negative character class. This can look confusing, but the characters allowed are simply reversed, so '[^a-z-[aeiou]]' indicates that consonants are *not* allowed, but vowels (and other characters) *are* allowed.

15.8   **Subexpressions**

A complete expression can be embedded within another expression, creating a **subexpression**. The embedded expression is enclosed by parentheses, '(' and ')'. On its own, however, a subexpression has no effect on the complete pattern. The following two examples are functionally identical:

```
abcde
```

```
a(bcd)e
```

At least two features are supported by this concept. A subexpression allows a sequence to be optional or repeatable and allows branches to be inserted into the middle of a larger expression.

Quantified groups

One reason for using a group is to give the enclosed tokens a quantifier. The whole group may be optional or repeatable. The same techniques are used as for single atoms:

```
a(bcd)?e
```

```
a(bcd){5,9}e
```

Note that the first example above is not equivalent to the expression 'ab?c?d?e'. The difference is that, in this case, the characters 'b', 'c' and 'd' must *all* be present (in that order) or must *all* be absent.

An ISBN code might be allowed to be incomplete if the publisher part of the code can be implied:

```
<pattern value="(0-201-)?[0-9]{5}-[0-9x]" />
```

Branching groups

A group is useful when several options are required at a particular location in the pattern, because a subexpression can contain branches. Consider the following example:

```
abc(1|2|3)d
```

This pattern matches the values 'abc1d', 'abc2d', and 'abc3d'. Of course, with only a single character in each branch, this is just an alternative for the more succinct pattern 'abc[123]d'. However, that much simpler technique cannot work for multicharacter scenarios. In the following example, the values allowed are 'abc111d', 'abc222d', and 'abc333d':

```
abc(111|222|333)d
```

Each branch is a complete expression, and may also contain subexpressions, though this is only needed when there are fixed characters before or after the embedded options:

```
...(...|aaa(...|...|...)zzz|...)...
```

An ISBN code for any book published in France (area code '2') or Poland (area code '83') is quite straightforward to express (though the following formulation unfortunately permits a missing or extra digit in the publisher or book code and does not prevent the hyphen that should separate these two parts from actually occuring before or after them both):

```
<pattern value=" (2|83)-[0-9-]{7,8}-[0-9x] " />
```

15.9 Character Class Escapes

There are various categories of **character class escape**. The simplest kind, **single character escape**, has already been discussed. This is an escape sequence for a single character that has a significant role in the expression language, such as '\{' to represent the '{' character (they are listed and discussed in more detail above). The other escape types are

- multicharacter escapes (such as '\S' (non-whitespace) and '.' (non-line-ending character));
- *general* category escapes (such as '\p{L}' and '\p{Lu}') and complementary *general* category escapes (such as '\P{L}' and '\P{Lu}');
- *block* category escapes (such as '\p{IsBasicLatin}' and '\p{IsTibetan}') and complementary *block* category escapes (such as '\P{IsBasicLatin}' and '\P{IsTibetan}').

Multicharacter escapes

For convenience, a number of single character escape codes are provided to represent very common sets of characters, including

- non-line-ending characters;
- whitespace characters and non-whitespace characters;
- initial XML name characters (and all characters except these characters);
- subsequent XML name characters (and all characters except these characters);
- decimal digits (and all characters except these digits).

The '.' character represents every character except a newline or carriage-return character. The sequence '.....' therefore represents a string of five characters that is not broken over lines. The simplest possible pattern for an ISBN code would be thirteen dots (ten digits and three hyphens):

```
<pattern value="............" />
```

The remaining multicharacter escape characters are escaped in the normal way: by a '\' symbol. They are all defined in pairs, with a lowercase letter representing a particular common requirement, and the equivalent uppercase letter representing the opposite effect.

The escape sequence '\s' represents any whitespace character, including the space, tab, newline and carriage-return characters. The '\S' sequence therefore represents any non-whitespace character.

The escape sequence '\i' represents any XML initial name character ('_', ':', or a letter). The '\I' sequence therefore represents any XML noninitial character. Similarly, the escape sequence '\c' represents any XML name character, and '\C' represents any non-XML name character.

The escape sequence '\d' represents any decimal digit. It is equivalent to '\p{Nd}' (see below). The '\D' sequence therefore represents any other character. The ISBN examples can now be shortened still further, and note that an escape sequence can even be placed within a character class, in this case to indicate that the check digit may be a digit instead of the letter 'x' (but note further that such escape sequences cannot be used to indicate the start or end of a range of characters):

```
<pattern value="\d*-\d*-\d*-[\dx]" />
```

The escape sequence '\w' represents all characters except punctuation, separators, and 'other' characters (using a mixture of techniques described above and below, this is equivalent to '[&#x0000;-&#x10FFFF;-[\p{P}\p{Z}\p{C}]]'), whereas the '\W' sequence represents only these characters.

Quantifiers can be used with these escape sequences. For example, '\d{5}' specifies that five decimal digits are required.

Category escapes

The escape sequence '\p' or '\P' introduces a **category escape** set. A category token is enclosed within curly brackets, '{' and '}'. These tokens represent predefined sets of characters, such as all uppercase letters (a general kind of category escape) or the Tibetan character set (a block from the Unicode character set).

General category escapes

A **general category escape** is a reference to a predefined set of characters, such as the uppercase letters, or all of the punctuation characters. These sets of characters have special names, such as 'Lu' for uppercase letters, and 'P' for all punctuation. For example, '\p{Lu}' represents all uppercase letters, and '\P{Lu}' represents all characters except uppercase letters.

Single letter codes are used for major groupings, such as 'L' for all letters (of which uppercase letters are just a subset). The full set of options is listed below:

L		**All Letters**
	Lu	uppercase
	Ll	lowercase
	Lt	titlecase
	Lm	modifier
	Lo	other
M		**All Marks**
	Mn	nonspacing
	Mc	spacing combination
	Me	enclosing
N		**All Numbers**
	Nd	decimal digit
	Nl	letter
	No	other
P		**All Punctuation**
	Pc	connector
	Pd	dash
	Ps	open
	Pe	close
	Pi	initial quote
	Pf	final quote
	Po	other
Z		**All Separators**
	Zs	space
	Zl	line
	Zp	paragraph
S		**All Symbols**
	Sm	math
	Sc	currency
	Sk	modifier
	So	other

C		All Others
	Cc	control
	Cf	format
	Co	private use

For details see http://www.unicode.org/Public/3.1-Update/UnicodeCharacter-Database-3.1.0.html.

Block category escapes

The Unicode character set is divided into many significant groupings such as musical symbols, Braille characters, and Tibetan characters. A keyword is assigned to each group, for example, 'MusicalSymbols', 'BraillePaṭterns', and 'Tibetan'.

The following table lists the full set of keywords in alphabetical order:

AlphabeticPresentationForms	Hebrew
Arabic	HighPrivateUseSurrogates
ArabicPresentationForms-A	HighSurrogates
ArabicPresentationForms-B	Hiragana
Armenian	IdeographicDescriptionCharacters
Arrows	IPAExtensions
BasicLatin	Kanbun
Bengali	KangxiRadicals
BlockElements	Kannada
Bopomofo	Katakana
BopomofoExtended	Khmer
BoxDrawing	Lao
BraillePatterns	Latin-1Supplement
ByzantineMusicalSymbols	LatinExtended-A
Cherokee	LatinExtended-B
CJKCompatibility	LatinExtendedAdditional
CJKCompatibilityForms	LetterlikeSymbols
CJKCompatibilityIdeographs	LowSurrogates
CJKCompatibilityIdeographsSupplement	Malayalam
CJKRadicalsSupplement	MathematicalAlphanumericSymbols
CJKSymbolsandPunctuation	MathematicalOperators

CJKUnifiedIdeographs	MiscellaneousSymbols
CJKUnifiedIdeographsExtensionA	MiscellaneousTechnical
CJKUnifiedIdeographsExtensionB	Mongolian
CombiningDiacriticalMarks	MusicalSymbols
CombiningHalfMarks	Myanmar
CombiningMarksforSymbols	NumberForms
ControlPictures	Ogham
CurrencySymbols	OldItalic
Cyrillic	OpticalCharacterRecognition
Deseret	Oriya
Devanagari	PrivateUse (three separate sets)
Dingbats	Runic
EnclosedAlphanumerics	Sinhala
EnclosedCJKLettersandMonths	SmallFormVariants
Ethiopic	SpacingModifierLetters
GeneralPunctuation	Specials (two separate sets)
GeometricShapes	SuperscriptsandSubscripts
Georgian	Syriac
Gothic	Tags
Greek	Tamil
GreekExtended	Telugu
Gujarati	Thaana
Gurmukhi	Thai
HalfwidthandFullwidthForms	Tibetan
HangulCompatibilityJamo	UnifiedCanadianAboriginalSyllabics
HangulJamo	YiRadicals
HangulSyllables	YiSyllables

A reference to one of these categories involves a keyword that begins with 'Is...' followed by a name from the list above, such as 'Tibetan'. For example, '\p{IsTibetan}' represents any Tibetan character and '\P{IsTibetan}' represents any character not from this set.

16. Shared and Derived Complex Types

A complex data type can be named, shared, and added to the target namespace. It can also be derived by restriction or extension from another data type. The other data type may be a complex data type or it may be a simple data type (thus allowing attributes to be added to an element with simple content).

16.1 Introduction

An element that requires attributes or has a content model that includes child elements must be created with the assistance of a **complex type** definition. Previous examples of complex type definitions have appeared within an element definition and have been tightly associated with the element concerned. They are considered to be **anonymous complex types** because they do not need to be referenced from elsewhere and therefore do not have to be given a referenceable name. But it is also possible for complex type definitions to be shared by many element declarations, and even from element declarations within other schema definitions. These complex types are defined outside of all element declarations and are given a name by which they can be referenced. They should perhaps be called '**named complex types**' (though this is not an official term).

Both anonymous and named complex types can be derived from other complex type definitions, and even from simple type definitions. A complex type can be

- an extended variant of a complex data type (adding elements and attributes);
- a restricted variant of a complex data type (removing or restraining the content of elements and attributes);
- a restricted variant of a complex data type that has a simple content model;
- an extended variant of a simple data type (adding attributes to a simple element).

16.2 Named Complex Types

A complex type definition can be shared if the `complexType` element is placed directly within the `schema` element. The **name** attribute gives the new complex type its identity:

```
<schema ...>
  ...
  <complexType name="eMailType">...</complexType>
  ...
</schema>
```

This new data type can then be referenced from an element definition in exactly the same way that a simple data type can:

```
<element name="EMail" type="E:eMailType" />
```

The name must be unique among all data type names, including simple data type names. However, the name can be the same as the name of another construct, such as an element declaration or group attribute definition.

Consider an anonymous complex type that is embedded within the EMail element:

```
<element name="EMail">
  <complexType>
    <sequence>
      <element ref="E:From" />
      <element ref="E:To" />
      <element ref="E:Title" />
      <element ref="E:Date" />
      <element ref="E:Message" />
    </sequence>
  </complexType>
</element>
```

The following example is equivalent:

```
<complexType name="eMailType">
  <sequence>
    <element ref="E:From" />
    <element ref="E:To" />
    <element ref="E:Title" />
    <element ref="E:Date" />
    <element ref="E:Message" />
  </sequence>
</complexType>

<element name="EMail" type="E:eMailType" />
```

But the advantage of this approach is that other element definitions could easily adopt the same content model:

```
<element name="ReceivedEMail" type="E:eMailType" />

<element name="SentEMail" type="E:eMailType" />
```

In this way a complex type can substitute for the `group` element, though this is not the real intention of this feature and the `group` element should be used instead for this simple sharing requirement. The `group` element also allows new structures to be built from smaller structures in a much more flexible manner.

The real advantage of naming complex data types is that they can be referenced by other complex data types that are based on them.

16.3   Additions to the Target Namespace

A named complex type can be referenced from other schema definitions. Indeed, a named complex type is automatically added to the target namespace for this purpose:

In the following example, an element in another schema definition refers to the defined complex type (see Section 13.4 for more on importing):

```
<element ... type="E:eMailType" />
```

As noted above, the main reason to create a named complex type is to allow other complex data types to base their own definitions on its characteristics. In this case, the other complex data types can be in schema definitions that target other namespaces.

Note that the namespace of the complex data type definition is usually irrelevant and transparent to document instance authors. One exception is these authors using the `xsi:type` attribute to directly select a data type. The only thing that matters to such authors is which namespace the element that adopts the data type belongs to.

16.4   Derivation from Complex Types

Just as a simple data type can be created from another simple data type by either extension or restriction of a 'base' type, a complex data type can also be derived by extension or restriction, though the specifics differ (and in the case of complex types, it is not actually essential that they be derived from another data type).

Complex content

The **complexContent** element specifies that a complex type is derived from another complex type:

```
<complexType name="myComplexType">
  <complexContent>
    . . .
  </complexContent>
</complexType>
```

When the `complexType` element contains this element, it can have no other content apart from an optional leading `annotation` element. Attribute declarations or references can still be added, but this is now done within elements embedded in the `complexContent` element.

Note that this feature is available to anonymous complex types, as well as to named complex types:

```
<element name="MyComplexElement">
  <complexType>
    <complexContent>
      . . .
    </complexContent>
  </complexType>
</element>
```

Also note that the name of the `complexContent` element is a little misleading because an element with complex content can always be created with simpler techniques, described earlier (see Chapter 6). Its real purpose is to specify that the element will include elements or attributes that have already been defined within an existing complex model, but with some minor modifications. A better name for this element might have been something like 'deriveModelFromComplexType'. It should also be observed that the word 'content' in the name is especially misleading, because the effect of the `complexContent` element is not constrained to the content of the element but may also affect attributes.

Mixed content

The `complexContent` element may hold a **mixed** attribute. If used, it overrides the setting for this attribute on the parent `complexType` element:

```
<complexType   ... mixed="true">
  <complexContent mixed="false">
    . . .
  </complexContent>
</complexType>
```

Extension or restriction

The `complexContent` element must contain either a single **restriction** element or a single **extension** element:

```
<complexType>
  <complexContent>
    <restriction>...</restriction>
  </complexContent>
</complexType>

<complexType>
  <complexContent>
    <extension>...</extension>
  </complexContent>
</complexType>
```

A value that conforms to a restricted data type is guaranteed to be a valid example of a value that conforms to the original data type (because nothing is added to the definition). The `restriction` element was seen before in Section 14.3, where it was used to restrict simple data types, but its content model is different in this new scenario.

An extended data type similarly prevents disruption of the original structure, by allowing only elements to be appended to the existing model.

16.5   Derivation by Extension

A complex type can be an extended variant of another complex type. An extension of a complex type always takes the form of new components simply appended to the end of the existing model. An implied `sequence` element encloses both models so as to enforce the rule that all models have a single topmost grouping construct. The **base** attribute on the **extension** element identifies the existing data type that populates the first part of the implied sequence:

```
<extension base="...">
  <sequence>
    <!-- ORIGINAL MODEL -->
    ...
    <!-- EXTENSION COMPONENTS -->
    ...
  </sequence>
</extension>
```

It does not matter if the original complex type had no model (because it was used to create empty elements).

Clearly, this technique is not suitable when simply appending new elements to a model would not reflect the actual requirement. It can therefore be used with typical datacentric documents, but not with typical narrative document models.

Neither the original data type nor the new data type can include the `all` element, because this element must always be at the top of a content model and therefore must not be embedded within even an implied `sequence` element.

If the original data type allows mixed content, the derived data type must also do so. If it does not, then the derived data type must also disallow mixed content.

An attribute wildcard can be added, but there are complications if the wildcard also appears in the original data type. In this case, a list of namespaces, along with '##local' and '##targetNamespace' keywords, is built from combining the lists in each of the wildcard definitions. If either contains the '##any' keyword, then this takes precedence. However, the keyword '##other' will have different meanings in each definition when the instances the keyword belongs to are in different namespaces. In this situation, the schema processor automatically replaces '##other' with '##any'.

16.6 Derivation by Restriction

A complex data type can be a restricted variant of another complex data type.

Elements

Creation of a restricted content mode is achieved by first replicating the original model, then tightening any relevant constraints in the copied model. For example, the email data type is derived by restriction, below, to create an email model that does not allow carbon-copy recipients:

```
<complexType name="eMailWithoutCCType">
  <complexContent>
    <restriction base="E:eMailType">
      <sequence>
        <element ref="E:From" />
        <element ref="E:To" minOccurs="1"
                            maxOccurs="unbounded" />
        <element ref="E:CarbonCopy" minOccurs="0"
                                    maxOccurs="0" />
        <element ref="E:Title" minOccurs="0" />
        <element ref="E:Date" />
        <element ref="E:Message" />
      </sequence>
    </restriction>
  </complexContent>
</complexType>
```

One reason for using this technique (rather than just informally copying the elements from the other type, then making any necessary adjustments) is that the processor can check that all of the base declarations are present and that nothing has been added or omitted. In particular, the processor can raise an error if the base type is amended, but the schema definition author forgets to reflect the changes in the restricted type. Other reasons for using this technique are discussed in Chapter 17.

Note that this feature is the primary reason for allowing the **maxOccurs** attribute to have a value of zero. In the example above, the 'eMailWithoutCCType' data type suppresses use of the CarbonCopy element (some schema processors require the minOccurs attribute to be present and set to zero too, even though it is already set to this value in the original declaration). Yet this capability is not essential, because an element that was optional in the original data type can be omitted entirely from the derived type instead.

An any element in the original data type can be replaced by a specific element that would be a valid match to the wildcard in the original data type.

When the data type that the new data type is to be derived from is itself an extension of a third type, then it is necessary to find the supertype so that its contribution to the model can be copied into the new type (this feature is not clever enough to find these declarations and copy them in automatically).

All the element references from the first two data types below are included in the third one because it is directly or indirectly derived from both of these data types:

```
<complexType name="eMailType">
  <sequence>
    <element ref="E:From" />
    <element ref="E:To" minOccurs="1"
                        maxOccurs="unbounded" />
    <element ref="E:Title" minOccurs="0" />
    <element ref="E:Date" />
    <element ref="E:Message" />
  </sequence>
</complexType>

<complexType name="eMailWithCCType">
  <complexContent>
    <extension base="E:eMailType">
      <sequence>
        <element ref="E:CarbonCopy"
                 minOccurs="0"
                 maxOccurs="unbounded" />
      </sequence>
    </extension>
  </complexContent>
</complexType>
```

```
<complexType name="eMailOneRecipientType">
  <complexContent>
    <restriction base="E:eMailWithCCType">
      <sequence>
        <element ref="E:From" />
        <element ref="E:To" minOccurs="1"
                            maxOccurs="1" />
        <element ref="E:Title" minOccurs="0" />
        <element ref="E:Date" />
        <element ref="E:Message" />
        <element ref="E:CarbonCopy" minOccurs="0"
                                    maxOccurs="0" />
      </sequence>
    </restriction>
  </complexContent>
</complexType>
```

Attributes

An attribute's data type can be changed to a valid subtype, a default value can be added, removed or changed, a fixed value can be added, and an optional attribute can be made either mandatory or prohibited.

A missing attribute definition does *not* imply that it is no longer wanted, but that it *is* wanted without modification. For an attribute to be removed the declaration must be included, and the **use** attribute must be set to '**prohibited**', though this is only allowed if the attribute was originally optional. This is clearly an equivalent technique to setting an element's maxOccurs attribute to zero.

The **anyAttribute** element *must* be omitted from the subtype if it is not wanted; there are no maxOccurs or use attribute alternatives here. When this definition is retained, the processing stringency setting can be changed, say, from 'lax' to 'strict' or from 'strict' to 'lax', and the namespace setting can be constrained from '##other' or '##any' to a specified namespace or list of namespaces. but not the other way around.

16.7 Simple Content

An element can be complex, in the sense that it contains attributes, while having content that does not include child elements but does include text that must conform to a simple data type. A complex data type can be restricted to having simple content, conforming to a data format that is derived from a *simple* data type, by the **simpleContent** element:

```
<complexType>
  <simpleContent>...</simpleContent>
</complexType>
```

A more appropriate name for the `simpleContent` element might have been 'deriveContentFromSimpleType'. Note that the word 'content' in the name refers to the allowed content of the element and does not refer to attributes, although attributes *are* declarable from within this element.

The data type that the content must conform to is derived, either by restriction or extension, from an existing simple data type. Just as for the complex equivalent (the `complexContent` element), this element must contain a single **extension** element or a single **restriction** element, though these child elements are used here in different ways:

```
<simpleContent>
  <extension>...</extension>
</simpleContent>

<simpleContent>
  <restriction>...</restriction>
</simpleContent>
```

An enclosing `complexType` element can have no other content apart from an optional leading `annotation` element. Attributes can still be added, but no longer directly within the `complexType` element. Also, the `complexType` element must not include the **mixed** attribute, because the referenced simple type already achieves the aim of allowing text to appear.

Extending a simple type

A `simpleContent` element can contain an **extension** element. The **base** attribute of this element must reference a simple data type:

```
<complexType>
  <simpleContent>
    <extension base="DOC:mySimpleType" />
  </simpleContent>
</complexType>
```

This simple example achieves nothing that cannot be achieved in an easier way. An element that included or referenced this complex type would have no child elements and no attributes. This classifies it as a simple element that could be defined much more easily as follows:

```
<element ... type="DOC:mySimpleType" />
```

But, while in this case the `extension` element cannot contain the elements that construct a content model (because simple data types cannot contain elements), it *can* still contain attribute definitions:

```
<simpleContent>
  <extension base="ChannelType">
    <attribute ref="PB:Owner" />
    <attributeGroup ref="PB:generalAttributes" />
    <anyAttribute namespace="##other"
                  processContents="lax" />
  </extension>
</simpleContent>
```

This example permits the following element to occur in a document instance:

```
<Channel Owner="BBC" Id="x123" >BBC 2</Channel>
```

Restricting simple content

It is not easy to find useful examples of the `restriction` element within the `simpleContent` element. It cannot be used to add attributes (unlike the `extension` element). However, it does have two relatively obscure purposes.

Just as with extensions, a restriction is based on a previously defined data type that is targeted by the **base** attribute. It would appear obvious that the referenced base data type must be a simple data type (either built in to the language or defined by a `simpleType` element) rather than by a complex data type. This is certainly the case when deriving by extension (as seen above), but is not necessarily true when deriving by restriction. There are two scenarios to consider.

The first possibility is that a referenced complex data type also has simple content, and that data type must be directly or indirectly derived from a simple data type (there must be a simple data type at the end of the chain, no matter how long the chain is).

The second, poorly supported and contentious, possibility is that a referenced complex type allows text to appear (as mixed content) and has child elements that can all be omitted. In the new data type, the elements are forced to be omitted and the remaining unconstrained text is tamed into conformance with the rules of a simple data type.

These two possibilities are explored further below.

Restricting a complex type with simple content

Earlier, it was shown that a complex type can be created as a restricted variant of another complex type. But that technique would not work if the referenced complex type used the technique shown above to specify that it has simple content. The following technique can be employed to create a restricted variant of another complex data type that in turn extends a simple data type. The **base** attribute must therefore refer to a complex data type, and the referenced complex data type must itself have a simple content model.

For example, the `extension` element could be used in the referenced complex type to add an attribute, and the new complex type could specify that this attribute is prohibited:

```
<complexType name="X">
  <simpleContent>
    <extension base="integer">
      <attribute name="Y" type="string" />
    </extension>
  </simpleContent>
</complexType>

<complexType name="Z">
  <simpleContent>
    <restriction base="DOC:X">
      <attribute name="Y" type="string"
                 use="prohibited" />
    </restriction>
  </simpleContent>
</complexType>
```

The `simpleType` element can be used instead of the `base` attribute on the `restriction` element and is useful for single-step creation of a restricted list:

```
<complexType name="eMailOneRecipientType">
  <simpleContent>
    <restriction>
      <simpleType>
        <list itemType="integer" />
      </simpleType>
      <length value="3" />
    </restriction>
  </simpleContent>
</complexType>
```

Restricting a complex type with mixed content

The second scenario is even more obscure. In fact, the standard cannot even decide whether it is valid (depending on which part of the standard is consulted). Some processors do not understand the following feature, and a future addendum or version of the standard must clarify whether or not they should.

Instead of the referenced complex type needing to have simple content, it can have complex content, but only when two conditions apply. The first condition is that the content model must be mixed. The second condition is that the elements that can be mixed with the text must all be optional. The following example can be derived because it meets both of these conditions:

```
<complexType name="mixedAndOptionalType"
             mixed="true">
  <sequence>
    <element ref="DOC:OptionalElement" minOccurs="0" />
  </sequence>
  <attribute ref="DOC:AnAttribute" use="optional" />
</complexType>
```

The derived simple content is created by eliminating the optional elements, which is done automatically in this context, then taming the text so that it conforms to a suitable data type. Because the source complex type does not refer to any data type, this can only be done by embedding a simpleType element that references the base data type needed (in this case as an unrestricted 'restriction' of the base type):

```
<complexType name="derivedFromMixedContent">
  <simpleContent>
    <restriction base="DOC:mixedAndOptionalType">
      <simpleType>
        <restriction base="integer" />
      </simpleType>
      <attribute ref="DOC:AnAttribute"
                 use="prohibited" />
    </restriction>
  </simpleContent>
</complexType>
```

The example above uses a restriction element within the embedded simple-Type element just to reference a suitable data type, but it could just as well enclose a real set of actual restrictions to create a customized data type or, indeed, the list or union elements instead.

Note that the original optional attribute is also prohibited in the derived complex type, which is a typical restriction activity. Indeed, the constraining of content on a complex data type that includes a number of attributes (whether they need to be modified or not) is perhaps the only useful purpose of this feature, though the use of an attribute group that is referenced by two unconnected data types might be thought to be just as effective and far less complex to implement.

This is the only scenario that allows both a base attribute and a simpleType child of the restriction element.

17. Advanced Inheritance Techniques

The concept of inheritance is an important characteristic of the object-oriented approach to software development that has become very popular in recent years. The XML Schema standard acknowledges the significance of inheritance and includes many features that either exploit or control the inheritance of data types.

17.1 Inheritance Concepts

For the benefit of those not already familiar with object-oriented techniques in general and the benefits of **inheritance** in particular, this is a good time to consider the principles of this concept, as well as the specific impact that inheritance techniques have on schema definition authors, document instance authors, and programmers of software applications that process document instances.

Specialization

Inheritance is a key component of the object-oriented concept. Inheritance creates an 'is-a' relationship between two objects. For example, a cat *is a* kind of animal and a car *is a* kind of vehicle. The cat and the car are examples of specialized forms of more generalized categories (animal and vehicle, respectively).

Specialization often takes the form of **extension** characteristics. For example, a cat shares basic characteristics with all other animals, such the ability to move spontaneously, but adds the specific characteristic of being able to catch mice. In addition to extensions, specialization often takes the form of **overriding** characteristics. For example, most cars have an internal combustion engine but some specialized cars run on batteries. However, overriding can only take the form of a **restriction** in the XML Schema standard, whereby some of the basic characteristics are removed or constrained. For example, a Manx cat is just like any other cat except that it loses the characteristic of having a tail. A car is normally able to hold passengers, but a racing car cannot.

A chain of specialization features involving both extensions and restrictions is conceivable. A Manx cat is a restricted form of cat, which is an extension of a generalized animal.

Inheritance in software

In object-oriented software languages, an object that contains attributes and methods (functions that operate within the object) belongs to a **class** that is also a **type** (interfaces are also types). But a class can derive its properties from another class and thereby inherit all of the original's attributes and methods (there is a 'class hierarchy'). The new **subtype** (or **subclass**) can then add additional attributes and methods and may also override methods by modifying the code that they contain to create more specialized functionality (the original type is considered to be the **supertype** (or **superclass**) of the new type). Typically, only extensions are allowed. For example, there are no characteristics of an animal class that do not apply to a cat class.

In the software fragment below, the variable called 'John' is an **object** that is assigned to type 'personType', and its 'age' property is set to '79'; this value is then retreived by a call to a method named 'getAge()':

```
personType John =
    new personType();         // John is 'personType'

John.age = 79;                // 'age' holds age value
int age = John.getAge();      // 'getAge' returns value
```

The same 'John' variable can hold an object of subtype 'olderPersonType', and this change is not expected to affect the ability to retrieve the age by the same 'getAge()' method. But the subclass might add a method called 'isRetired()' that discovers whether or not the person is retired:

```
personType John =
    new olderPersonType(); // John is 'olderPersonType'

John.age = 79;                // unaffected by change
int age = John.getAge();      // unaffected by change

boolean isRetired =
            John.isRetired() // extended feature
```

Backward compatibility

One of the main points of inheritance in modern software languages is that a subclass object can be assigned to a variable that is assigned to the supertype (as shown above). It does not matter if the assigned subtype object has additional constants, variables, and methods, and it does not even matter if the subtype overrides the behavior of some of the original methods, because these extensions do not remove or modify the core structures expected by software code that is expected to interpret or manipulate the object. The object is 'backward compatible.' Only when the variable is accessed by software that expects it to hold an object of the subclass are its extensions expected and used.

To a large extent, this principle of extending an existing type in such a way that software which is unaware of the additions will continue to recognize and interpret the content it understands is carried over to the XML domain by the XML Schema standard.

XML types

Despite its absence from the earlier DTD modeling language, the inheritance concept has been incorporated into the XML Schema standard. This is largely due to the relatively new use of XML in datacentric applications, in which it is exploited to help transfer complex data structures between databases (sometimes object-relational) and software applications (often written in object-oriented languages).

A data type may be a constrained form of text string that can occur in an attribute value or as the content of an element (a simple data type), or it may include attributes, a content model, or both (a complex data type).

Unusually, the XML Schema inheritance feature includes the concept of a subtype that is a **restriction**, rather than an extension, of the type it is derived from. A restriction of a data type (whether simple or complex) must be a valid subset of the original data type. This is really just a specialized form of overriding, and the concept of backward compatibility is maintained. A software application that is unaware that it is processing XML data that conforms to a restricted subtype does not need to know that the document instance author was constrained by this fact, and should not even notice that it is receiving values that are a subset of the range of values that it can cope with.

A **simple data type** is analogous to a primitive type in a programming language, and indeed many of the built-in simple data type names (such as 'boolean', 'integer', and 'string') are the same as the names of primitive types in many programming languages. But a **complex data type** can be very different from the more complex software reference types. At best an XML fragment is quite similar to a software object if the object contains only a set of primitive variables (a 'structure' or 'record', depending on the language in use):

```
public class eMail()
{
   String From = "";
   String To[] = new String[100];
   String Title = "";
   String Date = "";
   String Message = "";
}
```

```
<complexType name="eMail">
  <sequence>
    <element name="From"     type="string" />
    <element name="To"       type="string"
                             maxOccurs="100" />
    <element name="Title"    type="string" />
    <element name="Date"     type="string" />
    <element name="Message"  type="string" />
  </sequence>
</complexType>
```

In XML terms, an atomic attribute value or simple element text string content is equivalent to a field (a variable that is global to the class), but instead of methods XML only offers more complicated data types. Either way, a data type is still a single, self-contained unit that defines the domain from which valid values of that type can be drawn. And data types share with software objects the fundamental similarity that inheritance can eliminate redundant code (in this case, duplicate element or attribute declarations) and facilitate access by software with different levels of specialization.

Both simple data types and complex data types can be **extended**. Elements and attributes can be added to the end of a complex data type content model, ensuring that the original model is not disrupted in any way. However, the means by which simple types are extended breaks the conventions of software inheritance, in that union types and list types (introduced in Section 14.9 and Section 14.10, respectively) are not necessarily backward compatible with the types they are derived from.

Backward compatibility

Backward compatibility can be very important. Consider the program broadcast example and the possible introduction of specialized structures that add information specific to various categories of program, including an obvious fundamental divide into factual and fictional programs. First, though, it is necessary to introduce a data type from which these specialized types will be derived and which contains information that is relevant to all possible derivations:

```
<ProgramDetails>
  <CopyrightDate>1972</CopyrightDate>
  <Owner>MegaTVi Corp.</Owner>
</ProgramDetails>
```

A subtype for factual programs would add the `Narrator` or `Presenter` element:

```
<ProgramDetails>
  <CopyrightDate>1972</CopyrightDate>
  <Owner>MegaTVi Corp.</Owner>
  <Presenter>Kevin Smith</Presenter>
</ProgramDetails>
```

In the example above, the parent element remains the same as that employed by the base data type, but there is no reason why a more descriptive element could not be used instead (this feature is discussed later):

```
<FactualProgramDetails>
  <CopyrightDate>1972</CopyrightDate>
  <Owner>MegaTVi Corp.</Owner>
  <Presenter>Kevin Smith</Presenter>
</FactualProgramDetails>
```

The chain of inheritance can continue beyond two levels. For example, one category of factual programming might be biographical documentaries, and in this case the name of the subject of the documentary would be useful additional information. This time, instead of a new parent element being introduced, the reserved XML Schema xsi:type attribute is used to identify which derivation has been used (again, this is discussed later):

```
<ProgramDetails xsi:type="bioDocProgType">
  <CopyrightDate>1972</CopyrightDate>
  <Owner>MegaTVi Corp.</Owner>
  <Presenter>Kevin Smith</Presenter>
  <Subject>Winston Churchill</Subject>
</ProgramDetails>
```

Now imagine that three recipients of a document instance that contains the fragment above have different levels of interest in the content. The first recipient has developed processing software that is sensitive to biographical documentary programs and needs to extract the name from the Subject element. The second is unaware of the finer distinctions between factual program categories but still needs to distinguish between factual and fictional programs and to extract the name from the Presenter element when it is a factual program. The third is oblivious to all such distinctions but needs to know the copyright date and creator. All three programs should be able to extract the information that they need without difficulty, especially when the name of the container element does not change.

Naturally, the situation is more complex for the most generalized of the three programs when the element type is used to identify a subtype, as in the case of the FactualProgramDetails element above, because this program needs to be aware of the hierarchical relationships among the various alternatives in order to recognize that this is a stand-in element for an element that it does recognize (in this case the ProgramDetails element). This could only be achieved by interrogation of the schema definition.

17.2 Summary of Schema Inheritance Features

Chapter 14 showed how a new simple data type created by a schema definition author must derive its properties from another simple data type, and Section 16.4 showed how a new complex data type can also inherit its content model and attribute requirements. But these derivation mechanisms hardly scratch the surface of the extent to which the concept of **inheritance** has been adopted by the XML Schema language. In addition, it is possible to do the following:

- prevent a data type from being derived (by giving it a 'final' status)
- prevent a data type or element from being used, and thereby enforce the use of a derived type or element (by making it an 'abstract' component or by 'fixing' some facets of a simple data type)
- create elements that can be used in place of another element, wherever that element is allowed in the document model (by building a 'substitution group')
- grant document instance authors the ability to specify that the content of an element conforms to a data type that is derived from the data type formally assigned to that element (by using the xsi:type attribute)
- prevent document instance authors from selecting a derived data type, and prevent schema definition authors from creating a substitution group for a given element declaration

These concepts are discussed in depth below.

17.3 Final Types

The author of a data type may wish to prevent other schema definition authors from deriving new data types from it. Of course, one way to achieve this is to avoid naming the data type, which means embedding it within an element or attribute declaration. However, the author may also wish to make the data type global so that it can be referenced from various element and attribute declarations, and it must therefore be a named definition. It is not possible to hide a global data type from other schema definitions, but it *is* possible to bar derivations from it. A data type that cannot be derived from is known as a **final** data type; note that such a bar applies to the local schema definition, just as much as it does to other schema definitons that might import it.

The **final** attribute is empty by default. A number of keywords are allowed in this attribute value, though the options vary depending on the context, authors can specify several kinds of constraint by including multiple keywords in the value, separated by whitespace characters. But this attribute can be given the value '**#all**' in all circumstances, as an alternative to including all the other keywords described below. This keyword ensures that there cannot be derivations of any kind. It is therefore unnecessary, and illegal, to combine it with any of the other keywords.

Final complex types

In the **complexType** element, the `final` attribute may contain either the 'restriction' keyword or the 'extension' keyword, or its value may even be left as an empty text string. The presence of the '**restriction**' keyword ensures that the complex type cannot be derived by restriction. The presence of the '**extension**' keyword similarly ensures that the complex type cannot be derived by extension.

Both keywords may be present in the same attribute, but this is equivalent to simply using the '#all' keyword. The examples below are therefore equivalent:

```
<complexType ... final="#all">...</complexType>

<complexType ... final="restriction
                        extension">...</complexType>
```

Final simple types

When the `final` attribute is used on the **simpleType** element, the options are different. While the '#all' and 'restriction' keywords are used for the same purposes as before, the '**union**' and '**list**' keywords replace the 'extension' keyword. This means, for example, that it is possible to prevent a derived list from being created while still allowing a union to be partly derived from this data type:

```
<simpleType ... final="#all">...</simpleType>

<simpleType ... final="restriction">...</simpleType>

<simpleType ... final="union">...</simpleType>

<simpleType ... final="list">...</simpleType>
```

Unfortunately, multiple keywords are not allowed in this context. This prohibition might yet be deemed an error in the standard because of the inconsistency of allowing derivation by restriction but prohibiting derivation by extension. The keyword 'extension' is not allowed, '#all' would prevent restrictions too, and 'union list' is not allowed because this value is more than one keyword (though the `finalDefault` attribute on the `schema` element, which is discussed later, can do this). It is not legal, for example, to include the value 'restriction union' in order to allow derivation only by list.

Note that restricting a list data type creates a new list data type, which should not be allowed if the original list data type has a final setting that prevents derivations of type 'list', though many processors will not detect this condition and will therefore allow such a derivation.

Noninheritance of finality setting

The setting of a `final` attribute is not inherited by a derived data type. For example, a complex data type that is derived by extension from another complex data type that prevented derivation by restriction will itself be derivable by restriction.

Final elements

The `final` attribute may be used on the **element** element. The values '**#all**', '**restriction**', and '**extension**' are allowed in this context. The purpose of this feature in element declarations is to restrict schema definition authors in creating a substitution element that has a data type that is derived from the one assigned to this element (this is discussed in more detail later).

Default overriding

By default, a missing `final` attribute on any of the three elements to which it may be attached is interpreted as a string that contains none of the keywords described above, and therefore implies no constraints on derivation. If a schema definition author decides that the majority of definitions should be constrained in a particular way regardless of which constraint is desired, it appears to be necessary to add the attribute to all the relevant definitions:

```
<schema ...>
  <complexType ... final="restriction">
    ...
  </complexType>
  <complexType ... final="restriction">
    ...
  </complexType>
  <complexType ... final="restriction">
    ...
  </complexType>
  <complexType ... final="restriction">
    ...
  </complexType>
</schema>
```

However, instead of this tedious procedure, the **finalDefault** attribute can be used on the **schema** element to override the default setting. This attribute can hold the same keywords as described above. The following example is equivalent to the one above, but requires much less effort to create:

```
<schema ... finalDefault="restriction">
  <complexType ... >...</complexType>
  <complexType ... >...</complexType>
  <complexType ... >...</complexType>
  <complexType ... >...</complexType>
</schema>
```

As the attribute name suggests, this is only a default value. Individual definitions can still override it. In the following example, the second complex type definition cannot be derived at all, the third cannot be derived by extension (but it *can* be derived by restriction), and the fourth is not constrained in any way (an explicit empty value overrides the default setting and sets no constraints):

```
<schema ... finalDefault="restriction">
  <complexType ... > ... </complexType>
  <complexType final="#all" > ... </complexType>
  <complexType final="extension" > ... </complexType>
  <complexType final="" > ... </complexType>
</schema>
```

Note that the only time a `final` attribute with an empty string value needs to be added to an element is when a default is set, but the current definition is not to be restricted in any way (as in the final example above). An implicit `final` attribute, however, has a different meaning: that the default setting applies.

The value '**extension**' in the `finalDefault` attribute covers both the 'union' and 'list' extension options in simple type definitions. This is interesting because it is not possible to suppress both of these options and still retain the ability to restrict data types by using the `final` attribute on the individual definitions.

When a schema document is included into another schema document, the setting of the `finalDefault` attribute is not overridden, and so continues to apply to all the components in the included document, even when the including document has a different setting for this attribute.

17.4   Fixed Facets

Use of the `final` attribute to control derivation of simple data types is a rather blunt instrument when there may only be a desire to prevent overriding of particular facets. The **fixed** attribute can be added to most of the facet-related elements, including the **maxExclusive, minExclusive, maxInclusive, minInclusive, totalDigits, fractionDigits, length, minLength, maxLength**, and **whiteSpace** elements. The `pattern` and `enumeration` elements are excluded from this mechanism because it is not possible to enforce the use of a particular enumerated or pattern option in a derived type (though the subtype can explicitly contain a subset of enumerated or pattern options that it will support instead).

In the following example, the minimum value of the 'atLeastOneHundred' simple data type is set to '100', and derived types cannot change this setting to a higher value (a lower value derivation would not be allowed in any case):

```
<simpleType name="atLeastOneHundred">
  <restriction base="integer">
    <minInclusive value="100" fixed="true" />
  </restriction>
</simpleType>
```

As another example, a concrete implementation of the 'integer' data type would include the fractionDigits element with a fixed value of '0'. This makes sense because any type derived from the 'integer' data type should be a restricted form of integer:

```
<simpleType name="integer">
  <restriction base="decimal">
    <fractionDigits value="0" fixed="true" />
  </restriction>
</simpleType>
```

A fixed status on a facet is inherited. If a type called 'smallInteger' were created from the 'integer' data type (perhaps with a maximum value of '1000') and then another data type called 'verySmallInteger' were derived from this (perhaps setting the maximum to '100'), it could not reintroduce fraction digits.

Although it is possible to use the fixed attribute on the **length** element, there is little point in doing so. If a length is specified, then a derived data type cannot alter its setting either upward or downward, so the fixed attribute is redundant.

17.5 Abstract Data Types

Recall that it is possible to prevent a data type from being derived. At the other extreme, it is also possible to insist that a data type *must* be derived, thus preventing direct referencing from an element or attribute declaration. The term **abstract** describes something that has no 'concrete' existence (in this case, in a document model). An **abstract data type** can be derived to create a new, normal data type (a concrete data type).

The **abstract** attribute can be used on the **complexType** element, but it cannot be used on the simpleType element.

Utility types

Abstract types are considered to be **utility types** because they are *utilized* to create other data types. For example, if all email must be identified as incoming or outgoing email yet both kinds of email share some characteristics, such as the email title and message, then the following set of complex type definitions may be appropriate. The common characteristics are defined first, in an abstract data type:

```
<complexType name="eMailCommon" abstract="true">
  <sequence>
    <element ref="E:Title" />
    <element ref="E:Date" />
    <element ref="E:Message" />
  </sequence>
</complexType>

<complexType name="eMailIncoming">
  <complexContent base="eMailCommon">
    <sequence>
      <element ref="E:From" />
    </sequence>
  </complexContent>
</complexType>

<complexType name="eMailOutgoing">
  <complexContent base="eMailCommon">
    <sequence>
      <element ref="E:To" maxOccurs="unbounded" />
    </sequence>
  </complexContent>
</complexType>
```

Because the first definion is abstract, an element definition can refer to only one of the last two definitions. Any attempt to directly reference the 'eMailCommon' data type would raise an error:

```
<element name="EmailIn" type="E:eMailIncoming" />

<element name="EmailOut" type="E:eMailOutgoing" />

<!-- ERROR -->
<element name="Email" type="E:eMailCommon" />
```

Derivation rules

An abstract complex data type can be derived from either an abstract or concrete supertype. A chain of data types may therefore include several abstract data types that are interspersed with concrete data types. In the following example, only the data types called 'second' and 'fourth' can be used to help construct a document model (or, as explained later, be selected from within a document instance):

```
<complexType name="first" abstract="true">
  ...
</complexType>

<complexType name="second"> <!-- CONCRETE -->
  <restriction base="first">...</restriction>
</complexType>

<complexType name="third" abstract="true">
  <restriction base="second">...</restriction>
</complexType>
```

```
<complexType name="fourth"> <!-- CONCRETE -->
  <restriction base="third">...</restriction>
</complexType>
```

Software developers should note that although only single inheritance is allowed, groups can be used to partially overcome this limitation.

17.6 Substitution Data Type Selection

Although the schema definition author decides which data type to assign to an element, a document instance author can choose another data type when adding this element to their document. However, the selected data type must be derived from the data type originally assigned to the element. The **xsi:type** attribute allows the document instance author to select the data type. For example, the EMail element might be assigned to the 'eMailCommon' data type (no longer an abstract type in this scenario):

```
<element name="EMail" type="eMailCommon" />
```

The document instance author can select the 'eMailOutgoing' data type instead:

```
<EMail xsi:type="eMailOutgoing">...</EMail>
```

Consider the effect that this feature must have on XML authoring tools. Normally, when an element is selected, the appropriate list of attributes and possible child elements are immediately presented to the author. Delaying this action until the author has decided whether or not to select a derived data type would require the application to insist on an immediate answer to this question every time it arises, perhaps by popping up a dialog box that contains a list of alternative data types.

17.7 Blocking Derivation Usage

The **block** attribute can be used on the **element** element to prevent an element from being exploited in various extension features. The value '**#all**' ensures that the content of the element must always conform to the data type assigned to that element in the schema definition. The **xsi:type** attribute cannot then be used by a document instance author to select another data type that is derived from that data type.

But blocking all derivations is a rather blunt instrument. The '**restriction**' keyword prevents selection only of a data type derived by restriction from the base type, and the '**extension**' keyword similarly prevents selection only of a data type that is derived by extension.

Both the 'restriction' and 'extension' keywords may be present, but this does not quite mean the same thing as the '#all' keyword, because there is a third option, which needs to be explained. The block attribute can be added to an element declaration to block 'substitutions' (as explained later).

The **blockDefault** attribute on the schema element can be used to set a default block setting for all components. Note that when this attribute is used in an included schema document, its value still pertains to all of the relevant included components.

17.8   Substitution Elements

Use of the xsi:type attribute described above can be a clumsy method for document instance authors to select a derived content model. The author has to know in advance the name of the element, insert this element into the document instance, then select the xsi:type attribute, and choose from a list of allowed data types. This would be a test of both memory and patience and would require the author to learn about data types. It might be better if this author could simply choose a more appropriate element type instead (which hides from the author the fact that it conforms to another data type). This approach is supported by the **substitution** feature.

Head and substitution elements

Any declared element that is assigned to a named (global) data type can become the focus of the substitution feature, as the **head** of a set of related elements. Nothing is added to the declaration of this element to give it this status. Instead, all the other elements in the relationship simply refer to it. A global element type acquires its status as a head element as soon as at least one other global element declaration includes a **substitutionGroup** attribute with the name of this element as its value. For example, the ProgramDetails element would become a head element if the FactualProgDetails element referenced it (including the namespace prefix, provided that a namespace is targeted and is assigned to a prefix):

```
<element name="ProgramDetails">...</element>

<element name="FactualProgDetails"
          substitutionGroup="PB:ProgramDetails">
   ...
</element>
```

But this relationship would not be allowed if the data type assigned to the FactualProgDetails element was not the same as, or was not derived from, the data type assigned to the head element (either simple or complex). For example, the following definition would be unacceptable because the 'string' simple data type is not derived from the 'programDetails' complex data type:

```
<element name="ProgramDetails"
         type="programType">...</element>

<element name="FactualProgDetails"
         substitutionGroup="PB:ProgramDetails"
         type="string" /> <!-- ERROR -->
```

Substitution elements can be used in a document instance wherever the document model explicitly allows the head element to appear. Any occurrence attributes on the reference to the head element in the declaration of a context parent element apply to substitution elements. Indeed, if multiple occurrences are allowed, then a mixture of any of the elements in the group can appear.

Note that there is no concept of hierarchy within a single substitution group (though there can be a hierarchy of substitution groups, as discussed later). The BioDocProgDetails element declared below adopts the 'bioDocProgType' data type, which is a subtype of the 'factProgType' data type, yet this element is in no way subordinate to the FactualProgDetails element associated with that data type, and it refers directly to the ProgramDetails element in its substitution-Group attribute:

```
<element name="BioDocProgDetails"
         substitutionGroup="PB:ProgramDetails">
    ...
</element>
```

The actual relationships can be visualized as follows:

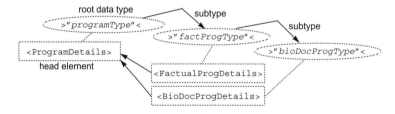

Benefits

The cost of this approach is that the document instance author has to learn more element names. But at least this author does not have to learn a list of allowed data type names and does not even have to be aware of the concept of data types. When a document instance author selects a substitution element, the appropriate derived data type is selected along with it.

Elements can be added to an existing substitution group in an imported schema definition, or a new substitution group can be created for an element that is declared in the imported schema definition (where it remains unaware of its new status).

Blocks on substitutions

The head element can be referenced from various other element declarations and therefore can appear in several places within the document structure, but it may not be appropriate to allow substitutions to occur within all of these contexts. It is therefore possible to prevent substitutions by adding the **block** attribute to a reference to a head element and giving it the value '**substitution**'.

```
<element name="headElem" block="substitution"/>
```

If an element must never be allowed to be the head of a substitution group, then the block attribute can be added to the declaration itself. This is a particularly useful way to prevent other schema definitions that import the current schema definition from declaring substitutions for it.

Final settings

The **final** attribute can be used on the **element** element to prevent schema definition authors from creating a substitute that is assigned to a derived data type. When the value '**#all**' is used, the element can only be at the head of a substitution group in which all of the substitution elements are assigned to the same data type as itself. When the value '**restriction**' is used, substitution elements can be assigned to data types that are derived by extension, but restricted data types are still forbidden. The converse is true when the value '**extension**' is used.

Abstract heads

The abstract attribute can be set to 'true' or '1' on the head element declaration to force its substitution. This is an appropriate technique when there is no obvious 'head' of a group of related elements. It makes clear the identical status of each of the elements that can be substituted for one another.

Groups instead of substitutions

There are times when the group element is a better option than the substitution feature. The group element must be used when

- some options need to have different occurrence settings;
- some options need to be elements defined in another document model that targets a different namespace;
- the element names of some of the options conflict with other element types, so local elements must be used;
- some of the elements need to be used in other places in a similar substitutable way (the substitutionGroup attribute cannot hold more than one head element reference).

However, with the grouping approach, control and coordination of the content models of the set of elements involved are lost, and the benefits of guaranteed backward compatibility that enforced inheritance brings are also lost.

Hierarchy

Although an element declaration can only refer to one head element, it can also be the head of another substitution group. Elements that can be substitutes for it can be substitutes for its own head element too. In this way, a hierarchy of substitution groups can be built.

Any element from any group can substitute for the element at the head of the top-most group. But this is not true of subgroups: Elements from outside a subgroup cannot substitute for the element at the head of the subgroup.

17.9 Comparison of Java and XML Inheritance Terminology

The following is a list of terms used in the Java programming language to describe inheritance-related features, and almost all of these terms also apply to other object-oriented programming languages. The same term is often used in the XML Schema standard to describe a similar concept, but in other cases the difference between these technologies makes the term irrelevant or twists its meaning beyond recognition:

Term	Java Programming Language	XML
abstract	A class that contains one or more abstract methods. A method that has no implementation.	A data type that cannot be selected to specify the allowed content of an element or attribute but that can be used to create data types which can be selected.
class	A type that defines the implementation of a particular kind of object.	A data type is the nearest equivalent.
class variable	A data item associated with a particular class as a whole, not with particular instances of the class. Also called 'static field'.	*(not applicable)*
constructor	A pseudo-method that creates an object. An instance method with the same name as its class. Invoked by the 'new' keyword.	*(not applicable)*
derived from	Class X is *derived from* class Y if class X extends class Y.	Data type X is *derived from* data type Y if data type X either extends or restricts data type Y.

Term	Java Programming Language	XML
encapsulation	The localization of knowledge within a module. Because objects encapsulate data and implementation, the user of an object can view it as a black box that provides services.	Not really applicable, though it could cover the localization of data within an element that may contain a single value or a substructure of other elements and attributes.
extends	Class X *extends* class Y to add functionality, either by adding fields or methods or by overriding methods of class Y. Class X is a subclass of class Y. An interface extends another interface by adding methods.	Data type X *extends* data type Y to add value options by adding elements and attributes, by allowing lists, or by including values defined by other data types (unions). Data type X *restricts* data type Y by reducing the range of values allowed or by removing optional elements and attributes.
field	A data member of a class.	This term is not used, but it could describe a value, attribute, or child element allowed by the data type.
final	A final class cannot be subclassed. A final method cannot be overridden. A final variable cannot change from its initialized value.	A final data type cannot be derived by restriction, extension, or both. A final head element cannot be referenced by an element that is assigned to a data type derived from the data type used by the head element.
hierarchy	A classification of class relationships in which each class except for the top one (known as the root) is a specialized form of the class above it. In the class hierarchy, the root is the Object class.	A classification of data type relationships, in which the 'anyType' type is the root data type and 'anySimpleType' is a subtype that is the root of all simple data types.
inheritance	The concept of classes automatically containing the variables and methods defined in their superclasses.	The concept of data types automatically containing the attributes and value or content model constraints defined in their supertypes. When complex types are derived by restriction, however, only attributes are automatically inherited (elements definition must be repeated).
instance	An object of a particular class, created with the 'new' operator followed by the class name.	An element instance in a document instance.
instance variable	Any item of data that is associated with a particular object. Each instance of a class has its own copy of the instance variables defined by the class.	This term is not used, but essentially any value of an element or attribute in an element instance that is associated with a particular data type.
member	A field or method of a class.	*(not applicable)*
method	A function defined in a class.	*(not applicable)*

Term	Java Programming Language	XML
object	The principal building block of object-oriented programs. Each object is a programming unit consisting of data (instance variables) and functionality (instance methods). An object must belong to a defined category, called its class.	An element or an attribute in a document instance that must belong to a defined category, called its data type.
overriding	Providing a different implementation of a method in a subclass of the class that originally defined the method.	A restricted data type overrides the base data type.
package	A group of types that can be included in a Java program. Package names ensure absence of conflicts when types from different packages have the same name.	The equivalent term might be 'library'. A separate schema document that targets a namespace and contains only data type definitions that can be imported into any schema definition. Namespace qualification ensures absence of name conflicts.
property	A characteristic of an object that users can set.	An attribute value or element content value, which document instance authors set.
root	In a hierarchy of items, the one item from which all other items are descended. The root class is called Object.	The 'anyType' data type.
subclass	A class that is derived from a particular class, perhaps with one or more classes in between.	See subtype.
subtype	If type X extends or implements type Y, then X is a *subtype* of Y.	If data type X extends or restricts data type Y, then X is a *subtype* of Y.
superclass	A class from which a particular class is derived, perhaps with one or more classes in between.	See supertype.
supertype	The supertypes of a type are all the interfaces and classes that are extended or implemented by that type.	The supertypes of a data type are all the data types that are extended or restricted by that type.
type	A class or interface.	A data type (simple or complex).

18. Document Modeling Techniques

The industry-standard models for many kinds of document can be used or can be adapted to incorporate the results of domain analysis or future-use analysis. Backward compatibility with an existing DTD model may be required. Comments, lists, and tables are common structures for which standard approaches exist. Special characters are also handled in a few ways. Finally, there are various methods of constructing a schema definition that represents the required model to be considered.

18.1 Industry-Standard Models

Many government organizations and industry standardization committees have produced standard schema definitions. There is a case for adopting such a standard for exchange of information with other organizations or simply for avoiding consideration of various design decisions (such as those discussed in later sections). But there are also disadvantages to this approach.

Advantages

Powerful reasons for considering the adoption of a standard model include the following:

- The model may have already stood the tests of time and stress.
- The model usually benefits from the wisdom of many expert contributors.
- The model usually benefits from the contribution of at least one XML expert.
- The costly and time-consuming task of developing a custom model is avoided.
- Freely available formatting and transformation stylesheets may exist.
- Extensive and professionally written documentation may already exist for the model.

In addition, consider the case of two organizations who want to both produce and exchange documentation:

- There are no arguments regarding who is going to build the model.
- The organizations have equal rights to the model.
- The recipient is at a particular advantage because this organization will have a data repository that understands the document structures (and stylesheets

already configured to present them) or software that can already interpret their contents.

- The model itself is already available to both parties and so does not have to be exchanged along with the data.

Disadvantages

Unfortunately, matters are rarely as simple as the arguments above imply. The exact needs of one organization will rarely match the exact needs of another. Each party will tend to make different decisions concerning the content of their data or documentation, even in tightly regulated industries, perhaps for reasons of commercial advantage or because their products differ in some detail. These factors tend to introduce three major drawbacks to using an industry-standard model:

- lack of required features
- surplus of undesirable elements and attributes
- too much freedom

The model may not be able to identify every feature of the documents produced by the implementor, in which case important information will either not be tagged at all or be tagged inappropriately, and such information will then be difficult to identify when it is required for indexing, styling, or extraction. Conversely (or simultaneously), the model may contain elements or attributes that will never be used by the implementor, and the presence of these elements or attributes on selection menus will both confuse authors and add unnecessary work for software developers (who may be unaware that they are not to be used).

A subtle combination of these two factors might be encountered. For example, if a standard model contains several elements to describe paragraph levels, such as Par0, Par1, and Par2, but the implementor only requires a single level of paragraph, then there are both unnecessary elements, which are to be ignored (Par1 and Par2), and an inappropriately named element for a simple paragraph, Par0, which would be better named 'Para' (or just 'P').

In an attempt to satisfy the varying needs of many organizations in the industry, the model rules may be too flexible and so fail to enforce an appropriate template. For example, the model may allow an author name to appear before or after a publication title and also allow it to be absent (if there is no author), despite there being an in-house style rule that states an author's name must always appear and that it must always precede the title. Every unnecessary degree of freedom will also add to the work of software filter developers and stylesheet designers. Worse still, more than one mechanism may be included to model a particular data structure because of compromises made by various contributors to the design during development of the model; and it would be unfortunate if document authors were able to choose a model at random, leading to inconsistencies that can cause categorization, extraction, and formatting problems later.

Adapting standards

The issues described above are not insurmountable and rarely constitute a reason for dismissing the standard model from consideration. A pragmatic approach can be adopted, taking account of the standard model, but modifying it to fulfill the actual need.

Although this approach undoubtedly hinders the transfer of documents between organizations that have modified the model in subtly different ways, at least some commonality will remain to help reduce confusion. For example, if the model contains an element named 'PriceCode', all modified versions of the model are likely to have retained this name (and not changed it to 'PC', for example).

The model designer should therefore compare the results of analysis against a suitable standard. Redundant elements should be removed, additional ones added, and loose occurrence rules tightened as appropriate.

This process is not as destructive as it first looks when one considers how to transfer data to an organization using the standard (or the organization's own variant of it). Tightening context and occurrence rules has no effect on the validity of the documents when they are parsed against the schema definition (the recipient's parser does not know or care that the documents were created according to a stricter data model). Also, removal of redundant elements usually has no implication beyond making them unavailable to document authors, provided that the elements were originally optional. Only the addition of new elements guarantees problems, and these can be resolved by either removing or renaming the elements before the data is transferred.

18.2 Analysis Techniques

When creating a new schema definition, schema definition authors must investigate the actual need. They do this by analyzing existing documents that will in the future have to conform to the model or by viewing relationship diagrams. But schema definition authors must also consider possible future needs.

Document analysis

Document analysis tends to be applicable to publication of applications of XML rather than the development of data exchange applications.

It is typically the case that a new XML-based publishing system replaces a system that adopted procedural markup principles, whether an old-fashioned typesetting system or a more modern DTP package. Existing books or documents will to some degree conform to in-house style guides (whether formally defined, loosely described in notes, or existing simply in the heads of senior editorial staff) and naturally form a good foundation for document analysis. The better the style guide and the more rigorously it has been applied, the easier it is to define a suitable model (and to convert these legacy documents to XML format too).

Studying existing documents reveals much about the required structure. However, an author or editor with widespread experience of the content of these documents should still be involved in the process. When the document collection is vast, only a small proportion of this material can realistically be assessed, and it is important that the selected material be representative of the whole collection. Another important principle to adopt is to be realistic about the technology and its capabilities. DTP operators have become accustomed to a degree of artistic freedom that cannot be sustained in a controlled XML environment (if such freedom is important, then XML is not a suitable way forward).

XML is usually implemented to improve the efficiency of publishing and of republishing to different target audiences on a variety of media. Software provides the necessary automation, but programs require predictable input. Utilities that locate, extract, manipulate, and display information from XML documents must be given manageable tasks to perform. In particular, regard must be given to the limitations of stylesheets and structure-oriented publishing products. Creating complex coding schemes to deal with document structures that appear infrequently may not be practical. One common example of such a problem is a small, vertically aligned fragment, as shown below. Perhaps these structures can be formatted more simply without any loss of legibility:

```
        300
          25.6
   and    1.3
```

For every feature identified in existing documents, the following set of questions may be asked, the answers to which form the basis of a document specification. Every object in the document is given a descriptive name and is assigned rules governing where and how often it may appear, and what it may contain:

- Does it always appear?
- May there be more than one?
- Must it always appear before (or after) some other feature?
- Does it deconstruct into smaller objects (to which these same questions apply)?
- Is some of the textual content always the same? If so, could it be generated automatically?

The term **template text** is sometimes used to describe presented material that is always the same, regardless of which document in the document class is being presented (the term **boilerplate text** is also used). The name of the document class itself, such as 'email' or 'program broadcast', or the name of the organization that created all the documents in this class ('ACME Corp.'), or even the prefix of all warnings ('Warning: ...'), are all possible examples of template text. There is no need to create models for template text. For example, if a presented document is always given a standard copyright notice, such as '© MegaTV Corp', there should *not* be an element to contain this text in the document model. In some cases, it may be necessary to actively discourage document instance authors from inadvertently adding template text (this issue is covered later).

UML model analysis

All or part of an XML document may consist of data extracted from a system or database that has been modeled with the *Unified Modeling Language* (UML) and, in particular, the class diagrams that this model incorporates (which are similar to entity relationship (E-R) diagrams). Such diagrams may be of use in helping to determine the XML data model. The reverse is also true; an existing XML document model may be used to help design the database schema, including the UML diagrams describing it. In either case, it is interesting to compare schema definitions with diagrams.

In a **one-to-one** relationship, one entity is related to one other entity. For example, a chapter may contain one title and that title belongs only to that chapter (note that the Chapter element is not mandatory to the Title element if the Title element may also be used elsewhere):

```
Chapter  ⊢ 0..1    1 ⊣  Title
```

```
<element name="Chapter">
  ... <element ref="Title" /> ...
</element>
```

If the Title element is not mandatory, this is indicated by the '0..1' multiplicity:

```
Chapter  ⊢ 0..1  0..1 ⊣  Title
```

```
<element name="Chapter">
  ... <element ref="Title" minOccurs="0" /> ...
</element>
```

In a **one-to-many** relationship, a single entity is related to many instances of another entity. For example, a Chapter element may (or perhaps must) contain at least one Para element:

```
Chapter  ⊢ 1    1..* ⊣  Para
```

```
<element name="Chapter">
  ... <element ref="Para" minOccurs="1"
                         maxOccurs="unbounded" /> ...
</element>
```

```
<element name="chapter">
  ... <element ref="para" minOccurs="0"
                         maxOccurs="unbounded" /> ...
</element>
```

The parent/child relationship is more strongly indicated when an aggregation is used and especially when a composition is used:

Alternative relationships can also be described in the UML class diagram. For example, a Chapter element may contain either a set of Para elements or a single Sections element (note that the Title element may be part of a chapter or a section):

```
<element name="Chapter">
  <complexType>
    <sequence>
      <element ref="Title" minOccurs="0"
                           maxOccurs="unbounded" />
      <choice>
        <element ref="Para" maxOccurs="unbounded" />
        <element name="Sections">
          <sequence>
            <element name="Section">
              <complexType>
                <sequence>
                  <element ref="Title" />
                  ...
                </sequence>
              </complexType>
            </element>
          </sequence>
        </element>
      </choice>
    </sequence>
  </complexType>
</element>
```

Future-use analysis

One major reason for adopting XML is the possibilities it offers for information reuse. Analysis should therefore not end at describing current practice unless it is certain that the data will never be put to any new purposes. The advent of electronic publishing has been a major factor in popularizing the generalized markup approach. Analysis must therefore include looking ahead to the features offered by these new publishing media and to possibilities for niche publications derived from subsets of the data.

One benefit of electronic publishing over traditional paper publishing is the capability of software to support hypertext links. The original document may contain obvious linking text, such as 'see section 9 for details,' but there may also be other, more subtle, links 'hidden' in the document structure. In both cases, it is necessary to determine a linking strategy, including a scheme for producing unique link values for each target object. The XLink and XPointer standards can be considered for this purpose.

The degree to which an element's content is organized into subelements is often termed its **granularity**. Grains can be coarse (like sugar) or fine (like flour). The issue of granularity is often raised at this point because future-use analysis tends to identify structures that need to be identified, but that have no distinctive visual appearance in existing printed publications. For example, while a person's name may be highlighted in the document, it is unlikely that the last name will be styled differently from the first name. Yet a future on-line publication or associated database may be envisaged that includes a list of names, sorted by last name. For automatic sorting, each part of the name should be tagged separately:

> The name *John Smith* is very popular in England.

```
The name <Name><F>John</F><S>Smith</S></Name> is
very popular in England.
```

18.3   Backward Compatibility with a DTD

The XML Schema standard is more powerful than the DTD feature of the XML standard. It has many more features, of which the most significant for this discussion are probably the concept of local element definitions and the unconstrained ordering model (as represented by the `all` element).

There are no concerns with using these powerful features when the documents that conform to a document model defined with a schema definition will always be processed by software that can read the schema definition. But if it is possible that some software applications will rely on a parser that can only work with DTDs, then backward compatibility becomes an issue.

It is relatively trivial to create a DTD representation of a model by automatically converting a schema definition into this form, provided the schema does not include any advanced features (see Section 22.3 for details of programs that can convert between DTDs and schema definitions).

Avoiding advanced features

The obvious solution is to avoid advanced features entirely.

Note that using the `minOccurs` and `maxOccurs` attributes with values other than '0', '1', or 'unbounded' can be modeled by a DTD, but ambiguities have to be acknowledged and handled:

```
<element name="List" ref="Item" minOccurs="2"
                                 maxOccurs="4" />
```

The following model is ambiguous:

```
<!ELEMENT List (Item, Item, Item?, Item?)>
```

It needs to be recast as follows:

```
<!ELEMENT List (Item, Item, (Item, Item?)?)>
```

Converting advanced features

The schema for schemas includes two local element declarations. Depending on the context, the `extension` and `restriction` elements have different content models. The DTD for schema definitions deals with the problem by allowing elements from either model to be included at the risk of authors using the wrong ones in a given context.

18.4 Element or Attribute Decision

In a few cases, there is no choice whether to use an element or an attribute for a given piece of information. For example, an attribute must be used to hold a value that conforms to the 'ID' data type. But more typically, a unit of information could be represented either by a child element or by an attribute. In some cases, either an element or an attribute would be equally well suited to the task, and even professional model designers would argue over some decisions. But in other cases, one or the other would be more suitable; here are some guidelines that may assist in making this decision.

An element should be chosen if the information

- is a subdivision of the element content rather than information about the content;

- is to be presented to an audience, rather than simply exchanged between software applications;
- contains substructures;
- is to some extent dependent on its location relative to other nearby values;
- could be a long text string;
- is allowed to be present or absent depending on the presence or absence of another value.

Candidate reasons for choosing an attribute include the following factors (which are really just the inverse of the factors listed above). The information

- describes the content of the element, rather than being a subdivision of the element content;
- is not usually presented to an audience;
- has no substructures;
- is not affected by its location relative to other nearby values;
- is always a short text string;
- is not affected by the presence or absence of other values;
- must be a single word or one option from a list of possible values.

Some of these factors are discussed in more depth later.

When a schema definition is to create the document model, an element is a better choice than an attribute because an element can

- use the `xsi:nil` attribute to specify that it is empty in a document instance (see Section 7.7);
- be part of a substitution group (see Section 17.8);
- use the `xsi:type` attribute to specify a derived data type in a document instance (see Section 17.6).

One additional reason for considering an attribute instead of an element is that a DTD might be needed by some software applications to validate document instances, and DTDs include a primitive data type assignment feature for attributes (see Section 19.4).

Components and metadata

Usually a distinction can be drawn between a value that is logically part of a larger value and a value that merely supports the existence of the larger value. For example, a month is part of a date, but an ISBN number is metadata that identifies a book. However, sometimes a value performs both of these roles, in which case either an attribute or an element container would be equally valid. For example, the title of a book is both part of the book and information about that book.

Note that the following factor is very closely related to this one.

Published output

When a document model is created for documents that could be described as narrative documents, then attributes are the natural choice for information *about* the document, while elements are the natural choice for content that will be presented to users. The very name 'attribute' makes the point clear because this word is synonymous with 'characteristic'. An attribute is not the thing itself, but a quality of that thing.

Metadata is information about the content of the document and is not itself part of the content. Thus stylesheet languages have tended to focus on the ability to format element content, more than on attribute values. Some products and stylesheet languages have limited or nonexistent capabilities for presenting attribute values. Instead, attribute values have often been used to help decide *how* to format the content.

Substructures

If the embedded information may itself contain substructures, then an element must be used because attributes are not capable of holding structured markup. For example, if the title of a book may contain subscript characters or emphasized words, it must be held in a `Title` element:

```
<Book>
  <Title>Qualities of H<Sub>2</Sub>O</Title>
  . . .
</Book>
```

The subscript start tag and end tag would not be recognized if inserted into an attribute value. Indeed, an error should be reported if any '<' symbols are found within an attribute value:

```
                    <!-- WILL NOT WORK -->
<Book Title="Qualities of H<Sub>2</Sub>O">
  . . .
</Book>
```

Sequential context significance

If the meaning of a value depends on its position relative to another value, it should be contained in an element rather than an attribute because elements can be given a sequential order that does not change, whereas attributes have no ordering significance and the order in which attributes appear within an element start tag can easily change during processing of the document instance.

Text length

Although, strictly speaking, there is no limit to the number of characters allowed in an attribute value, most software developed to parse, edit, or display the content of attributes expects to find short values. Long values may be difficult to work with at best and may crash the software at worst. Most XML-sensitive editors have primitive interfaces for attribute value editing and may truncate the data or at least make it necessary to scroll to see the whole value.

Dependency on other values

The presence or absence of an attribute on a given element cannot be used to determine the legality of another attribute being present or absent on the same element. For example, although the `notation` element of the XML Schema standard requires both the `public` and `system` attributes to be optional, it also requires at least one of them to be present, yet the schema for schemas cannot model this requirement. However, it would have been possible to use two child elements instead and to create a model that insists on at least one of these elements being present:

```
<choice>
  <sequence>
    <element ref="public" />
    <element ref="system" minOccurs="0" />
  </sequence>
  <sequence>
    <element ref="system" />
    <element ref="public" minOccurs="0" />
  </sequence>
</choice>
```

Restricted values

Another factor is not listed above but nevertheless deserves some attention. If the information must be constrained to one of a small set of possible values, then an attribute should probably be used. An attribute can enforce the restriction, and, with a typical XML-sensitive editor, the full set of options from which to choose can be presented to document authors. The XML Schema standard allows element content to be restricted in this way too, but the danger remains that a document will be processed by a tool that is only DTD-sensitive:

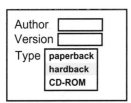

Uniformity of approach

The final factor is consistency. Following the recommendations above, a first draft of a model could be produced that consists almost entirely of elements or almost entirely of attributes (attached to elements, of course). At this point, it would be worth taking another look at the few remaining elements or attributes to see if the benefits of conformity with the rest of the model could outweigh the factors that originally determined the choices made. In an XML-sensitive editor, it is often inconvenient to switch between element inserting mode and attribute editing mode. Also, software that needs to process XML input (perhaps using the SAX or DOM interfaces) would be less complex if it only had to deal with elements or attributes instead of both.

18.5   Element Structures

In the designing of a document model, the number of elements needed is influenced by the following factors.

Appropriate granularity

It is said that the document has a **fine granularity** when the document uses elements to isolate and identify the smallest possible units of information. In the following example, the name of an actor is divided into the maximum number of useful subcomponents:

```
<Actor>
  <Salutation>Mr.</Salutation>
  <Initial>C</Initial>
  <LastName>Eastwood</LastName>
</Actor>
```

When less than the optimum number of elements are used, the document is said to have a **coarse granularity**. The following example illustrates an actor's name that could potentially be divided into smaller meaningful components (as shown above):

```
<Actor>Mr. C Eastwood</Actor>
```

The finer the granularity, the larger and more complex the document. When created manually, such documents are more expensive to produce. On the other hand, the document is 'richer,' as it is more amenable to analysis and processing.

Redundant element within element

The simplest possible content of an element is another single element that must be present:

```
<Actor><Name>Mr. C Eastwood</Name></Actor>
```

This kind of model is usually considered to be useless. If an element must only contain one instance of another element, then either the inner element or the outer element is redundant. The following alternative models would suffice:

```
<Actor>Clint</Actor>
```

```
<Name>Clint</Name>
```

```
<ActorName>Clint</ActorName>
```

There are only two circumstances in which an embedded element approach would be suitable. First, the model may be related to other models that will be familiar to those working with this model and include different or further content options. In this case, consistency with the normal approach is recommended to avoid confusion. Second, the model may be expected to become more complex in the future, and this approach allows other child elements to be added later without confusing either software or document instance authors with the sudden introduction of a container element.

Possible list containers

When an element repeats to create a compact sequence of elements of the same type, it is worth considering the benefits of adding a container element. For example:

```
<Actors>
  <Actor>Clint Eastwood</Actor>
  <Actor>Kevin Bacon</Actor>
  <Actor>Kevin Costner</Actor>
</Actors>
```

The container element helps in a number of circumstances. First, it facilitates identification of the last listed element when it needs special processing or formatting (such as not being followed by a comma). Second, a search engine can create a targeted searchable zone that encompasses all the text in these elements. Third, it becomes possible to copy or move all the elements in a single operation within an XML-based word processor.

Containers or headings

Most document types include the concept of chapters, sections, or parts and often allow a number of division levels (this book comprises chapters that contain optional sections and subsections). Two approaches can be taken to tagging such documents, each having advantages and disadvantages.

The first approach will be familiar to those who have developed Web pages by using HTML tags. This approach simply marks headings with tags that indicate the level. In the case of HTML, these tags are named H1, H2, H3, H4, H5, H6, and H7. The level number applies an appropriate style to the heading, usually varying the point size so that readers can easily see where each level starts and ends.

The second approach also tags the headings, but this time using a single element type, such as Header or Title, regardless of the level concerned. In addition, an element is used to enclose the heading and the following material that it covers, such as a Part, Chapter, or Section element. This approach requires more tagging but has some benefits.

Conceptually, the second approach is the better one. It follows the principle that all significant components of a document should be explicitly and unambiguously identified. A section of a document is a significant component, so it should be properly enclosed by a suitable element. These elements set boundaries that can be used by search engines to delimit searchable zones and by database software to extract sections.

If the same element type is used for all levels of a hierarchical document structure, such as Section instead of Part, Chapter, Section, and SubSection, then it becomes much easier to promote or demote sections because no retagging is required. The only downside is that it becomes harder for an author working on the text to see what level a specific fragment is at. A text editor that can automate the numbering of headings or differentiate the style of headings by their context can be used, however. (The format of a Title element in a Section element would differ from a Title element in a Section element that is within another Section element.)

Legally overlapping structures

There are occasions when it is absolutely essential that ranges of data that span structures must be identified and isolated despite the strict rules concerning proper element nesting defined in the XML standard. For example, it is common practice in technical documentation for text that has changed since a previous release of the document to be marked as 'revised text,' perhaps by a vertical bar in the margin. Yet such text may begin partway through one paragraph and end in the middle of the next.

Breaking the range into smaller pieces is always possible, but doing so would add a number of tags to the document and would also destroy the significance of the complete unit (if there *is* any significance to the grouping). Instead, pairs of empty elements can be employed to describe a block of text that spans element structures. In the example below, the empty Revision element indicates the start of a block of revised text, and the empty RevisionEnd element indicates the end of the block. The parser is unaware of the particular significance of the two empty elements, so it cannot object to their use to define the boundaries of a range of text that does not fit into the formal document structure:

```
<Para>In this paragraph there is
some <Revision/>revised text.</Para>
<Para>This text is also changed,
but<RevisionEnd/> this text is not.</Para>
```

In this paragraph there is
some **revised text.**

This text is also changed,
but this text is not.

This mechanism can be used to extract arbitrary ranges of material, but only for non-XML processing because the embedded structures will be invalid when taken out of context. The following example fragment is not well formed, because the fragment begins with an empty element, followed by text and an end tag, and only the first half of the following paragraph:

```
<Revision/>revised text.</Para>
<Para>This text is also changed, but <RevisionEnd/>
```

An alternative approach would be to place the range information elsewhere and perhaps use the XPointer standard to define the range, but that approach assumes the use of tools that can hide the mechanism from document authors.

Generatable text

Sometimes a mixed content model is only considered because it will allow punctuation or other text to appear that could in principle be omitted from the document entirely. Consider the following document instance fragment that depends on the existence of a mixed content model for the Actors element:

```
<Actors><Actor>Penny Smith</Actor>,
<Actor>John Carter</Actor> and
<Actor>Peter Frederickson</Actor></Actors>
```

Clearly, the comma and 'and' connectors could be generated by an XSLT stylesheet as a preliminary step to presenting this information, and they should not even be allowed in the XML document. The model should therefore be:

```
<element name="Actors">
  <complexType>
    <element ref="Actor" maxOccurs="unbounded" />
  </complexType>
</element>
```

The document should then reflect this model (note that the elements can be formatted more sensibly without confusion too):

```
<Actors>
  <Actor>Penny Smith</Actor>
  <Actor>John Carter</Actor>
  <Actor>Peter Frederickson</Actor>
</Actors>
```

18.6 Devising Element and Attribute Names

The XML standard places few constraints on the names of elements and attributes. The schema author can create names that are one character in length or a hundred characters in length, and uppercase and lowercase letters can be freely mixed. It is tempting to just allow imagination and individuality to take their course, but some conventions are worth considering.

Standardizing case

A document model looks unprofessional if there is no consistency in the use of lowercase letters and uppercase letters in element and attribute names. In addition, such inconsistencies are likely to lead to errors when stylesheet authors and software developers need to remember and refer to these elements and attributes:

```
<COMPANY>ACME</COMPANY>
<president>J Smith</president>
```

The use of lowercase letters is in vogue today because uppercase names tend to be harder to read and too obtrusive. In theory, lowercase names are also better because they are more likely to be exact string matches with words in the document text and so make smaller documents when they are compressed.

Short names and long names

Element and attribute names can be of any length, from a single character to, in theory, a string of infinite length. In practice, such names vary in length, and in each case two conflicting principles must vie for attention.

Traditionally, short names, often consisting of just one or two characters, served the purpose of reducing keystrokes (when using standard text editors before XML editors were available) and minimizing memory and disk storage space (when both were expensive and very limited). But the obvious problem with short names is that their meanings are far from obvious. When a document model consists of many elements and attributes, the learning curve and demands on human memory are high.

Today, with more memory and disk space available and element tags more likely to be created by selection from a menu, the benefits of meaningful names has risen to prominence.

Despite this, there are still at least two good reasons for using short element and attribute names. First, because they reduce the size of XML documents, these documents are transmitted over networks quickly. Second, when an XML document is edited with the tags showing (to make editing easier), the tags do not take up too much screen real estate.

One good compromise is to make the names of commonly used elements short. For example, the name 'P' is used for paragraphs if they are very common, but the name 'CompanyPresident' is used, rather than 'CP', if it is used infrequently. This approach simultaneously provides a significant benefit to the size of the XML document (most element tags present in a document have short names) while reducing the need to memorize cryptic names for the other, less frequently used elements.

Distinguishing multiple words

When some element or attribute names are composed of two or more words, it is common practice to indicate where each word begins. After all, the name 'companyvicepresident' is not easy to read and interpret. This problem is particularly vivid when abbreviations, such as 'compvpres', are used.

One technique that is quite common employs the underscore character, '_', to separate the words, as in 'company_vice_president' or 'comp_v_pres'. But these separators add to the length of the name. A widely used alternative approach uses uppercase letters to start each word, as in 'CompanyVicePresident' or 'CompVPres'. However, the first letter does not need to be emphasized in this way, so it is also common practice to find names such as 'companyVicePresident' or 'compVPres'. This final approach follows popular software conventions and is therefore recommended when the content of specific elements or attributes is going to be copied into or out of programming language variables, because the same names can be used. Note that the XML Schema standard adopts this technique, with element names such as 'complexType' and 'whiteSpace' (but with exceptions, such as 'appinfo').

While many people think that using an uppercase letter for each subsequent word is the most appropriate approach, it does not discount the use of underlines too. When a name is composed of multiple words divided into two or more phrases, then underlines could be used to separate the phrases. This approach makes groups of related elements more obvious:

```
<Seller_FullName>
<Seller_Address>
<Seller_ItemCode>

<Buyer_FullName>
<Buyer_Address>
<Buyer_TimeOfPurchase>
```

However, this technique should not be needed if an ancestor element indicates the context:

```
<Seller>
  <FullName>...</FullName>
  <Address>...</Address>
  <ItemCode>...</ItemCode>
</Seller>
<Buyer>
  <FullName>...</FullName>
  <Address>...</Address>
  <TimeOfPurchase>...</TimeOfPurchase>
</Buyer>
```

Reusing element names

When a number of elements in the document structure have a similar purpose, it is a good idea to use the same element name for them all. This means that there will be a smaller number of element names for people to learn. The context is used, when necessary, to give the element a more refined meaning. For example, this book contains many titles—book title, chapter titles, section titles, subsection titles, and table titles:

```
<Book>
  <Title>Book Title</Title>
  ...
  <Chapter>
    <Title>Chapter Title</Title>
    ...
    <Table>
      <Title>Table Title</Title>
      ...
    </Table>
    ...
    <Section>
      <Title>Section Title</Title>
      ...
      <SubSection>
        <Title>Subsection Titles</Title>
        ...
      </SubSection>
      ...
    </Section>
    ...
  </Chapter>
  ...
</Book>
```

There are two reasons why identical content models may be considered important to using this approach. First, with a DTD, one cannot create multiple element declarations with the same name but with different content models. Second, even when a DTD is not used, document authors and software developers can be confused by working with elements that have identical names but different capabilities. For these two reasons, then, it may be better to use separate names when the content models differ from the majority of cases (such as 'TableTitle' for tables and 'Title' for all other cases).

Names should differ if zoned searches might need to be done on the content of some of these elements and the search engine chosen is unable to use the wider context to determine which element content to search.

Names and references

When two attributes are being used to hold an identifier and as an identifier reference, it is good practice to give them different names. Instead of using, for example, 'ChapterName' for both attributes, make the name 'ChapterNameReference' for the referencing attribute. This name still makes it clear that it relates to the name of a chapter but now also makes it clear that this attribute is not declaring a new name, but simply referring to an existing declaration.

18.7 Comments

The XML standard includes special comment markup, as in the following example:

```
<!-- This is a comment. -->
```

However, it is often a good idea to include a `Comment` element in the document model (XML comments are often lost during transformations and parsing):

```
<Comment>This is a comment.</Comment>
```

A `Comment` element will be treated like any other element; it can be easily suppressed when the comment is not to be seen, such as when an XSLT stylesheet is used:

```
<Template Name="comment"><!-- SUPPRESS --></Template>
```

It is also possible to create classes of comment by using an appropriate attribute. One use of this technique is to isolate text that needs further treatment:

```
<Para>The
<Comment Type="UnknownWord">watchamacallit</Comment>
is very important.</Para>
```

When comments are used for this purpose, it may be necessary to declare two comment elements with different content models: one for use as an inline comment and one for use as a wrapper of paragraph-level objects.

18.8   Lists

Lists are just complex enough to raise a few specific issues regarding their design.

List structure

It is almost always a good idea to surround a set of elements that define list items with another element that defines the scope of the entire list (see the more general points about containers above):

```
<List>
  <Item>Item one</Item>
  <Item>Item two</Item>
  <Item>Item three</Item>
</List>
```

This approach is particularly important when the same element type is used for items in both numbered and nonnumbered (also known as 'random', 'bulleted', or 'unnumbered') lists because the enclosing element then specifies how the items are to be interpreted. It also identifies the point at which one list ends and another one starts when no other elements lie between them:

```
<NumberedList>
  <Item>Item one</Item>
  <Item>Item two</Item>
  <Item>Item three</Item>
</NumberedList>
<BulletedList>
  <Item>An item</Item>
  <Item>Another item</Item>
  <Item>Yet another item</Item>
</BulletedList>
```

At least two items

Some purists state that a list should only be created if there are going to be at least two items in the list. This constraint can be specified in the model:

```
<element name="Item" minOccurs="2" />
```

However, a list that is to be completed later might well contain a single item initially, and the constraint would then be unacceptable.

Simple or complex content

An important decision to make about list items is whether they can hold more than a single paragraph of text. If they are constrained to a single paragraph, then a mixed content model is needed. But if there is a possibility that an item needs to contain more than a single paragraph or to contain other structures such as notes and warnings, tables, or even embedded sublists, then the content model should not allow direct entry of text. Either a simple paragraph should be used by the document instance author or a special element, perhaps called 'Text', could be used. Alternatively, two elements could represent items: one that contains only text and one that contains complex structures:

```
<Item>Only text here</Item>
<LargeItem>
  <Para>First paragraph.</Para>
  <Para>Second paragraph.</Para>
</LargeItem>
```

Embedded sublists

A relatively minor modeling issue arises when a list item is allowed to contain a complete further list and this is a common requirement. It is usual to indent embedded lists to show that the items are all part of a single item in the outer list.

But a simple model cannot constrain document authors to a maximum number of list levels, so there is a danger that an author will use more levels than allowed for by a given stylesheet. The only way to overcome this problem is to predefine list elements with a level indicator as part of the name. In the following example, authors are constrained to use no more than three levels of list:

```
<element name="List1">
  <complexType>
    <sequence>
      <element ref="DOC:Item1" minOccurs="1"
                               maxOccurs="unbounded" />
    </sequence>
  </complexType>
</element>

<element name="Item1">
  <complexType>
    <choice minOccurs="0" maxOccurs="unbounded">
      <element ref="DOC:Para" />
      <element ref="DOC:List2" />
    </choice>
  </complexType>>
</element>

<element name="List2">
  <complexType>
    <sequence>
      <element ref="DOC:Item2" minOccurs="1"
                               maxOccurs="unbounded" />
    </sequence>
  </complexType>
</element>

<element name="Item2">
  <complexType>
    <choice minOccurs="0" maxOccurs="unbounded">
```

```
          <element ref="DOC:Para" />
          <element ref="DOC:List3" />
      </choice>
    </complexType>
</element>

<element name="List3">
  <complexType>
    <sequence>
      <element ref="DOC:Item3" minOccurs="1"
                              maxOccurs="unbounded" />
    </sequence>
  </complexType>
</element>

<element name="Item3">
  <complexType>
    <choice minOccurs="0" maxOccurs="unbounded" />
      <element ref="DOC:Para" />
    </choice>
  </complexType>
</element>
```

For example:

```
<List1>
  <Item1>
    <Para>First level list.</Para>
    <List2>
      <Item2>
        <Para>Second level list.</Para>
      </Item2>
    </List2>
  </Item1>
</List1>
```

Alternatively, local content models could be used to constrain the content of a single 'Item' element, depending on which level of list contains it:

```
<element name="List">
  <complexType>
    <sequence>
      <element name="Item" minOccurs="1"
                           maxOccurs="unbounded">
        <complexType>
          <choice>
            ...
            <element name="List">
              <complexType>
                <sequence>
                  <element name="Item"
                          minOccurs="1"
                          maxOccurs="unbounded">
                    ...
                  </element>
                </sequence>
```

```
          </complexType>
        </element>
          . . .
      </choice>
    </complexType>
  </element>
</sequence>
</complexType>
</element>
```

However, that this method is not backward compatible with DTDs may be a consideration.

Custom and definition lists

If edits to lists after initial publication of a document are not allowed to affect the number of existing items in the list, then automatically numbered lists are not the solution. For example, when a new item is inserted between item '5' and item '6', it may be that the new item has to be numbered '5b' in order to avoid renumbering the later items. This is common practice when there may be references in the text to a specific item such as 'see item 6 for details.' In such a case, the model needs to include a list type that does not predefine the numbers of each item.

Using the same technique required to provide custom lists, many document models can also include a 'definition list' type. This is also known as a 'glossary list' type since it is often used for glossaries. These lists are actually more akin to two-column tables with fixed column widths and the first column set to be much narrower than the second. In the first column, a term that requires clarification appears. In the second column, the clarification (or 'definition') itself appears. Typically, the term is constrained to simple text, but the definition can be large and possibly include multiple paragraphs:

```
<DefList>
  <Item>
    <Term>XML</Term>
    <Def><Para>eXtensible Markup Language</Para></Def>
  </Item>
  <Item>
    <Term>HTML</Term>
    <Def><Para>HyperText Markup Language</Para></Def>
  </Item>
</DefList>
```

HTML lists

It is common practice to use element names invented for HTML in other DTDs. The names OL (Ordered List), UL (Unordered List), and LI (List Item) are often seen. For definition lists, HTML defines the DL (Definition List), DT (Definition Term), and DD (Definition Description) elements.

18.9 **Tables**

Industry standards play an important role in defining models for constructs that are difficult to render on screen or paper, and the most common example of this is tabular matter. Structures like paragraphs, lists, and warnings form a simple linear sequence, but table cells are arranged into a two-dimensional grid. A rendering application must recognize the elements that represent column or row boundaries. Other complications include border lines, cells that span adjoining rows and columns, and the various ways in which text can be aligned within each cell. These typical table features can be described by additional elements or attributes, but if every document model designer adopted a different approach, then an application that is required to present the information in a tabular format would have little chance of being able to interpret the markup.

CALS and HTML tables

Recognition of this problem in the SGML community led to the establishment of a *de facto* standard. From a few competing models, widespread use of applications that supported DTDs developed for the U.S. Department of Defense meant that the **CALS table** model was the inevitable winner. This table model requires the use of specific elements including `table`, `thead`, `tbody`, `tfoot`, `row`, and `entry`.

This model also influenced the approach taken to add table support to HTML. Introduced in HTML 2.0, this model has been extended in later versions and is now quite similar to the CALS model. The HTML model is rapidly becoming the new *de facto* standard. Certainly, this model is retained in XHTML and other HTML-derived standards.

Meaningful element names

Although nothing prevents the creation of XML elements that reflect the names of HTML table elements such as `Table`, `Tr` (table row), `Th` (table header), and `Td` (table data), the freedom to use names that are more meaningful to the content of the cells remains an important XML principle.

For example, when the table contains a list of product codes and prices, the following structure may be deemed more appropriate:

```
<Prices>
  <Prod><Code>XYZ-15</Code><Price>987</Price></Prod>
  <Prod><Code>XYZ-22</Code><Price>765</Price></Prod>
</Prices>
```

In this example, the information is sufficiently well identified for product details to be automatically located and extracted, and the price of a specific product can be located. The content can also be presented in a number of different ways. Nevertheless, the most obvious presentation format is a tabular structure. Close study of the elements reveals that the `Prices` element is analogous to the HTML `Table` element, the `Prod` element encloses a single row of data, and the `Code` and `Price` elements both translate into individual cells.

CSS mappings

An application must be informed of the specific significance of each of these elements. This can be achieved with a stylesheet. Fortunately, the CSS 2 specification includes property values that map an element name to a table part role. The values 'table', 'table-row', and 'table-cell' can be assigned to the display property:

```
Prices { display:table }
Prod   { display:table-row }
Code   { display:table-cell }
Price  { display:table-cell }
```

XYZ-15	987
XYZ-22	765

Care should be taken to adopt a row-oriented approach, as shown in the example above, so that the elements can be easily mapped to the HTML model. It is not possible to map elements in a structure that takes a column-oriented approach, as in the example below:

```
<Table>
  <Products>
    <Code>XYZ-15</Code>
    <Code>XYZ-22</Code>
  </Products>
  <Prices>
    <Price>987</Price>
    <Price>765</Price>
  </Prices>
</Table>
```

Another reason for avoiding this approach is that it is more likely to separate related items (such as a product code and the price for that product), a characteristic that complicates analysis and extraction of these items.

18.10   Representing Special Characters

A common difficulty that arises when a DTD is replaced with a schema definition to model a set of existing document instances is that special characters are traditionally handled in way that is inconsistent with the use of a schema definition.

An entity declaration in a DTD for the 'é' character might assign the name 'eacute' to this character and might also stipulate the value that this entity should be converted to during the parsing process:

```
<!ENTITY eacute "&#233;">
```

A document instance would include a reference to this entity:

```
The Caf&eacute; is open
```

The parsed document would have the entity replaced (in this case, by a character reference):

```
The Caf&#233; is open
```

Finally, this would be interpreted by the rendering application:

The Café is open

Entity sets

Parameter entities are commonly used in DTDs to incorporate separate files that contain lists of entities for characters that are difficult or impossible to enter directly from the keyboard, such as 'é'. Several sets of entities have been defined by the ISO and are usually called in as follows:

```
<!ENTITY % ISOnum
    PUBLIC "ISO 8879:1986//ENTITIES Numeric and Special
            Graphic//EN" SYSTEM "ISOnum.ent">
<!ENTITY % ISOlat1
    PUBLIC "ISO 8879:1986//ENTITIES Added Latin 1//EN"
    SYSTEM "ISOlat1.ent">
<!ENTITY % ISOgrk1
    PUBLIC "ISO 8879:1986//ENTITIES Greek Letters//EN"
    SYSTEM "ISOgrk.ent">
<!ENTITY % ISOpub
    PUBLIC "ISO 8879:1986//ENTITIES Publishing//EN"
    SYSTEM "ISOpub.ent">

<!-- merge-in the external entities -->

%ISOnum;
%ISOlat1;
%ISOgrk1;
%ISOpub;
```

One possible solution is to duplicate the above definitions and references in each document instance, in the internal subset of a now nonexistent DTD, or perhaps just a single definition and reference to a grouping file:

```
<!DOCTYPE Book [
  <!ENTITY % ISOcharacterSets SYSTEM "ISOcharSets.ent">
  %ISOcharacterSets;
]>
<Book>...</Book>
```

Apart from the document instance maintenance issue, the other problem with this technique is that a parser might attempt to validate the document against a DTD and report errors because none of the elements in the document are defined.

Empty placeholder elements

Another approach is to replace all character-based general entities in the document instances with empty elements:

```
The Caf<Eacute/> is open
```

But instead of creating numerous empty elements to represent each character, a single element could be used that includes an attribute to identify the character:

```
The Caf<Char Name="eacute" /> is open
```

However, this technique requires that a transformation is performed to convert the empty elements into characters (or escape sequences conforming to the needs of the markup language concerned, such as 'é' for 'é' in the case of HTML). Also, an existing DTD would not work with these documents, though the DTD could be updated to also use empty elements for these characters.

Actually, there are benefits to adopting this approach because it is easier to preserve character references when a document instance undergoes a series of transformations.

Note, however, that attribute values cannot include elements, so if this technique is adopted, then this is a good reason for choosing to store information in an element instead of an attribute.

18.11   Schema Document Construction

Once the conceptual model of a document type has been defined, the only remaining task is to construct the schema definition that reflects this model. Various approaches can be taken, from authoring the schema definition in a text editor to using a product designed specifically for this task. Depending on the approach taken, certain options become available or certain problems arise.

Schema development tools

Applications developed specifically to construct schema definitions tend to be very good at preventing invalid models from being created and at presenting the models to authors in a friendly visual fashion:

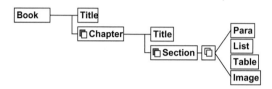

However, these products usually have to export the model ('save as XSD') when it is complete, and the author typically has little or no control over the formatting of the schema document. This may not matter, but it can be problematic if another author has to later edit the definition, using more basic tools.

As an alternative, a standard XML word processor can be used to construct the schema definition. In this case, the schema for schemas (at http://www.w3.org/2001/XMLSchema.xsd) or a DTD for schemas (see Chapter 20) can be used.

Model-building techniques

The XML Schema standard includes many alternative techniques to achieve the same aims, and these techniques can be combined in either elegant or inelegant ways. Various experts will recommend their own favored approach, but a few general pointers are worth considering.

Those familiar with DTDs will naturally tend to use equivalent techniques. This means using global element declarations and local attribute declarations, and either not using named data type declarations at all or simply using them to serve the same role as parameter entities (to avoid repetition of identical structures). This approach shares with DTDs the weakness that document instance authors may have too much freedom to create arbitrarily small documents, with any element from the model employed as the root element.

A radically different approach uses local element declarations for all but the intended root element, thus ensuring that document authors always create complete documents. In this scenario, named data types are typically used for all content models. When used to define local element declarations with the same name, they serve to show how these elements are really just the same element. The only problem with this technique is that the document model largely consists of a single huge element structure that can be difficult to read and modify with standard editing tools.

General entities for schema management

When a text editor or standard XML word processor is used to create a schema definition, the fact that an XML Schema document can include general entities, just as any document instance can, can be exploited to help build the component definitions. But some uses of this technique do not appear to work with some parsers, and only the safest uses are described below.

An entity can be used to provide the name of an element or attribute. In the following example, the entity declaration holds the name of an element, to be used to name it in the definition for that element and in all references to it:

```
<!DOCTYPE xsd:schema [
  <!ENTITY elemName "Para">
]>

<xsd:schema ...>

  <xsd:element name="&elemName;" ...>

  <xsd:element name="Book">
    <xsd:complexType>
      <xsd:sequence>
        <xsd:element ref="&elemName;" minOccur="0" />
      </xsd:sequence>
    </xsd:complexType>
  </xsd:element>

</xsd:schema>
```

For an entire element to be included in the entity, the namespace declaration must be repeated in this element, and even then, some parsers do not cope with this technique:

```
<!DOCTYPE xsd:schema [
  <!ENTITY element "<xsd:element xmlns:xsd="..." ...>">
]>

<xsd:schema ...>

  &element;

</xsd:schema>
```

19. DTD Models

The best source of information from which to create a schema definition model often takes the form of an existing DTD model, which may exist only in hardcopy form. In other situations, it may be necessary to ensure that a new schema definition does not use features that are unavailable in DTDs, because a DTD will need to be created from it for use with software that is not schema sensitive. In either case, it is necessary to understand DTD syntax and concepts.

A DTD for schema definitions is provided in Chapter 20.

19.1 Background

The XML standard includes a document modeling language, called the **DTD (Document Type Definition)** feature. This standard has a long history, is now very widely used, and arguably has a continued role to play.

Document models can be translated from one form to another. Because the XML Schema standard is backward compatible with DTDs, a DTD can always be automatically converted into a schema definition. However, the reverse is not always true, due to the limitations of DTDs.

The SGML standard upon which XML is based introduced the concept of DTDs, and indeed a DTD is officially required for all document instances that conform to that language.

Although XML DTDs are optional and are simpler than SGML DTDs, they are still important, even now that alternatives are available. While it could be argued that the success of the XML Schema standard, coupled with its backward compatibility with DTDs, implies that the earlier technology is now redundant, this need not be the case. It is certainly not true in the short term, because DTDs have some strengths over schema definitions and other alternatives. Specifically, the DTD modeling language

- is the most widely supported, and is almost always supported in full;
- is a small language that facilitates very fast validation;
- offers a convenient, terse syntax for modeling documents and individual elements, allowing experts to experiment with and absorb the details of a model very quickly.

Also, even though the XML Schema standard was released about two years ago (at the time of this writing, 2003), support for it is still patchy. Also, because of its complexity, many supporting tools have interpreted the specification wrongly or have interpreted it differently from other tools because the standard contains mistakes or vague rules. These problems will disappear in time, but a policy of reliance on this standard is perhaps premature.

19.2   Declarations

DTDs are constructed from a number of declarations. Declarations vaguely resemble XML element tags. They start with a left angle bracket, followed immediately by an exclamation mark:

```
<! ... >
```

There is always an initial keyword in a declaration. The most significant keyword for building document models is '**ELEMENT**', and all keywords must be in uppercase:

```
<!ELEMENT ... >

<!ATTRIBUTE ... >
```

There is no concept of a data type in this language (apart from a very crude scheme that applies only to attribute values), so there is no declaration for creating data types. However, there are declarations that define attributes, notations, and entities, and others that isolate segments of a DTD to create optional scenarios.

19.3   Element Declarations

An element declaration creates an element type and specifies its content model. The element type name appears first:

```
<!ELEMENT MyElement ... >
```

Empty elements

An empty element is signified by the '**EMPTY**' keyword at the end of the instruction:

```
<!ELEMENT MyEmptyElement EMPTY >
```

A document instance can include the element as a single empty element tag or as a pair of tags. This is a feature of the XML standard itself.

Any child elements

An element that can contain any other element defined in the DTD contains the '**ANY**' keyword:

```
<!ELEMENT MyANYElemcnt ANY >
```

Note that this is equivalent to using the any element in a schema definition, except that it cannot be used as part of a sequence: it must be the entire model. It also stands in for any number of elements, but not text, and it cannot be used to allow elements from other namespaces.

Explicit content models

All the remaining options require a content model to be included. A content model must consist of at least one group, which is indicated by enclosing parentheses ('(' and ')'):

```
<!ELEMENT MyElement (...) >
```

A sequence of elements can be specified by a list of the allowed child elements, in the correct order, with commas (',') between the names:

```
<!ELEMENT EMail (From, To, Title, Data, Message)>
```

The document instance author can be made to choose one child element from a list of options. In this case, the names of the allowed elements are separated by vertical bar ('l') characters:

```
<!ELEMENT Book (Parts | Chapters)>
```

Embedded models

Sequence and choice connectors cannot be mixed in the same model, so the following example is not legal. In any event, such a model, if allowed, would be ambiguous. It would not be clear whether the D element is an alternative to the C element alone or an alternative to the entire sequence:

```
(A, B, C | D)
```

Subgroups must be used to avoid ambiguity. Both of the scenarios discussed above are covered by these examples. The first example makes the D element an alternative to the C element above, and the A and B elements are both required. The second example makes the D element an alternative to a sequence of A, B, and C elements:

```
(A, B, (C | D))
((A, B, C) | D)
```

Both of the examples above are valid; this can be confirmed by the observation that neither includes both connector types directly within the same group.

Optional and repeatable elements and models

An element reference can be made optional by appending the '?' symbol, repeatable by appending the '+' symbol, and both optional and repeatable by using the '*' symbol. In the following example, the From element is required, the To element must occur at least once, the CarbonCopy element may repeat or be omitted entirely, the Title element is optional, and the Date and Message elements are required:

```
(From, To+, CarbonCopy*, Title?, Date, Message)
```

An entire group, including the outer group, can be qualified in the same way:

```
(... (...)? ...)*
```

When a choice group is given a '*' or '+' qualification, then any of the choices can be selected in any order, any number of times (including none):

```
(Para | List | Table)+
```

```
<Table>...</Table><Para>...</Para><Para>...</Para>
```

Note that these concepts replicate, in part, the minimum and maximum occurrence features of the XML Schema language. The '?' symbol is equivalent to setting the minimum to '0' and the maximum to '1', the '+' symbol is equivalent to setting the minimum to '1' and the maximum to 'unbounded', and the '*' symbol is equivalent to setting the minimum to '0' and the maximum to 'unbounded'.

Arbitrary occurrence requirements (such as a minimum of three chapters and maximum of six) cannot be set, though element references can be repeated to set the minimum number of times and further optional references can be used up to the maximum. However, the following model is not quite legal:

```
(Chapter, Chapter, Chapter,
 Chapter?, Chapter?, Chapter?)
```

While this model appears to indicate a minimum of three occurrences and a maximum of six, it is in fact ambiguous (see Chapter 8). Instead, the following model is needed:

```
(Chapter, Chapter, Chapter,
 (Chapter, (Chapter, Chapter?)?)?
 )
```

This model makes it clear that if, for example, a fourth `Chapter` element is present, then it must correspond to the fourth reference to this element in the content model (the outer optional group has been used).

Text and mixed content

An element can contain text. The '**#PCDATA**' keyword represents zero or more characters, so it is not necessary to add a qualifier to allow multiple characters:

```
<!ELEMENT Para (#PCDATA)>
```

```
<Para>This paragraph can only contain text.</Para>
```

Text can be mixed with elements (in a mixed content model) but only in one very specific way. It is necessary to allow the text to occur before, after, and between the elements and the elements must be able to occur any number of times, including not at all. The following model type must be used, and the '#PCDATA' keyword must appear first in the declaration:

```
<!ELEMENT Para (#PCDATA | Emph |
                ImportantTerm | InlineExample)*>
```

```
<Para>A <ImportantTerm>mixed content</ImportantTerm>
element can contain text <Emph>and</Emph>
child elements.</Para>
```

Note that this is clearly much more limited than mixed models in schema definitions, whereby the elements can be given a specific sequence as well as individual occurrence options.

Note the line break in the example content model above. These characters are acceptable whitespace characters along with tabs and spaces.

19.4   Attribute Declarations

Attribute declarations are separate from element declarations, but each one is nevertheless tightly associated with a specific element (they are not shareable). The keyword '**ATTLIST**' is followed by the name of the element to which the list of attributes will be assigned:

```
<!ELEMENT Para (...)>

<!ATTLIST Para ......
               ......
               ...... >
```

Typically, each attribute is defined on a separate line of the declaration. The name of the attribute is followed by its type, then by the specification that it is *either* optional ('**#IMPLIED**') *or* required ('**#REQUIRED**'), and then is *either* fixed ('**#FIXED**') and followed by its permanent value *or* has a default value enclosed by quotation marks:

```
<!ATTLIST Para Security  (normal | secret)  "normal"
               Id         ID                 #REQUIRED
               Author     CDATA              #IMPLIED>
```

The keywords 'ID' and 'CDATA', plus a number of other alternatives, are also available as simple data types in schema definitions (and are introduced and briefly discussed in Section 7.5 and Section 7.6).

19.5 Entities for Sharing Definitions

Parameter entities can be used to help reuse shared components across several declarations. A parameter entity is similar to a general entity, except that the percent symbol, '%', replaces the ampersand symbol, and this symbol is also added in the entity declaration. For example, the Id and Version attributes can be added to several elements:

```
<!ENTITY % generalAttributes "Id       ID    #REQUIRED
                              Version CDATA #IMPLIED" >

<!ATTLIST Book   ...
                 %generalAttributes;>

<!ATTLIST Title ...
                 %generalAttributes;>

<!ATTLIST Para   ...
                 %generalAttributes;>
```

Parameter entities also commonly incorporate separate files that contain lists of entities for characters that are difficult or impossible to enter directly from the keyboard (such as 'é', which is typically represented by an entity called 'eacute'). Several sets of entities have been defined by the ISO and are usually called in as follows:

```
<!ENTITY % ISOnum
   PUBLIC "ISO 8879:1986//ENTITIES Numeric and Special
          Graphic//EN"
   SYSTEM "ISOnum.ent">
<!ENTITY % ISOlat1
   PUBLIC "ISO 8879:1986//ENTITIES Added Latin 1//EN"
   SYSTEM "ISOlat1.ent">
<!ENTITY % ISOgrk1
   PUBLIC "ISO 8879:1986//ENTITIES Greek Letters//EN"
   SYSTEM "ISOgrk.ent">
```

```
<!ENTITY % ISOpub
    PUBLIC "ISO 8879:1986//ENTITIES Publishing//EN"
    SYSTEM "ISOpub.ent">

<!-- merge-in the external entities -->

%ISOnum; %ISOlat1; %ISOgrk1; %ISOpub;
```

See Section 18.10 for a discussion on how to handle such characters when a schema definition is used instead of a DTD.

19.6   Notations

Entities can refer to external files that contain data that conform to a format other than XML. When this happens, the parser must not attempt to validate the data, and the application that receives the parsed document needs to know something about the format so that it can pass the data to another application that can interpret it.

An entity can be used to name and locate an external data file that conforms to a format other than XML. The entity declaration includes the '**NDATA**' keyword, which is followed by the name of the data format. This name is defined in a notation declaration that includes the '**NOTATION**' keyword:

```
<!NOTATION gif SYSTEM "gifViewer.exe">

<!ENTITY boat SYSTEM "boat.gif" NDATA gif>
```

The foreign data format may be text based and happen not to conflict with XML markup, so a chunk of data conforming to this format could be inserted into an element without confusing a parser. In this scenario an attribute is needed on the element to tell the application what kind of data it holds (for the same reason as above):

```
<Formula Format="TeX">-$${ \Gamma (J^psi ...</Formula>
```

In this example, the Format attribute of the Formula element is assigned to the '**NOTATION**' type:

```
<!ATTLIST Formula    Format NOTATION
                            (TeX | LaTeX | TROFF)>
```

Note that a schema definition likewise has to assign a list of valid notations whenever an attribute is assigned to the 'NOTATION' data type. It is also stressed in the standard that this data type should only be applied to attributes values (not element content). Also, despite some confusion caused in part by an error in the schema for schemas, the public identifier is not required in a notation component definition but either a system or public identifier is needed (and both can be present).

19.7   Suppressed DTD Fragments

Some DTDs are designed to incorporate multiple document models, although only one model can be active at any one time. Alternative models are suppressed by conditional sections that enclose element and attribute declarations. A conditional section includes an initial keyword that specifies whether or not that section contains declarations that are wanted. The keyword '**INCLUDE**' signifies that the material is wanted, and the keyword '**IGNORE**' siginifies that the material is to be ignored.

In the following example, a model that wraps individual parts or chapters of a book in a Parts or Chapters element is included, and a document model that dispenses with this layer in the document structure is suppressed:

```
<![INCLUDE[
  <!ELEMENT Book     (Parts|Chapters) >
  <!ELEMENT Parts    (Part+)>
  <!ELEMENT Chapters (Chapter+)>
]]>

<![IGNORE[
  <!ELEMENT Book (Part+|Chapter+) >
]]>
```

In the example above, the model can be changed by swapping the keywords, but this can be a tedious task when the DTD contains many interdependent conditional sections. Parameter entities can be used in place of the keywords so that a single edit to an entity declaration can switch on or switch off many conditional sections simultaneously:

```
<!ENTITY % simpleModel "IGNORE" >
<!ENTITY % complexModel "INCLUDE" >

<![%simpleModel;[ ... ]]>
<![%complexModel;[ ... ]]>

<![%simpleModel;[ ... ]]>
<![%complexModel;[ ... ]]>
```

19.8   Namespace Handling

A DTD can model documents that belong to a namespace, even though this modeling language is not namespace aware (the Namespaces standard was developed after the XML standard was released).

A DTD does not recognize the significance of a colon in a name. The following declaration is valid, but as far as the DTD is concerned, this is just declaring an element type called 'DOC:a':

```
<!ELEMENT DOC:A (#PCDATA)>
```

```
<DOC:A>This may be namespace qualified, but the DTD
does not know it.</DOC:A>
```

Nevertheless, this declaration works, provided that a namespace-qualified document instance uses the same prefix that is hard-coded into the DTD.

When a DTD is converted to a schema definition, the prefixes must be removed from the names, and any attribute definitions for attributes that define a namespace (such as 'xmlns' and 'xmlns:xyz') must be removed.

20. DTD for Schema Definitions

The DTD included in this chapter illustrates the structure of schema definitions in terms familiar to DTD authors and can be used with a DTD-sensitive XML word processor to create schema definitions.

20.1 Background

The 42 elements defined in the XML Schema standard can be used to build a schema definition. The following DTD illustrates the document model for these elements and is usable for validating or authoring a schema definition using tools that are not yet schema-capable.

This DTD can be used to validate XML Schema definitions that do not use a namespace prefix. If this DTD will be used to construct schema definitions for documents that do not use namespaces, then it must be edited to use prefixes. The schema definition author should add 'xsd:' to the start of all element names, both where they are declared and wherever they are referenced.

Comments have been added to the DTD to assist with analysis of the content model. Each element declaration is given a number that represents its location in the DTD relative to other elements (shown in the second column of the first table below). This number is used to reference the declaration whenever that element is used in a content model. Comments under each content model reflect the model structure but replace the element names with their assigned number.

20.2 Element Hierarchies

The following table shows the parents and children of each element in the DTD:

Elements	Location in DTD	Child of (in DTD order)	Contains (in DTD order)
all	08	02 complexType 05 extension 07 group 28 restriction	06 element 24 annotation

Elements	Location in DTD	Child of (in DTD order)	Contains (in DTD order)
annotation	24	*(almost all)*	25 appinfo 26 documentation
any	11	09 choice 10 sequence	24 annotation
anyAttribute	12	02 complexType 05 extension 14 attributeGroup 28 restriction	24 annotation
appinfo	25	24 annotation	*(any element and text)*
attribute	13	01 schema 02 complexType 05 extension 14 attributeGroup 28 restriction	24 annotation 27 simpleType
attributeGroup	14	01 schema 02 complexType 05 extension 14 attributeGroup 22 redefine 28 restriction	12 anyAttribute 13 attribute 14 attributeGroup *(recursive)*
choice	09	02 complexType 05 extension 07 group 09 *(recursive)* 10 sequence 28 restriction	06 element 07 group 09 choice *(recursive)* 10 sequence 11 any 24 annotation
complexContent	03	02 complexType	05 extension 28 restriction
complexType	02	01 schema 06 element 22 redefine	03 complexContent 04 simpleContent 07 group 08 all 09 choice 10 sequence 12 anyAttribute 13 attribute 14 attributeGroup 24 annotation
documentation	26	24 annotation	(any element and text)
element	06	01 schema 08 all 09 choice 10 sequence	02 complexType 15 unique 16 key 17 keyref 24 annotation 27 simpleType
enumeration	40	28 restriction	24 annotation

Elements	Location in DTD	Child of (in DTD order)	Contains (in DTD order)
extension	05	03 complexContent 04 simpleContent	07 group 08 all 09 choice 10 sequence 12 anyAttribute 13 attribute 14 attributeGroup
field	19	15 unique 16 key 17 keyref	24 annotation
fractionDigits	36	28 restriction	24 annotation
group	07	01 schema 02 complexType 05 extension 09 choice 10 sequence 22 redefine 28 restriction	08 all 09 choice 10 sequence 24 annotation
import	21	01 schema	24 annotation
include	20	01 schema	24 annotation
key	16	06 element	18 selector 19 field 24 annotation
keyref	17	06 element	18 selector 19 field 24 annotation
length	37	28 restriction	24 annotation
list	29	27 simpleType	24 annotation 27 simpleType
maxExclusive	31	28 restriction	24 annotation
maxInclusive	33	28 restriction	24 annotation
maxLength	39	28 restriction	24 annotation
minExclusive	32	28 restriction	24 annotation
minInclusive	34	28 restriction	24 annotation
minLength	38	28 restriction	24 annotation
notation	23	01 schema	24 annotation
pattern	42	28 restriction	24 annotation
redefine	22	01 schema	02 complexType 07 group 14 attributeGroup 24 annotation 27 simpleType

Elements	Location in DTD	Child of (in DTD order)	Contains (in DTD order)
restriction	28	03 complexContent 04 simpleContent 27 simpleType	07 group 08 all 09 choice 10 sequence 12 anyAttribute 13 attribute 14 attributeGroup 27 simpleType 31 maxExclusive 32 minExclusive 33 maxInclusive 34 minInclusive 35 totalDigits 36 fractionDigits 37 length 38 minLength 39 maxLength 40 enumeration 41 whiteSpace 42 pattern
schema	01	*(none)*	02 complexType 06 element 07 group 13 attribute 14 attributeGroup 20 include 21 import 22 redefine 23 notation 27 simpleType
selector	18	15 unique 16 key 17 keyref	24 annotation
sequence	10	02 complexType 05 extension 07 group 09 choice 10 sequence 28 restriction	06 element 07 group 09 choice 10 sequence *(recursive)* 11 any 24 annotation
simpleContent	04	02 complexType	05 extension 28 restriction
simpleType	27	01 schema 06 element 13 attribute 22 redefine 27 list 30 union	24 annotation 28 restriction 29 list 30 union
totalDigits	35	28 restriction	24 annotation
union	30	27 simpleType	24 annotation 27 simpleType
unique	15	06 element	18 selector 19 field 24 annotation
whiteSpace	41	28 restriction	24 annotation

20.3 **Attributes**

Many of the elements listed above contain attributes, and some contain attributes
with the same names and meanings:

Attributes	Elements applied to (in alphabetical order)
abstract	09 complexType 06 element
attributeFormDefault	01 schema
base	05 extension 28 restriction
block	09 complexType 06 element
blockDefault	01 schema
default	13 attribute 06 element
elementFormDefault	01 schema
final	02 complexType 06 element 27simpleType
finalDefault	01 schema
fixed	13 attribute 06 element 36 fractionDigits 37 length 31 maxExclusive 39 maxLength 33 maxInclusive 32 minExclusive 38 minLength 34 minInclusive 35 totalDigits 41 whiteSpace
form	13 attribute 06 element
id	*all elements*
itemType	29 list
maxOccurs	08 all 11 any 09 choice 06 element 07 group 10 sequence
memberType	30 union

Attributes	Elements applied to (in alphabetical order)
minOccurs	08 all 11 any 09 choice 06 element 07 group 10 sequence
mixed	03 complexContent 09 complexType
name	13 attribute 14 attributeGroup 09 complexType 06 element 07 group 16 key 17 keyref 23 notation 27 simpleType 15 unique
namespace	11 any 12 anyAttribute 21 import
nillable	06 element
processContents	11 any 12 anyAttribute
public	28 notation
ref	13 attribute 14 attributeGroup 06 element 07 group
refer	17 keyref
schemaLocation	20 include 21 import 22 redefine
source	25 appInfo 26 documentation
substitutionGroup	06 element
system	28 notation
targetNamespace	01 schema
type	13 attribute 06 element
use	13 attribute

Attributes	Elements applied to (in alphabetical order)
value	40 enumeration 36 fractionDigits 37 length 31 maxExclusive 39 maxLength 33 maxInclusive 32 minExclusive 38 minLength 34 minInclusive 42 pattern 35 totalDigits 41 whiteSpace
version	01 schema
xmlns	01 schema
xmlns:target	01 schema
xml:lang	26 documentation
xpath	19 field 18 selector

20.4   Complete DTD

The complete DTD:

```
<!-- DTD for XML Schemas -->

<!-- This DTD is suitable for schema definitions that
     target a namespace (the xmlns:target attribute
     in the Schema element should be changed to
     reflect the prefix needed). For it to work for
     non-namespace schema definitions, a prefix must
     be added to all of the element names. -->

<!-- CONTENTS -->
<!-- (01) schema -->
<!-- (02) ComplexType -->
<!-- (03) ComplexContent -->
<!-- (04) simpleContent -->
<!-- (05) extension -->
<!-- (06) element -->
<!-- (07) group -->
<!-- (08) all -->
<!-- (09) choice -->
<!-- (10) sequence -->
<!-- (11) any -->
<!-- (12) anyAttribute -->
<!-- (13) attribute -->
<!-- (14) attributeGroup -->
<!-- (15) unique -->
<!-- (16) key -->
<!-- (17) keyref -->
```

```
<!-- (18) selector -->
<!-- (19) field -->
<!-- (20) include -->
<!-- (21) import -->
<!-- (22) redefine -->
<!-- (23) notation -->
<!-- (24) annotation -->
<!-- (25) appinfo -->
<!-- (26) documentation -->
<!-- (27) simpleType -->
<!-- (28) restriction -->
<!-- (29) list -->
<!-- (30) union -->
<!-- (31) maxExclusive -->
<!-- (32) minExclusive -->
<!-- (33) maxInclusive -->
<!-- (34) minInclusive -->
<!-- (35) totalDigits -->
<!-- (36) fractionDigits -->
<!-- (37) length -->
<!-- (38) minLength -->
<!-- (39) maxLength -->
<!-- (40) enumeration -->
<!-- (41) whiteSpace -->
<!-- (42) pattern -->

<!-- (01) Schema -->

<!ELEMENT schema
     (import*, (include | redefine | annotation)*,
     ((simpleType | complexType | element | attribute |
      attributeGroup | group | notation ),
      annotation*)*)>
<!-- (21, (20 | 22 | 24)*,
     ((27 | 02 | 06 | 13 |
      14 | 07 | 23),
      24*)*)
-->
<!ATTLIST schema
    targetNamespace       CDATA   #IMPLIED
    version               CDATA   #IMPLIED
    xmlns                 CDATA
       #FIXED 'http://www.w3.org/2000/10/XMLSchema'
    xmlns:target          CDATA   #IMPLIED
    finalDefault          CDATA   ""
    blockDefault          CDATA   ""
    id                    ID      #IMPLIED
    elementFormDefault    (qualified |
                          unqualified) "unqualified"
    attributeFormDefault (qualified|unqualified)
                                  "unqualified">


<!-- (02) ComplexType -->
<!--           (referenced by 01 06 22 ) -->
<!-- mixed is disallowed if simpleContent used, and
```

```
            overridden if complexContent has one too. -->
<!-- If anyAttribute appears in one or more referenced
     attributeGroups and/or explicitly, the
     intersection of the permissions is used -->
<!ELEMENT complexType
     (annotation?, (simpleContent | complexContent |
                   ((all | choice | sequence | group)?,
                    (attribute | attributeGroup)*,
                    anyAttribute?)))>
<!-- (24?, (04 | 03 | 24)*,
     ((08 | 09 | 10 | 07)?,
      (13 | 14)*,
      12?)))
-->
<!ATTLIST complexType
     name      CDATA           #IMPLIED
     id        ID              #IMPLIED
     abstract  (true|false|1|0) #IMPLIED
     final     CDATA           #IMPLIED
     block     CDATA           #IMPLIED
     mixed     (true|false)    "false">


<!-- (03) ComplexContent -->
<!--           (referenced by 02 ) -->

<!ELEMENT complexContent (restriction | extension)>
<!-- (28 | 05) -->
<!ATTLIST complexContent mixed (true|false) #IMPLIED
                         id    ID             #IMPLIED>


<!-- (04) SimpleContent -->
<!--           (referenced by 02 ) -->

<!ELEMENT simpleContent (restriction | extension)>
<!-- (28 | 05) -->
<!ATTLIST simpleContent
     id     ID          #IMPLIED>


<!-- (05) Extension -->
<!--           (referenced by 03 04 ) -->
<!-- an element is declared either by:
     a name and a type (either nested or referenced via
     the type attribute) or by a ref to an existing
     element declaration -->
<!-- when used in SimpleContent element, only
     attribute-related elements allowed in content -->
<!ELEMENT extension
     ((all | choice | sequence | group)?,
      (attribute | attributeGroup)*, anyAttribute?)>
<!-- ((08 | 09 | 10 | 07)?,
     (13 | 14)*, 12?)
-->
<!-- when used in ComplexContent element, base
```

```
        attribute must reference a complex data type;
        when used in SimpleContent element, base attribute
        must reference a simple data type -->
<!ATTLIST extension
     base  CDATA        #REQUIRED
     id    ID           #IMPLIED>


<!-- (06) Element -->
<!--          (referenced by 01 08 09 10 ) -->
<!-- simpleType or complexType allowed only
     if there is no type or ref attribute -->
<!ELEMENT element
     (annotation?,
      (complexType | simpleType)?,
      (unique | key | keyref)*)>
<!-- ref not allowed at top level -->
<!-- (24?,
     (02 | 27)?,
     (15 | 16 | 17)*)
-->
<!ATTLIST element
     name                CDATA            #IMPLIED
     id                  ID               #IMPLIED
     ref                 CDATA            #IMPLIED
     type                CDATA            #IMPLIED
     minOccurs           CDATA            #IMPLIED
     maxOccurs           CDATA            #IMPLIED
     nillable            (true | false |
                          1 | 0)          #IMPLIED
     substitutionGroup   CDATA            #IMPLIED
     abstract            (true | false |
                          1 | 0)          "false"
     final               CDATA            #IMPLIED
     block               CDATA            #IMPLIED
     default             CDATA            #IMPLIED
     fixed               CDATA            #IMPLIED
     form                (qualified |
                          unqualified)    #IMPLIED>


<!-- (07) Group -->
<!--          (referenced by 01 02 05 09 10 22 28 ) -->
<!-- default and fixed are mutually exclusive -->
<!-- type and ref are mutually exclusive.
     name and ref are mutually exclusive, one is
     required -->
<!-- In the absence of type and ref, type defaults to
     type of substitutionGroup, if any, else the
     ur-type (unconstrained) -->
<!ELEMENT group
     (annotation?, (all | choice | sequence)?)>
<!-- (24, (08 | 09 | 10)? )
-->
<!ATTLIST group
     name           CDATA   #IMPLIED
```

```
    ref             CDATA     #IMPLIED
    minOccurs       CDATA     #IMPLIED
    maxOccurs       CDATA     #IMPLIED
    id              ID        #IMPLIED>


<!-- (08) All -->
<!--            (referenced by 02 05 07 28 ) -->
<!ELEMENT all (annotation?, element*)>
<!ATTLIST all
    minOccurs       (1)       #IMPLIED
    maxOccurs       (1)       #IMPLIED
    id              ID        #IMPLIED>


<!-- (09) Choice -->
<!--            (referenced by 02 05 07 09 10 28 ) -->
<!ELEMENT choice
    (annotation?,
     (element | group | choice | sequence | any)*)>
<!-- (24?,
      (06 | 07 | 09 | 10 | 11)*)
-->
<!ATTLIST choice
    minOccurs       CDATA     "1"
    maxOccurs       CDATA     "1"
    id              ID        #IMPLIED>


<!-- (10) Sequence -->
<!--            (referenced by 02 05 07 09 10 28 ) -->
<!ELEMENT sequence
    (annotation?,
     (element| group| choice | sequence | any)*)>
<!-- (24?,
      (06 | 07 | 09 | 10 | 11)*)
-->
<!ATTLIST sequence
    minOccurs       CDATA     "1"
    maxOccurs       CDATA     "1"
    id              ID        #IMPLIED>


<!-- (11) Any -->
<!--            (referenced by 09 10 ) -->
<!-- an anonymous grouping in a model, or a top-level
    named group definition, or a reference to same -->
<!-- If order is 'all', group is not allowed
    inside.
    If order is 'all' THIS group must be alone
    (or referenced alone) at the top level of a
    content model -->
<!-- If order is 'all', minOccurs and maxOccurs
    must equal 1 on element/any inside -->
<!-- Should allow minOccurs equal 0 inside
    order="all" -->
```

```
<!ELEMENT any (annotation?)>
<!--         (24?) -->
<!-- namespace is interpreted as follows:
     ##any     any nonconflicting WFXML at all
     ##other   any nonconflicting WFXML from
               namespace other
               than targetNamespace
     ##local   any unqualified nonconflicting
               WFXML/attribute
     ##targetNamespace  the target namespace
     ##targetNamespace ##local may appear in the above
               list, with the obvious meaning -->
<!ATTLIST any
     namespace       CDATA                    "##any"
     processContents (skip | lax | strict)    "strict"
     minOccurs       CDATA                    "1"
     maxOccurs       CDATA                    "1"
     id              ID                       #IMPLIED>


<!-- (12) AnyAttribute -->
<!--         (referenced by 02 05 14 28 ) -->
<!ELEMENT anyAttribute (annotation?)>
<!--               (24?) -->
<!ATTLIST anyAttribute
     namespace       CDATA                    "##any"
     processContents (skip | lax | strict)    "strict"
     id              ID                       #IMPLIED>


<!-- (13) Attribute -->
<!--         (referenced by 01 02 05 14 28 ) -->
<!-- simpleType only if no type or ref attribute -->
<!-- ref not allowed at top level, name used at top
     level -->
<!ELEMENT attribute (annotation?, simpleType?)>
<!--               (24?, 27) -->
<!-- type and ref are mutually exclusive.
     name and ref are mutually exclusive, one is
     required -->
<!-- name and use are mutually exclusive -->
<!-- type attribute and simpleType content are
     mutually exclusive -->
<!ATTLIST attribute
     name      CDATA                     #IMPLIED
     id        ID                        #IMPLIED
     ref       CDATA                     #IMPLIED
     type      CDATA                     #IMPLIED
     use       (prohibited | optional |
               required)                 #IMPLIED
     default   CDATA                     #IMPLIED
     fixed     CDATA                     #IMPLIED
     form      (qualified | unqualified) #IMPLIED>


<!-- (14) AttributeGroup -->
```

```
<!--          (referenced by 01 02 05 14 22 28 ) -->
<!ELEMENT attributeGroup
     (annotation?, (attribute | attributeGroup)*,
     anyAttribute?)>
<!-- (24?, (13 | 14)*,
     12?)
-->
<!-- ref used if no content and no name.
     ref used if not top level -->
<!-- better reference mechanisms -->
<!ATTLIST attributeGroup
     name          CDATA          #IMPLIED
     id            ID             #IMPLIED
     ref           CDATA          #IMPLIED>


<!-- (15) Unique -->
<!--          (referenced by 06 ) -->
<!ELEMENT unique (annotation?, selector, field+)>
<!--          (24?, 18, 19+) -->
<!ATTLIST unique
     name          CDATA          #REQUIRED
     id            ID             #IMPLIED>


<!-- (16) Key -->
<!--          (referenced by 06 ) -->
<!ELEMENT key (annotation?, selector, field+)>
<!--         (24?, 18, 19+) -->
<!ATTLIST key
    name          CDATA          #REQUIRED
    id            ID             #IMPLIED>


<!-- (17) Keyref -->
<!--          (referenced by 06 ) -->
<!ELEMENT keyref   (annotation?, selector, field+)>
<!--          (24?, 18, 19+) -->
<!ATTLIST keyref
     name          CDATA          #REQUIRED
     refer         CDATA          #REQUIRED
     id            ID             #IMPLIED>


<!-- (18) Selector -->
<!--          (referenced by 15 16 17 ) -->
<!ELEMENT selector (annotation?)>
<!--          (24?) -->
<!ATTLIST selector
     xpath         CDATA          #REQUIRED
     id            ID             #IMPLIED>


<!-- (19) Field -->
<!--          (referenced by 15 16 17 ) -->
<!ELEMENT field (annotation?)>
```

```
<!--              (24?) -->
<!ATTLIST field
     xpath    CDATA       #REQUIRED
     id       ID          #IMPLIED>


<!-- (20) Include -->
<!--         (referenced by 01 ) -->
<!-- Schema combination mechanisms -->
<!ELEMENT include (annotation?)>
<!--              (24?) -->
<!ATTLIST include
     schemaLocation  CDATA     #REQUIRED
     id              ID        #IMPLIED>


<!-- (21) Import -->
<!--         (referenced by 01 ) -->
<!ELEMENT import (annotation?)>
<!--              (24?) -->
<!ATTLIST import
     namespace       CDATA     #IMPLIED
     schemaLocation  CDATA     #IMPLIED
     id              ID        #IMPLIED>


<!-- (22) Redefine -->
<!--         (referenced by 01 ) -->
<!ELEMENT redefine
     (annotation | simpleType | complexType |
     attributeGroup | group)*>
<!-- (24? | 27 | 03 |
     14 | 07)*)
-->
<!ATTLIST redefine
     schemaLocation  CDATA     #REQUIRED
     id              ID        #IMPLIED>


<!-- (23) Notation -->
<!--         (referenced by 01 ) -->
<!ELEMENT notation (annotation?)>
<!--              (24?) -->
<!ATTLIST notation
     name     CDATA       #REQUIRED
     id       ID          #IMPLIED
     public   CDATA       #REQUIRED
     system   CDATA       #IMPLIED>


<!-- (24) Annotation -->
<!--         (referenced by 01 02 06 07 08 09 10 11 12
                           13 14 15 16 17 18 19 20 21
                           22 23 27 28 29 30 31 32 33
                           34 35 36 ) -->
<!-- Annotation is either application information
```

```
           or documentation -->
<!ELEMENT annotation (appinfo | documentation)*>
<!--                  (15 | 16)* -->


<!-- (25) Appinfo -->
<!--          (referenced by 24 ) -->
<!-- User must define annotation elements in internal
     subset for this to work -->
<!ELEMENT appinfo ANY> <!-- too restrictive -->
<!ATTLIST appinfo
     source    CDATA       #IMPLIED
     id        ID          #IMPLIED>


<!-- (26) Documentation -->
<!--          (referenced by 24 ) -->
<!ELEMENT documentation ANY> <!-- too restrictive -->
<!ATTLIST documentation
     source    CDATA       #IMPLIED
     id        ID          #IMPLIED
     xml:lang  CDATA       #IMPLIED>


<!-- (27) SimpleType -->
<!--          (referenced by 01 06 13 ) -->
<!-- name is required at top level -->
<!ELEMENT simpleType
     (annotation?, (restriction | list | union))>
<!-- (24?, (28 | 29 | 30)) -->
<!ATTLIST simpleType
     name      NMTOKEN     #IMPLIED
     final     CDATA       #IMPLIED
     id        ID          #IMPLIED>


<!-- (28) Restriction -->
<!--          (referenced by 03 04 27 ) -->
<!-- restriction is shared between simpleType and
     simpleContent and complexContent
     (in XMLSchema.xsd).
     %complexRestriction; is for when this
     is restricting a complex type. -->
<!-- when used in ComplexType element,
     base attribute must always reference a complex
     type;
     when used in SimpleContent element, only part of
     %complexRestriction can be used to suppress
     attributes) -->
<!ENTITY % complexRestriction
          "(all | choice | sequence | group)?,
           (attribute | attributeGroup)*,
           anyAttribute?">
<!--      (8 | 9 | 10 | 7)?,
          (13 | 14),
          12?
```

```
-->

<!--
   OVERLY RESTRICTIVE SEQUENTIAL MODEL BELOW IS
   INTRODUCED TO MODEL FOLLOWING CONSTRAINTS ...
   whiteSpace    - 0 or 1

   minInclusive - 0 or 1  \ mutually exclusive
   maxInclusive - 0 or 1  /
   minExclusive - 0 or 1  \ mutually exclusive
   maxExclusive - 0 or 1  /

   totalDigits    - 0 or 1
   fractionDigits - 0 or 1

   length        - 0 or 1 \ mutually exclusive
   maxLength     - 0 or 1 /
   minLength     - 0 or 1 /

   pattern       - 0 to unbounded
   enumeration   - 0 to unbounded
-->
<!ENTITY % simpleRestriction
              "(simpleType?, whiteSpace?,
               (minInclusive|minExclusive)?,
               (maxInclusive|maxExclusive)?,
               totalDigits?, fractionDigits?,
               (length | (minLength?, maxLength?))?,
               pattern*, enumeration*)">
<!--          (27?, 41?,
               (34|32)?,
               (23|31)?,
               35?, 36?,
               (37|(38?, 39?))?,
               42*, 40*) -->


<!-- base attribute and simpleType child are mutually
     exclusive, one is required. -->
<!ELEMENT restriction
     (annotation?,
      (%complexRestriction;|%simpleRestriction;))>
<!-- (24?,)
     (.../...))
-->
<!ATTLIST restriction base    NMTOKEN    #IMPLIED
                      id      ID         #IMPLIED>


<!-- (29) List -->
<!--          (referenced by 27 ) -->
<!-- itemType and simpleType child are mutually
     exclusive, one is required -->
<!ELEMENT list (annotation?, simpleType?)>
<!--           (24?, 27?) -->
<!ATTLIST list itemType  NMTOKEN  #IMPLIED
```

```
                      id          ID        #IMPLIED>


<!-- (30) Union -->
<!--           (referenced by 27 ) -->
<!-- At least one item in memberTypes or one simpleType
    child is required -->
<!ELEMENT union (annotation?, simpleType*)>
<!--           (24?, 27*) -->
<!ATTLIST union id              ID        #IMPLIED
                memberTypes     NMTOKEN   #IMPLIED>


<!-- (31) MaxExclusive -->
<!--           (referenced by 28 ) -->
<!ELEMENT maxExclusive (annotation?)>
<!--                   (24?) -->
<!ATTLIST maxExclusive value CDATA       #REQUIRED
                       id    ID          #IMPLIED
                       fixed (true|false) #IMPLIED>


<!-- (32) MinExclusive -->
<!--           (referenced by 28 ) -->
<!ELEMENT minExclusive (annotation?)>
<!--                   (24?) -->
<!ATTLIST minExclusive value CDATA       #REQUIRED
                       id    ID          #IMPLIED
                       fixed (true|false) #IMPLIED>


<!-- (33) MaxInclusive -->
<!--           (referenced by 28 ) -->
<!ELEMENT maxInclusive (annotation?)>
<!--                   (24?) -->
<!ATTLIST maxInclusive value CDATA       #REQUIRED
                       id    ID          #IMPLIED
                       fixed (true|false) #IMPLIED>


<!-- (34) MinInclusive -->
<!--           (referenced by 28 ) -->
<!ELEMENT minInclusive (annotation?)>
<!--                   (24?) -->
<!ATTLIST minInclusive value CDATA       #REQUIRED
                       id    ID          #IMPLIED
                       fixed (true|false) #IMPLIED>


<!-- (35) TotalDigits -->
<!--           (referenced by 28 ) -->
<!ELEMENT totalDigits (annotation?)>
<!--                  (24?) -->
<!ATTLIST totalDigits value CDATA        #REQUIRED
                      id    ID           #IMPLIED
                      fixed (true|false)  #IMPLIED>
```

```
<!-- (36) FractionDigits -->
<!--          (referenced by 28 ) -->
<!ELEMENT fractionDigits (annotation?)>
<!--                  (24?) -->
<!ATTLIST fractionDigits value CDATA        #REQUIRED
                         id    ID           #IMPLIED
                         fixed (true|false) #IMPLIED>


<!-- (37) Length -->
<!--          (referenced by 28 ) -->
<!ELEMENT length (annotation?)>
<!--          (24?) -->
<!ATTLIST length value CDATA        #REQUIRED
                 id    ID           #IMPLIED
                 fixed (true|false) #IMPLIED>


<!-- (38) MinLength -->
<!--          (referenced by 28 ) -->
<!ELEMENT minLength (annotation?)>
<!--          (24?) -->
<!ATTLIST minLength value CDATA        #REQUIRED
                    id    ID           #IMPLIED
                    fixed (true|false) #IMPLIED>


<!-- (39) MaxLength -->
<!--          (referenced by 28 ) -->
<!ELEMENT maxLength (annotation?)>
<!--          (24?) -->
<!ATTLIST maxLength value CDATA        #REQUIRED
                    id    ID           #IMPLIED
                    fixed (true|false) #IMPLIED>


<!-- (40) Enumeration -->
<!--          (referenced by 28 ) -->
<!-- This element can be repeated -->
<!ELEMENT enumeration (annotation?)>
<!--              (24?) -->
<!ATTLIST enumeration value CDATA #REQUIRED
                      id    ID    #IMPLIED>


<!-- (41) WhiteSpace -->
<!--          (referenced by 28 ) -->
<!ELEMENT whiteSpace (annotation?)>
<!--              (24?) -->
<!ATTLIST whiteSpace value CDATA        #REQUIRED
                     id    ID           #IMPLIED
                     fixed (true|false) #IMPLIED>
```

```
<!-- (42) Pattern -->
<!--          (referenced by 28 ) -->
<!-- This element can be repeated -->
<!ELEMENT pattern (annotation?)>
<!--              (24?) -->
<!ATTLIST pattern value CDATA #REQUIRED
                  id    ID    #IMPLIED>


<!-- END END END -->
```

21. Namespaces

Namespaces are fundamental to the XML Schema standard. This is partly because schema definitions can validate documents that use namespaces, and partly because namespaces are used in schema definition documents too. This chapter describes namespaces in general, particularly for the benefit of readers who have not previously encountered them or are not adept in their use.

See Section 4.3 for more on how document instances that employ namespaces reference schema definitions, and see Chapter 12 for more on how schema definitions are selected in response to the presence of namespace-related markup in a document instance.

21.1   Before Namespaces

Before discussing namespaces, it is necessary to take a close look at XML documents that do not use this standard and establish some terminology that will help distinguish between these different kinds of XML document.

Local elements

An XML document that does not make any use of namespaces might be called a 'traditional document,' or a 'basic document.' These documents consist entirely of elements that implicitly belong to the model for that document if there *is* a model, or simply to the document itself if there is no model. Every element is a **local element**:

```
<LocalRootElement>
  <LocalElement>
    <LocalEmptyElement />
  </LocalElement>
</LocalRootElement>
```

In keeping with this definition, the XML Schema standard includes the keyword '##local' for use in the namespace attribute of the any element where it stipulates that elements that do not belong to any namespace can be inserted into the document instance.

Contextual identification

If two local elements have the same name, they are either indistinguishable from each other or, at best, the contextual location of each element is taken into consideration to establish their respective meanings. Two elements with the same name must have the same attributes and content model when defined in a DTD but may have different attributes and content models when using a schema definition to specify a location context in each case. However, they still belong to the same document model, and in this sense they are both still local to the non-namespace document.

Caution: the XML Schema standard uses the term 'local element' to describe an element that is defined for use only in a given contextual location. This meaning should not be confused with the definition of this term above.

Foreign elements and fragments

The well-formed nature of XML documents makes insertion of a **foreign element** into a document relatively easy. Nothing prevents an element declared in one document model from including elements that have been declared in another:

```
<LocalRootElement>
  <LocalElement>...</LocalElement>
  <ForeignElement />
  <LocalElement>...</LocalElement>
</LocalRootElement>
```

When a foreign element directly enclosed within a local element contains further structures, the term **foreign fragment** may be more appropriate. The element at the root of a fragment marks the boundary between local elements and foreign elements. However, this term is typically also applied to simple elements and empty elements:

```
<LocalRootElement>
  <LocalElement>...</LocalElement>
  <ForeignFragment><ForeignElement/></ForeignFragment>
  <LocalElement />
  <ForeignFragment>text</ForeignFragment>
  <LocalElement />
  <ForeignFragment />
  <LocalElement>...</LocalElement>
</LocalRootElement>
```

21.2 The Need for Namespaces

A software application that interprets an XML document normally relies on the names of elements to identify the specific units of information that it is interested in. Mixing fragments in the way described above raises some issues because the name alone cannot be relied on.

The first problem is to identify which document model each element belongs to. The element name might be considered sufficient to identify the model, but in practice, an application would have to hold a list of elements from each domain in order to distinguish between them. This would certainly be inconvenient, but not as serious as the impact that the second problem has on this issue.

The second problem is how to avoid duplication of element and attribute names, because nothing prevents different models from including elements with the same name. XML does not allow two element types to have the same name (ignoring local declarations in schema definitions for the moment), because it would then be impossible to identify which one is intended when an element with this name is found in a document instance.

As an illustration of the second problem, consider a document model that describes musical compositions and includes elements that identify the composer, the title of the composition, and the name of the person who provided a particular score (arrangement). Another document model describes the performance of a musician in a competition and includes the score that the individual obtained for the performance. In this scenario, both models have an element named Score:

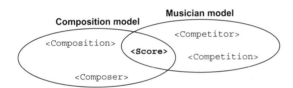

The possibility that a document will contain elements with the same name from different models is called a **collision problem**. If a single document were to contain both sets of elements, there would be two Score elements in the document, causing a collision.

```
<CompetitionEntry>
  <Competition>Piano</Competition>
  <Competitor>J Smith</Competitor>
  <Score>57<Score>
  <Composer>George Gershwin</Composer>
  <Composition>Rhapsody in Blue</Composition>
  <Score>Ferde Grofé</Score>
</CompetitionEntry>
```

While a person could easily identify the meaning of each Score element by studying its respective contents, it is far less easy for software to reliably draw the same kind of conclusions.

Unambiguous identification of elements is therefore needed to do the following:

- enable a parser to identify which model an element belongs to, in order to use the appropriate document model to validate it

- enable an application to identify the elements that require special treatment (and perhaps call another, specialized application to interpret and act upon the information that they contain)

These issues are relevant to attributes as well as to elements.

Clearly, the solution is to somehow **qualify** each element instance in such a way as to make its origins clear.

21.3 The Namespaces Standard

The **Namespaces in XML** standard provides a mechanism for building documents from fragments defined in multiple document models. It was produced by the W3C and gained recommended status in January 1999. The standard can be found at http://www.w3.org/TR/REC-xml-names.

A **namespace** identifies elements and attributes that are declared in a single document model. A namespace is a controlled environment in which all element names are unique. Any reference to a named element within a given namespace is therefore unambiguous.

In the following example, it is possible to reference the unique element called 'Score' in either of the two namespaces simply by qualifying the name by adding the name of the namespace ('Score element in Music namespace' or 'Score element in Competition namespace'):

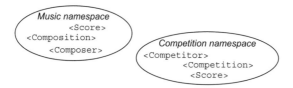

This concept also applies to attribute names, but only in special circumstances. An attribute that is assigned to a specific element (a **local attribute**) is arguably not relevant to this feature, but an attribute that can be used on any element, including elements from other namespaces (a **global attribute**), is certainly relevant.

A namespace-qualified document usually has no local elements but often does have elements from another namespace. In this circumstance, authors can avoid confusion by distinguishing between a **native element** and a foreign element. Native elements are those elements that belong to the same namespace as the root element of the whole document.

Note that the Namespaces standard refers only to element and attribute names, but the XML Schema standard introduces data types, groups, and attribute groups, thereby allowing an element or attribute declaration in one schema definition to use a data type, content model, or set of attributes that are defined in another schema definition.

The term **qualified document** refers to a document that conforms to a namespace. At least one element (the root element) acknowledges that it belongs to the namespace, and typically some or all of the remaining elements contain similar acknowledgements (they are **qualified**).

Many industry standards use namespaces. For example, the XSLT standard allows the mixing of formatting instructions with target document element tags, and the XLink standard requires linking role attributes to be added to elements belonging to any document model.

21.4   Namespace Partitions

In other computing disciplines, a namespace is a set of unique names, each one having a single meaning. But it can be observed that a DTD does not require attribute names to differ from element names, allows an element to contain an attribute with the same name, and further allows the same attribute name to appear, with different attribute types, in different elements. An XML namespace must therefore be partitioned into at least three subspaces to make it behave more like namespaces in other disciplines, in which the whole point of a namespace is that it contains a set of unique names:

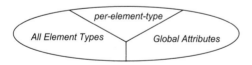

The 'All Element Types' partition holds the unique set of element names: all elements declared in a DTD or globally declared elements in a schema definition.

The 'Global Attributes' partition holds a unique set of attribute names. A DTD cannot identify global attributes (because every attribute must be explicitly assigned to an element in the same model) but *can* do so in a schema definition (all globally declared attributes can be assigned to this partition).

The 'per-element-type' partition holds a separate embedded miniature namespace for each element type that appears in the first partition containing the local attributes declared for use only in that element.

The following namespace includes X and Y elements and also X and Y global attributes. These names do not conflict because they are in different partitions. Both elements have an associated X attribute, but these names also do not conflict with each other or with anything else because they are in different miniature namespaces:

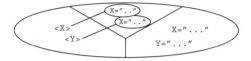

It could be argued that the XML Schema standard adds further partitions to contain data type names, element groups, and attribute groups and that it exploits the existing miniature namespaces to hold local elements (which are similar in concept to normal attributes).

But namespaces do not exist as physical entities. There is no namespace definition markup language and no namespace file, object, or interface. Arguably, a namespace is so closely associated with a document model that it can be said to be defined by the DTD or schema definition for the relevant model as a byproduct of the definitions it contains. But namespaces are really just a concept. This fact alone has led to much unnecessary confusion. Even the namespace partitioning system outlined above is just an opinion and is not included in the normative part of the standard. For example, many argue that local attributes are not in the namespace at all, but are simply associated with an element that is in the namespace. This is an irrelevant argument, in practical terms, because an application already knows which elements and attributes it expects to encounter, and a schema definition already contains the declarations it will accept, so validation of a document instance cannot be affected by such a debate.

21.5 Namespace Identification

Every namespace must have an identifier so that it can be referenced whenever it is needed. This identifier must also be unique so that a reference to a namespace can never be confused with a reference to a different namespace.

Namespace names

Most standard document models can be associated with a specific location on the Web. For example, XHTML is defined at http://www.w3.org/1999/xhtml. Because these Web addresses must be unique, the string of characters that constitutes an address can be considered to be a suitable **namespace name**. Note that a namespace name is always case sensitive, even if it is actually a Web address that happens to be case insensitive.

Although the standard allows the name to be any URI (Uniform Resource *Identifier*), the name will usually be a URL (Uniform Resource *Locator*). But, despite this fact, the reference is treated only as a useful and well-known text string, not as the locator of an actual resource of any kind. Of course, it might be considered convenient if a URL locates a DTD or XML Schema definition, points to documentation for such a model, or is a RDDL (Resource Directory Description Language) document, but this cannot be relied upon. A namespace-sensitive application is only expected to compare the URL against a list of URLs for document models that it can meaningfully process. Though less popular at this early stage, a URN (Uniform Resource *Name*) can be used in place of a URL.

The XML Schema standard defines three namespaces, using three URLs, including the 'http://www.w3.org/2001/XMLSchema-instance' namespace. This namespace happens to contain only four attributes (theoretically, in the Global Attributes partition):

```
http://www.w3.org/2001/XMLSchema-instance
noNamespaceSchemaLocation="..."
schemaLocation="..."
                          nil="..."
                     type="..."
```

Namespace prefixes

Elements and attributes from different namespaces can be distinguished from each other within a document instance by a **namespace prefix** added to their names. The prefix is separated from the rest of the element or attribute name by a colon. The original name is now properly known as the **local part** of the full name:

*prefix***:***local_part*

Note that in the XML Schema standard this mechanism distinguishes data type, group, and attribute group names imported from document models that target different namespaces.

It having been noted that URLs are a good way to uniquely identify a namespace, it must also be said that they are not suitable for use as element and attribute prefixes. First, they tend to be quite long, as in the schema namespace example above. More importantly, they often contain characters that are not allowed in element and attribute names. The following example would not be acceptable for both of these reasons (the colon is reserved for namespace identification, and the '/' character is illegal):

```
<Value
  http://www.w3.org/2001/XMLSchema-instance:nil="true">
</Value>
```

To solve these problems, the standard includes a mechanism for defining short, legal prefixes. For example, XHTML paragraph elements and XSLT template elements are typically given the following prefixes:

```
html:html
html:p
html:ol

xsl:stylesheet
xsl:template
xsl:apply-templates
```

The two main XML Schema standard namespaces typically have the following prefixes, with 'xsd' standing for 'XML Schema Definition', and 'xsi' standing for 'XML Schema Instance':

```
xsd:schema
xsd:simpleType
xsd:element

xsi:nil
xsi:type
xsi:schemaLocation
```

The following attribute name is both valid and concise, unlike the earlier example:

```
<Value xsi:nil="true"></Value>
```

A prefix should not include a colon and must not begin with the letters 'xml...', in any letter case, so 'XmlX' would not be a suitable prefix. The prefix 'xml' has a fixed association with a special namespace (as explained later).

Local prefix assignment

It cannot be left to the developers of document models or the inventors of namespaces to define the prefix to be used, because the collision problem could easily reemerge in a different guise. This time, it is the prefixes that could collide. For example, a fictional organization called 'XML Software International' might create a document model and associated namespace and wish to use 'xsi' as a prefix to reflect the company name, yet this would conflict with the prefix for one of the XML Schema namespaces. To avoid such conflicts, the document instance author can control prefix names. This author is expected (though not trusted) to ensure that each prefix is unique within the confines of that document instance. For example, the author might use the prefixes 'xsi1' and 'xsi2' to avoid the conflict just described or might use a little more imagination ('tom' and 'jerry').

21.6   **Absence of Namespaces**

The Namespaces standard is an optional addition to the XML standard. XML documents existed before the release of the Namespaces standard, and they remain legal today. Indeed, it is still possible to create XML documents that do not include namespaces, or to only use namespaces for contained fragments. Furthermore, compliant XML processing tools are not required to be sensitive to namespaces (and the DTD modeling language remains insensitive to namespaces).

The term **unqualified document** can be used to avoid the repeated use of the phrase 'a document that does not belong to any namespace.' This definition does not preclude the presence of fragments within the document that *do* belong to a namespace, and the term still applies even if the root element is the only element that is not qualified.

At least some of the elements in an unqualified document (including the root element) are simply outside all namespaces, as if floating in limbo. They are not in a 'null' namespace as some suggest (in part because this would constrain such elements to form a unique list):

An element that does not belong to a namespace has an **unqualified name**. It has no namespace prefix and should not have a colon in the name. But the absence of a prefix alone does not prove that the element does not belong to a namespace. This is because a qualified element can be **implicitly qualified** (the prefix is absent) instead of being **explicitly qualified**.

Note that a schema definition that does not specify a target namespace creates unqualified elements and attributes (it creates a document model for unqualified documents).

21.7   **Namespace Declarations**

A document instance includes a **namespace declaration** in order to do the following:

- declare that elements or attributes belonging to a namespace *may* be present in the document
- identify the namespace that these elements belong to

- specify the prefix that needs to be added to element names in order to map these elements to the namespace

An attribute with a name that begins '**xmlns:**...' declares a namespace. The value of this attribute is a reference to the namespace concerned. The remainder of the attribute name is the prefix that is to stand in for this name. This can be confusing at first because an element or attribute name *prefix* is determined by this attribute's *suffix*. In the following example, the HTML 4.0 namespace is referenced and given the prefix 'X':

```
<X:html xmlns:X="http://www.w3.org/1999/xhtml">
  ...<X:P>An HTML paragraph.</X:P>...
</X:html>
```

Such attributes must never be declared in a schema definition (though they must be declared in a DTD) because they do not belong to the document type being defined (they do not belong to any model).

The 'http://www.w3.org/2000/xmlns/' namespace is the official namespace for the 'xmlns' attribute and all attributes that have the 'xmlns:' prefix (the URL happens to point to an HTML document that describes the purpose of this namespace). No other prefix can be associated with this namespace. The purpose of this namespace is to allow these vital attributes to be treated like any other attribute that needs to be associated with a namespace. For example, the DOM (Document Object Model) interface requires this.

The following example of an unqualified XML document contains three qualified elements:

```
<CompetitionEntry xmlns:M="...">
  <Competition>Piano</Competition>
  <Competitor>J Smith</Competitor>
  <Score>57</Score>
  <M:Composer>George Gershwin</M:Composer>
  <M:Composition>Rhapsody in Blue</M:Composition>
  <M:Score>Ferde Grofé</M:Score>
</CompetitionEntry>
```

Note that the XML Schema standard copes with such documents by allowing a parser that includes a schema processor to switch from one schema definition to another. Only one schema definition is 'active' at any one time. Whenever the schema processor encounters an element from a different namespace, it may be allowed to switch in the appropriate schema definition and then continue to validate the content against the new document model. But such switching is strictly under the control of the active schema definition (until the end tag of the 'root' element of the fragment it was called in for is reached).

The schema definition specifies exactly where it is possible to insert document fragments that belong to another namespace. The any element and anyAttribute element (discussed in Section 12.4 and Section 12.6, respectively) allow any element or attribute from another namespace to appear, and the import feature allows specific foreign elements or attributes to appear.

Multiple declarations

An element may contain more than one namespace declaration. Of course, an element is not allowed to contain two attributes with the same name, but there is actually no conflict here because each namespace must be assigned to a different prefix (even a nonvalidating, namespace-unaware parser would report an error if the same prefix was assigned to two or more namespaces on the same element):

```
<D:Document xmlns:D="http://MyCorp/document"
            xmlns:X="http://www.w3.org/TR/REC-html40">
 ...<D:Description>...</D:Description>...
 ...<X:Td>An HTML table cell.</X:Td>...
 ...<D:Summary>...</D:Summary>...
</D:Document>
```

Namespace scope

While namespaces may be declared on the root element, as in the examples above, they can also be specified on other elements. When this is done, the declaration has only a **local scope**. It is not relevant to elements before, after, or above the element containing the namespace declaration. Only the `table` and `td` elements are affected in the example below:

```
<Document>
  <Description>...</Description>
  <X:table xmlns:X="http://www.w3.org/1999/xhtml">
   ...<X:td>An HTML table cell.</X:td>...
  </X:table>
  <Summary>...</Summary>
</Document>
```

The declaration comes into effect immediately. Its scope includes the element it is declared within. Indeed, one reference to the declaration (the element name prefix in the start tag of the element containing the declaration) precedes the declaration itself (as the prefix of the `table` start tag above shows), though this is not a problem because a parser will read the entire start tag including its attribute declarations before any namespace processing or checking is performed.

The ability to place multiple declarations on the root element can be very convenient. As the music competition example demonstrates, it is often a good idea to keep the declarations on the root element because they might otherwise be needed on every element. The example below is unnecessarily overburdened by namespace declarations:

```
<CompetitionEntry>
  <C:Competition xmlns:C="...">Piano</C:Competition>
  <C:Competitor xmlns:C="...">J Smith</C:Competitor>
  <C:Score xmlns:C="...">57</C:Score>
  <M:Composer xmlns:M="...">
    George Gershwin
  </M:Composer>
  <M:Composition xmlns:M="...">
    Rhapsody in Blue
  </M:Composition>
  <M:Score xmlns:M="...">Ferde Grofé</M:Score>
</CompetitionEntry>
```

21.8 Default Namespace

A document can become difficult to read when every element has a prefix, and the extra characters in the names certainly add to the document size. Fortunately, the standard includes the concept of a **default namespace**, which eliminates the need for prefixes. However, this feature raises some complications, especially when unqualified elements are also present.

Element defaults

Elements can belong to a default namespace. Authors enable this by declaring the namespace, using an attribute named '**xmlns**', with no suffix and no colon:

```
<Document xmlns="file:///DTDs/document.dtd"
          xmlns:X="http://www.w3.org/1999/xhtml">
  ...<Description>...</Description>...
  ...<X:td>An XHTML table cell.</X:td>...
</Document>
```

In the example above, the Document and Description elements are still qualified, but **implicitly qualified** rather than **explicitly qualified**.

When this feature is used, qualified elements look just like unqualified elements. This can cause confusion when both are present in the same document instance. In the following example, the root element is not qualified but the embedded element is, and only the location of the namespace declaration provides any hint as to what is going on:

```
<Unqualified>
  <Qualified xmlns="..."> ... </Qualified>
</Unqualified>
```

Note that to add to the potential confusion, the XML Schema standard includes the concept of unqualified local elements. In fact, a schema processor always assumes that an element that has no prefix is a local element, provided that there is a local element declaration with a matching name. But the any element's namespace attribute value can override this assumption, especially if it is given the value '##local' (though '##any' is just confusing). However, when processing such a document without accessing the schema definition, an application could be forgiven for assuming that the local elements are actually part of a surrounding unprefixed namespace.

Overriding defaults

The default namespace can be changed at any point in the document hierarchy. This is an ideal technique when a sufficiently large fragment from another namespace occurs. In the following example, the second XHTML fragment is assigned to the default namespace, temporarily replacing the original assignment to the other namespace:

```
<Document xmlns="file:///DTDs/document.dtd"
          xmlns:X="http://www.w3.org/1999/xhtml">
   ...3
   ...<Para>A normal paragraph.</Para>...
   ...<X:td>An HTML table cell.</X:td>...
   ...<Description>...</Description>...

   ...<html xmlns="http://www.w3.org/1999/xhtml">
      ...<td>An HTML table cell.</td>...
   ...</html>
   ...
   <Summary>...</Summary>
</Document>
```

It would still be possible to explicitly qualify some or all of the elements in the second fragment because the prefixed declaration is still in scope:

```
<Document xmlns="file:///DTDs/document.dtd"
          xmlns:X="http://www.w3.org/1999/xhtml">
   ...
   ...<html xmlns="http://www.w3.org/1999/xhtml">
      ...<td>An HTML table cell.</td>
         <X:td>An HTML table cell.</X:td>...
   ...</html>
   ...
</Document>
```

However, employing two definitions for the same namespace in this way is only really useful for explicitly qualifying attributes when they are used on elements from other namespaces and elements from the same namespace adopt the default namespace (see below).

21.9 Attributes

Namespaces apply to attributes as well as to elements, though there are some subtle complications to be aware of.

Attribute from current namespace

When an attribute belongs to the same namespace as the element containing it, there is no need to include the prefix on the attribute. Indeed, it must not be included. In the following example, the Version attribute belongs to the Document element, even though it does not carry the prefix:

```
<D:Document Version="2.3"
           xmlns:D="file:///DTDs/document.dtd"
   ...
</D:Document>
```

This rule has some significant implications. First, these attributes cannot belong to a document model representing any unqualified elements in the document because it would then be impossible to distinguish between attributes from different domains. Second, if a default namespace is in effect, attributes without a prefix are *not* considered to belong to that namespace as elements without a prefix would be. For this reason, the default namespace should not be used for a document model containing attributes that may need to be attached to elements from other namespaces.

In fact, there has been some confusion about whether such attributes even belong to the namespace of the containing element. It is a widely held view that an attribute without a prefix is deemed *not* to belong to the namespace; it is simply the job of the application processing the XML data to recognize its origins and treat it accordingly. But an appendix to the standard includes an example showing that an attribute would conform to the same namespace as the element it belongs to rather than to no namespace at all, and the suggested namespace partitioning system also indicates their inclusion. However, there is little practical difference since both interpretations become irrelevant when processing occurs.

Note that the XML Schema standard makes it clear that, by default, attributes defined as part of an element definition are not assigned to the target namespace. Only global attributes (with unique names) are definitely assigned. However, there is some confusion about whether local attributes that are forced to include a prefix do get assigned to the namespace. But if they do, they must still be hidden in the per-element-type partition because they cannot be guaranteed to be unique.

Attribute from other namespace

Attributes from one namespace can be used on elements from another. The attribute names contain the same prefixes as the elements (if any) from the same namespace.

The following example of a House element contains two Style attributes. The first one is a foreign HTML attribute that formats the content of the element (in this case, coloring the text red). The second one is from the property namespace and explains what kind of property the House element describes. It has no prefix because it belongs to the same namespace as the element it is on:

```
<property:House  html:Style="color:red"
                      Style="Georgian" >
...
</property:House>
```

Note that when a schema definition is used to create a document model, only globally declared attributes can be used in this way.

21.10 Combined Qualified and Unqualified Elements

Documents may contain a mixture of elements that belong to one or more namespaces and elements that do not belong to any namespace. In fact, many XML documents are namespace free, in particular, the vast number of XML documents that were created before the Namespaces standard was released.

Unqualified document containing qualified fragments

Documents that do not belong to a namespace may contain fragments that do belong to a namespace:

```
<UnqualifiedDocument>
  <Unqualified>...</Unqualified>

  <X:Qualified xmlns:X="TheNamespace">
    <X:Qualified>...</X:Qualified>
  </X:Qualified>
</UnqualifiedDocument>
```

The namespace declaration can also be placed on the root element in this circumstance. The fact that the root element is not itself qualified is not important, and this approach is desirable when several fragments belong to the same namespace:

```
<UnqualifiedDocument xmlns:X="TheNamespace">
  <Unqualified>...</Unqualified>

  <X:QualifiedRoot>
    <X:Qualified>...</X:Qualified>
  </X:QualifiedRoot>

  <Unqualified>...</Unqualified>

  <X:QualifiedRoot>
    <X:Qualified>...</X:Qualified>
  </X:QualifiedRoot>
</UnqualifiedDocument>
```

The ability to use the default namespace for an embedded fragment is unaffected in this scenario, but such use cannot occur if the namespace declaration was placed on the root element. The reason is that all elements with no prefix would then be deemed to be in the declared namespace:

```
<UnqualifiedDocument>
  <Unqualified>...</Unqualified>

  <QualifiedRoot xmlns="MyNamespace">
    <Qualified>...</Qualified>
  </QualifiedRoot>
</UnqualifiedDocument>
```

Nevertheless, the fact that unqualified elements and default namespace-qualified elements look the same can be confusing (and gets even more confusing when non-prefixed local elements from a schema definition are added to the mix, as discussed in Section 9.4).

Qualified document containing unqualified fragments

Documents that belong to a namespace may contain fragments that do not belong to a namespace. When the document uses a namespace prefix, the unqualified elements are easily recognized since those elements that do not have this prefix:

```
<X:QualifiedDocument xmlns:X="MyDocNamespace">
  <X:Qualified>...</X:Qualified>

  <Unqualified>
    <Unqualified>...</Unqualified>
  </Unqualified>
</X:QualifiedDocument>
```

Note that an XML Schema may place a different interpretation on such elements (they may be locally defined elements without a prefix).

Default qualified document containing unqualified fragments

The technique just described above can even be applied when the default namespace is used. The boundary is detected by the presence of an overriding default namespace declaration that has an empty value. The empty string means that no namespace is in effect for unqualified elements:

```
<QualifiedDocument xmlns="MyDocNamespace">
  <Qualified>...</Qualified>

  <Unqualified xmlns="">
    <Unqualified>...</Unqualified>
  </Unqualified>
</QualifiedDocument>
```

21.11 **XML Namespace**

A namespace exists that is associated with the XML standard itself. The 'http://www.w3.org/XML/1998/namespace' namespace contains three special attributes and differs from all other namespaces in one very significant respect.

The reason why other namespaces cannot be assigned to the prefix 'xml' is that this prefix is 'hard coded' to the XML namespace. The important consequence of this enforced association is that the namespace declaration becomes redundant. It is no longer needed because the prefix alone is sufficient to identify the namespace concerned. This means that even software applications that are not namespace aware can readily detect these significant attributes.

Note that an XML Schema definition for an unqualified document model must still handle this namespace like any other, for example, by importing a schema definition targeted at this namespace and referencing the attributes wherever they are needed in this model. A schema definition for the XML namespace exists at http://www.w3.org/2001/xml.xsd.

22. Next Steps

There is plenty of information on the Internet concerning XML, document modeling in general and the XML Schema standard in particular. This chapter includes links to XML sites, relevant software, further reading, existing document models, and relevant mailing lists.

22.1 Introduction

The tables in this chapter contain links to Web resources (URLs) and descriptions of these resources.

URLs

There are a number of things to note about the URLs:

- They should all have an 'http://' prefix (though browsers will tend to add this automatically).
- Because of space constraints, many of the longer URLs are wrapped over two or more lines, but they must be considered to be a single line of text, and a space must *not* be inserted where a URL is split across lines.
- Many of them will undoubtedly become obsolete over time (in some cases by the time this book has been published).

Descriptions

Quoted italic explanatory text is taken from reviewer and vendor descriptions of sites and products; the accuracy of this text has not been checked or endorsed by the author of this book.

22.2 General XML Sites

The XML Schema standard is dependent on other XML-related standards, and these standards are discussed on various Web sites.

XML portal sites

The following table includes XML-related Web sites that are likely to include relevant news and product reviews (later tables may refer to specific pages within these sites that target more specific categories of information):

www.w3.org	According to the site, "*The World Wide Web Consortium (W3C) develops interoperable technologies (specifications, guidelines, software, and tools) to lead the Web to its full potential. W3C is a forum for information, commerce, communication, and collective understanding.*"
www.xml.org	According to the site, "*www.XML.org was formed ... to minimize overlap and duplication in XML languages and XML standard initiatives by providing public access to XML information and XML Schemas. Today XML.org has ... emerged as a valuable and leading resource to technologists, developers and businesspeople developing purpose-built XML languages.*"
www.xml.com	This is "*a web site covering essential news, issues, opinions and programming advice from the XML developer community.*"
www.xmlhack.com	This is "*a web site covering essential news, issues, opinions and programming advice from the XML developer community.*"
www.xml.coverpages.org www.xml.coverpages.org/schemas.html	OASIS provides the cover pages as "*a public resource to document and encourage the use of open standards that enhance the intelligibility, quality, and longevity of digital information*"

Related standards

The XML Schema standard relies on or references a number of other standards:

www.w3.org/xml	XML
www.w3.org/TR/REC-xml-names	Namespaces in XML
www.w3.org/TR/xpath	XPath
www.unicode.org	Unicode

22.3 Relevant Software

In general, this book does not discuss particular products, in part because this might imply that the mentioned products are superior to competing offerings (even when a product really just happens to be one that the author uses), and in part because new products and new versions of existing products quickly become obsolete. However, the following tables list some applications and tools that have a high profile at the time of this writing.

Schema-building assistance tools

The following tools assist with the creation of XML Schema documents by providing a development environment, by analyzing a schema definition for errors and inefficient techniques (which is much more useful than simply responding to errors raised by validating parsers as they attempt to read the schema definition to validate a document instance), or by presenting a schema definition in a graphical format that naturally reveals some of the common problems that can occur with document models:

www.xml.com/pub/r/1107	XML Schema Quality Checker – "... *is a tool that analyzes an XML Schema and reports any improper usage of XML Schema Language. The program will perform a schema-wide check when multiple schema documents are connected, and has a batch mode available for automating larger jobs.*"
puvogel.informatik.med.uni-giessen.de/lumrix	XSBrowser – "... *is able to document / instantiate a given DTD (REC-xml-19980210) or XML schema (REC-xmlschema-1-20010502). The XSBrowser aims at creating a human readable document model from a given DTD or XML schema.*"
www.bluetetra.com/xsddoc/	XsdDoc – "... *is a documentation tool that automatically generates detailed reports from XML Schema definitions. XsdDoc transforms plain XML files into cross-referenced and hyperlinked HTML documents for easy website publication and collaboration among developers.*"
www.sysonyx.com/products/xmlarchitect	xmlArchitect – "...*the largest feature of xmlArchitect is* [its] *unique ability to display a tree view of the XML Document that the schema is attempting to define. Through this tree view, users can watch how their changes to the schema will affect their document. They can also make direct changes in the xml tree view and xmlArchitect will automatically update the schema.*"

Schema language converters

The following tools convert DTDs to schema definitions or convert between these and other languages. Such tools can save time and help avoid the inevitable errors that occur when models are manually translated:

www.syntext.com/products	Dtd2Xs – this product "... *allows to convert complex, modularized XML DTDs and DTDs with namespaces to XML Schemas. As an example of Dtd2Xs conversion check out DocBook XML Schema generated from XML DocBook DTD V4.2, and XSL-FO Schema generated from XSL-FO DTD.*"

puvogel.informatik.med.uni-giessen.de/ lumrix	Convert DTD to schema definition – "*... can map meaningful DTD entities onto XML Schema constructs (simpleType, attributeGroup, group), i.e. the XML document model is not anonymized. In addition, the translator can map DTD comments onto XML Schema documentation nodes in various ways.*"
www.thaiopensource.com/relaxng/ trang.html	Trang – Converts between DTD, XML Schema, and Relax NG.
msdn.microsoft.com/library/ default.asp?url=/downloads/list/ xmlgeneral.asp	Convertor for XDR (old Microsoft schema language) to XML Schema definition.

Validation during parsing

Validating XML parsers now tend to have support for validation against a schema definition instead of a DTD (or can even validate against both if the document references both a DTD and a schema definition):

msdn.microsoft.com/library/ default.asp?url=/downloads/list/ xmlgeneral.asp	Microsoft platform MSXML command-line parser
xml.apache.org/xerces2-j/index.html	Any Java platform Apache parser
xml.apache.org/xerces2-c/index.html	Multiplatform Apache C++ parser

Validation

Some tools simply validate an XML document for compliance against a schema definition, but do not parse the content for handing over to an application for processing:

http://apps.gotdotnet.com/xmltools/ xsdvalidator/	Online schema validator

XML Schema-sensitive document instance editors

Advanced XML-sensitive word processors and text editors are now including interactive validation and author guidance, based on a schema definition rather than a DTD:

www.corel.com	XMetaL
www.arbortext.com	Epic Editor
www.xmlspy.com	xmlspy

22.4   **Further Reading**

This section includes links to reading material on developing schema definitions.

Alternative explanations

Although this book covers all features of the XML Schema language, it is sometimes beneficial to have access to other explanations (that include different examples or approaches to illustrating a concept):

www.xml.com/pub/a/2000/11/29/ schemas/partterns.html	Using design patterns to build schema definitions

Other modeling languages

XML Schema is not the only XML document modeling language. Others can be used in place of schema definitions or can complement them:

www.w3.org/TR/REC-xml	DTD (Document Type Definition) – part of the XML standard itself
www.relaxng.org	RelaxNG
www.ascc.net/xml/resource/schematron	Schematron

Schema modeling best practices

Some online material focuses on "best practices" (the advice given on these sites is not necessarily the view of the author of this book):

www.xfront.com/ BestPracticesHomepage.html	This advice *"was developed collaboratively by The MITRE Corporation and members of the xml-dev list group."*
www.xml.com/pub/a/2002/11/20/ schemas.html	An attempt to define an effective subset of the language

22.5   **Existing Document Models**

Creation of a new document model often involves extending, modifying, or subsetting an existing industry-standard model (some of the following links are to parts of general XML sites listed earlier).

Document model libraries

The following links are to registries of common document models:

www.oasis-open.org	This site *"is a not-for-profit, global consortium that drives the development, convergence and adoption of e-business standards. Members themselves set the OASIS technical agenda, using a lightweight, open process expressly designed to promote industry consensus and unite disparate efforts. OASIS produces worldwide standards for security, Web services, XML conformance, business transactions, electronic publishing, topic maps and interoperability within and between marketplaces."*
www.xml.org/xml/registry.jsp	Covers: Defense, EGovernment, Financial Services, Human Resources, Insurance, Localization, Printing and Publishing, Retail, Security, Tax/Accounting and Other Industries.

Popular document models

High-profile document model standards include:

www.oasis-open.org/docbook/xml	DOCBOOK – the standard model for books
www.w3.org/MarkUp	XHTML – the XML-compliant version of the popular HTML language used on the Web

Popular document model fragments

Standards have emerged for specific structures within complex documents:

www.oasis-open.org/specs/a503.htm	OASIS subset of CALS Table model – *"... an Exchange subset of the full CALS table model DTD described in OASIS Technical Memorandum TM 9502:1995. This Exchange subset has been chosen as being a useful subset of the complete CALS table model such that, if an application's tables are tagged according to this subset, there is a high probability that the table will be interoperable among the great majority of OASIS vendor products."*
www.w3.org/Math	MathML – *"... is a low-level specification for describing mathematics as a basis for machine to machine communication. It provides a much needed foundation for the inclusion of mathematical expressions in Web pages."*
www.dublincore.org	Dublin Core metadata – *"The Dublin Core Metadata Initiative (DCMI) is an organization dedicated to promoting the widespread adoption of interoperable metadata standards and developing specialized metadata vocabularies for describing resources that enable more intelligent information discovery systems."* View schema at www.dublincore.org/schemas/xmls/qdc/2003/04/02/dc.xsd.

22.6   **Mailing Lists**

Questions and responses from other schema developers can be a very enlightening way to discover how to use the XML Schema standard in the real world:

lists.w3.org/Archives/Public/ xmlschema-dev/	Archive of the official W3C mail list for XML Schema discussions
www.xml.org/xml/xmldev.shtml	This *"serves as an open, unmoderated list supporting XML implementation and development. XML-DEV emphasizes active participation through code development, creation of protocols and specifications, and other material contributions such as reference resources."*
groups.yahoo.com/group/xml-doc	This is *"a place where writers, developers, product and service vendors, and others discuss the application of XML, SGML, and related technologies to structured authoring, particularly authoring of documentation for computer software and hardware."*

22.7   **About the Author**

The author of this book has a personal Web site and has published a number of other books:

www.bradley.co.uk	The author's own Web site
www.awprofessional.com	Addison-Wesley (publisher of this book)
www.aw.com/catalog/academic/product/ 0,4096,0201419998,00.html	The Concise SGML Companion
www.aw.com/catalog/academic/product/ 0,4096,0201770598,00.html	The XML Companion (3rd edition)
www.aw.com/catalog/academic/product/ 0,4096,0201770830,00.html	The XSL Companion (2nd edition)

Index

NOTE: This index identifies terms introduced in the main text (where they are displayed in bold).

THE XML COMPANION, THIRD EDITION

BY NEIL BRADLEY

©2002 • ISBN 0-201-77059-8

If you're a current or potential XML user looking for just one reference to get you up to speed on XML with clarity, comprehensive coverage, and precision, then this book will be your essential and constant companion. Whether you're a programmer, analyst, or consultant involved in the management, processing, transfer, or publication of XML data and documents, all your questions will be answered here. Apart from the core chapters on the XML standard itself, this book concentrates on related standards developed by the W3C and on the two most popular applications of this technology: document publishing and data exchange.

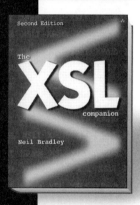

THE XSL COMPANION, SECOND EDITION

BY NEIL BRADLEY

©2002 • ISBN 0-201-77083-0

This new edition of the very popular and successful *XSL Companion* covers all the features of the new XSLT standard. The XSLT standard is now firmly established as a companion to XML for all manner of transformation needs. Experience with using this standard to solve serious practical problems has resulted in more explanatory material and suggestions on how to exploit it to the fullest.

THE CONCISE SGML COMPANION

BY NEIL BRADLEY

©1997 • ISBN 0-201-41999-8

This book is the essential desktop/briefcase reference for busy SGML practitioners. Neil Bradley's philosophy: "to get to the point quickly and stick with it until it's been fully explained."

Addison
Wesley

Register
Your Book

at www.awprofessional.com/register

You may be eligible to receive:

- Advance notice of forthcoming editions of the book
- Related book recommendations
- Chapter excerpts and supplements of forthcoming titles
- Information about special contests and promotions throughout the year
- Notices and reminders about author appearances, tradeshows, and online chats with special guests

Contact us

If you are interested in writing a book or reviewing manuscripts prior to publication, please write to us at:

Editorial Department
Addison-Wesley Professional
75 Arlington Street, Suite 300
Boston, MA 02116 USA
Email: AWPro@aw.com

Addison-Wesley

Visit us on the Web: http://www.awprofessional.com